TIME FOR CHANGE

WHOLE FOODS FOR WHOLE HEALTH!

DANIELLE BUSSONE

WHAT PEOPLE ARE SAYING ABOUT "TIME FOR CHANGE"

"Time For Change" is a comprehensive, engaging and passionate book by an intrepid woman who fought through years of catastrophic medical events. By continuous reading, research, and diligently listening to her body, Bussone has found her way back to good health by means of a plant-based diet. Here she shares her story, her research findings, her contagious enthusiasm, her wonderful cooking methods and vegan recipes. This book is also a fervent cry against pesticides, genetically modified and highly processed foods. — Patricia Kandle, MD

Until Danielle Bussone introduced me to a plant-based lifestyle, I suffered from chronic crippling migraines, often lasting over fifteen days. I was an avid carnivore, a triathlete with a terrible diet, and a college kid who didn't sleep enough. Unwilling as I was to embrace a vegan diet, I managed to restrict myself for two days to "give it a go." Forty-eight hours later, I was migraine-free! Meat looked wholly unappetizing; I felt stronger, slimmer, faster, harder, and was refreshed after a full night's sleep. Danielle could tell you exactly what it is about plants that revitalizes the human body, but for me, her book, freedom from debilitating headaches, and a fitter body is enough to keep me motivated!
— *Catherine Deborah Davidson-Hiers, College Student*

Horrific. Heroic. A must read for anyone who has to deal with doctors and hospitals. — Bill Kaiser, Author of "Bloodroot" and "Hellebore: A Novel of Reconstruction."

This book shouts, "Wellness happens!" An intelligent and enjoyable read for both laypersons and medical professionals. "Time For Change" offers a vegan lifestyle that creates and sustains vitality. Ms Bussone has done her research. Everyone should read this book! — Teresa Wood, DDS

Danielle's story of adopting a vegan diet to recover her health is an inspiration. "Time For Change" offers a strong foundation to the benefits of a plant-based diet and is filled with delicious recipes to whet your appetite. This book is a must-have for every pantry and bookshelf! - Vegan Athlete, Kate Strong — 2014 World Champion Women's Long-Distance Triathlon

Danielle "stirs" an inspirational story of transitioning to veganism, a glossary of terms for new vegans, numerous delicious multicultural cooking recipes, awesome tips towards healthy living and more in this one-stop Go Vegan book for beginners and seasoned vegans. Vegan Athlete, — Omowale Adewale, Super Middleweight Boxing Champion

Turning to a healthy, whole foods plant-based diet can raise many questions and a few eyebrows. Danielle Bussone, in her well written and information-packed book "Time For Change," helps to make the transition in a well-informed and healthy manner. This book answers many of the questions often asked of individuals living a whole food plant-based lifestyle, such as "Where do you get your protein?" Each chapter is filled with personal insights and guidance. Thank you Danielle for pouring your heart and soul into this book! — Lisa Harris, Naturopath and Author of "Rebuilding the Temple: A Practical Guide to Health and Wellness"

TIME FOR CHANGE
WHOLE FOODS FOR WHOLE HEALTH!

Published by Danrich Publishing, LLC

Neither the publisher nor the author is engaged in rendering professional advice or services and makes no claims to medical authority. The ideas and suggestions in this book are not intended as a substitute for consulting with a physician. All matters of health require medical supervision. Neither the author nor the publisher shall be liable or responsible for any loss or damage allegedly arising from any information or suggestion in this book.

The recipes in this book are to be followed exactly as written. Neither the author nor the publisher is responsible for specific health or allergy needs that may require medical supervision or for any adverse reactions to these recipes.

ISBN-13: 978-0615794792

Book design by Danielle Bussone
Photography by Danielle Bussone and Richard Bussone
unless otherwise specified

PRINTED IN THE UNITED STATES OF AMERICA

DANRICH
PUBLISHING

To Rich, my heart.

TIME FOR CHANGE

WHOLE FOODS FOR WHOLE HEALTH!

by DANIELLE BUSSONE

TABLE OF CONTENTS

INTRODUCTION

A person's life can change in the blink of an eye. I was healthy, strong and energetic. Or so I thought. Throughout our marriage, Rich and I led physically active lives. We rode bicycles, enjoyed skiing, rollerblading and long hikes. I went to the gym and worked out with weights and became intimate with the stair master. Still, I was significantly overweight. I had just come to accept that I would always be heavy and to consider my weight a birthright. My mother was heavy, her mother and sisters were heavy. They all looked alike to me. I thought I was stuck with this genetic inheritance. It didn't help that I loved to cook and to eat rich foods.

After Rich retired as a dentist with the Air Force, we spent ten years converting a tobacco barn into a house. We did most of the work ourselves, a learn-as-you-go project, paying for it a board at a time, having a blast. We hammered nails, planed and sawed long boards, carried heavy sheets of plywood and drywall and scrambled up and down scaffolding.

I muscled heavy rocks in place to build the walls lining my garden. We crawled all over the walls and roof of that barn as it finally took shape and became our home. At night, Rich and I regularly fell into bed exhausted. Good times.

Suddenly, I wasn't healthy anymore. A time bomb in my liver, a series of failed medical procedures followed by uncommon medical complications converged to create a perfect storm that altered my life forever.

The following pages may be difficult to read. I felt it was necessary to include them so you can understand just how bad things became before my medical nightmare was behind me and I began to recover. Changing to a healthy, plant-based diet turned my life around. This is not an exaggeration. In ONE DAY I was free of gastric pain that had made my life intolerable. I've also lost a great deal of weight without limiting the amount of food I eat.

This book is not about weight loss, though weight loss is a natural side effect of a plant-based diet. It is about regaining health and giving your body the nutritional support it needs to not only survive but to thrive.

This is my story.

1

A RECIPE FOR DISASTER

"Are you sitting down?" My primary care physician called me with the results of an ultrasound I had recently undergone due to a nagging pain I was experiencing underneath my right scapula.

Oh, dear, this doesn't sound good. She told me that the ultrasound showed several small masses and she suspected I had liver cancer. We would need to do a biopsy to know for sure.

"If I have liver cancer, I'm pretty much toast, right?" I waited to hear some words reassuring me that this wasn't as bad as it sounded.

"Yes," she said frankly.

Oh, shit.

I had a meltdown before they put me under anesthesia. For years Rich and I had been in the habit sharing a bottle of wine in the evening. It was our one guilty pleasure and we enjoyed it. The nurse asked me if I was a social drinker.

"We get a lot of social drinkers in here who are surprised to discover they have liver cancer," she said.

I burst into tears. *Have I done this to myself?*

The radiologist who was performing the punch biopsy said to me in the most kind and gentle voice, "Danielle, if you have cancer it is not your fault. There is so much we are learning about cancers. We even know now that some cancers are contagious."

I recall seeing his face beaming down at me when I awoke from the anesthesia.

"You won't remember this, but you don't have cancer," he said.

I did remember. I didn't have cancer. Later he told me I was his miracle patient. He said that only one out of 500 patients whose images presented like mine turn out to be benign. My liver tissue was relatively healthy. I had some fatty liver tissue but even that was not excessive, especially considering the fact I was considerably overweight. The tumors were hepatic adenomas, benign liver tumors that are believed to be caused by long-term use of birth control pills. Most physicians I've spoken to are not even aware of this consequence of taking birth control pills. Liver doctors are certainly aware of it. These tumors have become so commonplace with the baby boomer generation that the liver docs refer to them as "hormonomas." They are very slow growing, often taking 20 years to become symptomatic. Even though they are benign, they can turn into cancerous tumors as they progress. They also become more painful as they fill with blood and stretch. Eventually, they reach a size in which rupture becomes a concern. Once one of these tumors rupture, bleeding to death is an immediate threat. We decided to do nothing, watch it for a while and see if they continued to grow.

In the fall I was out riding horses with my friend, Nina Beth, in the mountains of Appalachia. The wind whipped my bangs from my face as I galloped to join her. I was riding Slick, an intelligent, mountain savvy Tennessee walking horse Nina Beth had lent me for the day. Nina Beth looked back at me from astride her quarter horse, Clifford, and said, "Danielle, wipe that dirt off your forehead!"

"It's a mole!" I shouted back at her, laughing. I have had this tiny mole on my forehead since birth but I noticed in recent years it was growing. I had shown it to several doctors over the past three years and they all told me it was nothing. For Nina Beth to see it from the back of a horse several lengths away made me realize it was bigger than I thought.

I made an appointment with my doctor to have it evaluated. She agreed with the other doctors that it was nothing to be concerned about. I insisted on having a dermatologist look at it. One of the previous doctors who had seen it was a dermatologist, but I thought it was time to have another pair of eyes on it. He examined it carefully and assured me it was harmless.

Something about it though, kept nagging at me. I couldn't let it rest. I had heard on medical segments on the news that if a mole grew to the size of a pencil eraser, it should be removed. This mole had always been about the size of a pencil point, now it was larger than a pencil eraser. I called the doctor's office again and told the receptionist that I was not satisfied with my exam and I wanted the doctor to do it again. She immediately scheduled me for a follow-up visit the very next day.

The doctor looked at me with a quizzical expression and asked me what the problem was.

"I want you to take the damned thing off."

He did as I asked. I felt a surge of relief and returned home feeling as though I had dodged a bullet. I didn't think I had cancer, but I felt as if I had averted potential cancer.

A couple of weeks later, Rich and I were preparing to go to dinner with some friends, including Nina Beth, Charlie, (who is a plastic surgeon) and some other horse people. Just as I was heading out the door, the phone rang. It was my dermatologist. He awkwardly informed me that my lab results were back and my mole was a melanoma. He expressed how surprised he was at the news. The doctor told me he thought it was an "in situ" melanoma, Latin for "in place." This meant the cancer was only on the very outer surface of the mole and had not infiltrated the interior of the mole nor my skin. While I was comforted somewhat to know this, I had no illusions as to the seriousness of this diagnosis. Rich and I had lost two friends in recent years from melanoma. One of them, Dan, was a dermatologist. So, I knew very well that this was not good news.

I am not placing the blame for this on my doctors. If anything is to blame it is growing up as an active, fair-skinned child in the blazing summers of the Mississippi Gulf Coast. Melanomas do not always follow a typical pattern. I'm sure this mole really did look benign. Dan, an expert in the field, had not believed his own mole was a melanoma.

Our instincts are our internal guidance systems. We ignore them at our own peril. For three years my instincts had told me that something was not right with this mole and I deferred to the opinion of doctors over my own misgivings. Had I not finally listened to my intuition, that nagging voice in my head telling me something wasn't right, that melanoma would have undoubtedly metastasized into my brain and by now I would probably be dead.

The standard care for any melanoma is a wide excision to ensure that all the cancer is removed. An escaped renegade cell could cause a deadly recurrence, which is most likely what happened to Dan. Charlie performed the excision, leaving me with a nasty scar that formed a backwards "S" shape in the middle of my forehead from my scalp to just over my eyebrows. It was pretty hideous during the healing stages. Happily, the next biopsy showed no signs of the melanoma. It had all been removed during the initial biopsy. The dermatologist had been right about that. Fortunately, my bangs have a very strong forward growth and cover the scar fairly well. I've come to regard it as a mark of survival.

With two cancer scares behind me, the pain underneath my right shoulder blade was becoming increasingly intense. An MRI showed that either the adenomas had either experienced significant growth since my punch biopsy or the initial ultrasound had not adequately represented the tumors' true size. Since they had reached the point where rupture was a possibility, especially since they were symptomatically painful, my doctor recommended the tumors be surgically removed.

I was referred to a general surgeon with an outstanding reputation. He, in turn, referred me to a young liver and kidney surgeon who was to amputate the left lobe of my liver, where the three tumors were located.

The liver is an organ that, fortunately, regenerates. It would not regrow the left lobe, but the right lobe would become larger to compensate for the missing part of the left lobe. I was astonished to learn it only takes five weeks to regrow a liver.

It appeared the operation was successful and the surgeon only had to amputate half of the left lobe. Interestingly, within each of the liver tumors were many more tumors. The largest tumor had more than 20 small tumors inside of it. The liver surgeon assured me that the operation went well and I would recover completely.

Well… that didn't happen.

The next ten days saw my condition deteriorate conspicuously. I became so jaundiced I was unrecognizable, my skin a sickly yellow-brown color. I was weak and getting weaker. The liver surgeon couldn't figure it out. It was obvious I was dying. Rich was beside himself. I had numerous CT scans, X-rays, blood tests and a myriad of other tests that revealed nothing useful. I was given blood transfusions. I couldn't eat anything. Doctors from other specialties were called in to consult on my case. Finally, ten days following my initial surgery, a gastroenterologist suggested a series of imaging tests to rule out possibilities. They were all extremely painful, requiring I lay on my injured abdomen to have the scans performed. The final test revealed the problem. The liver surgeon had mistakenly severed my common bile duct. A human being cannot survive without this crucial piece of anatomy.

An emergency repair was performed by the same liver surgeon. Since I could not live without my common bile duct, he had to create a new one. To do this the surgeon had to perform a procedure called a Roux-en-Y hepatico-jejunostomy. He essentially had to cut a section of my small bowel, loop it up and attach it to the liver forming a new bile duct from my intestines. The relief I felt from this surgery was instantaneous. I ignored the voices surrounding me, asking questions of me as I regained consciousness. *Leave me alone. Let me enjoy this.* I wanted to revel in my body's reawakening to life.

The next day my surgeon informed me of what he had done. He told me the Roux-en Y permanently corrected the issue and I would have no further problems.

Well… that didn't happen either.

I was released from the hospital once I could eat solid food and my drainage tube had stopped draining bile, which indicated the liver was probably no longer leaking and had sealed properly. All my tests looked good. However, by the time I arrived home I began to feel sick. I started throwing up. I called my surgeon to let him know. He had left town for the Christmas holidays and his partner, who had assisted my surgeon in my initial operation, returned my call. I told him that I had a fever, was in considerable pain and had become very sensitive to smells, that everything was making me vomit. Prior to my medical issues, Rich and I had been working on a building project, converting a tobacco barn into a house. I was suddenly extremely sensitive to the smell of drywall. I told the doctor I thought I had been released from the hospital prematurely. I was feeling very ill and I felt I needed to be readmitted.

His answer nearly floored me.

"We are not going to use the hospital as a hotel room."

I called him often in the following five days to tell him about my worsening condition. He essentially blew me off. "Call me when you can't stand the pain anymore," he said.

I slept in a window seat Rich and I had built. It is roughly twelve feet long and the width of a twin bed. We used two twin bed mattresses as cushions for it, placing them head to toe. The windows overlooked the woods on our property, the branches of the trees were draped in snow and shimmered in the moonlight. It felt surreal to me that everything outside seemed so pristine and peaceful while internally my body was engaged in violent turmoil. Since any unnecessary movement caused me a great deal of pain, I couldn't sleep in our queen bed with Rich. I slept on one of the twin mattresses and Rich slept on the other so he could be with me without disturbing me with his movements. He awoke at all hours of the night to take my temperature, give me medication, and help me to the bathroom. I could see the stress wearing on him.

I knew what kind of trouble I was in when my beloved "Monsters" (the collective name I've given my rough and tumble animals, two cats and two dogs) began treating me with kid gloves. Tempest, my oldest kitty, has never been an overtly affectionate cat. During those terrible five days of suffering, she curled up with me, molding her furry body against my fevered abdomen as if by osmosis she could will her vitality into me. She would not leave my side except occasionally to eat and visit her litter box. Camper, my golden canine of questionable breeding, kept a silent stony vigil at the side of my bed. Phoenix, an 85 pound mix between a Samoyed and "some big red dog" periodically crossed the room and pressed a cold, wet nose against my face and neck, as if to evaluate my condition. D'Artagnan, a small densely muscled cat whose tread presses the full weight of his body into each step approached me light as a feather, barely letting me know he was resting on my thigh. I didn't know he could do that. Each day they stayed with me, waiting, worrying and keeping watch as my condition deteriorated by the hour. There were times when the pain was so great and I just felt so sick I wondered if I would still be alive the next morning.

Finally, Rich called and informed my liver doctor I was going to the ER and he damned well needed to meet me there and figure out what was wrong. When I arrived I was given another CT scan. Apparently, the drain in my abdomen that they had removed before releasing me from the hospital had not actually quit draining, it had just been clogged up. For a week bile had been dumping directly into my abdominal cavity and I had developed an abscess. My liver doctors, the same doctors who had created this situation in the first place, had sent me home with an active infection and refused to listen to me when I complained of severe pain.

I was hospitalized again, for another sixteen days. From the time of the original surgery to the time I was finally released and able to function, I spent a total of five weeks in the hospital. For virtually all of that time I could not eat. What I was able to choke down remained in my stomach only seconds. I was not fed intravenously for fear of an infection setting in. The smell of ice was enough to make me vomit. When the last IV antibiotic was removed the nausea abated, my appetite returned, and I was able to eat again.

I feel I have to round out this experience with a note about how well I was treated at the hospital. The nurses were excellent and were so kind and compassionate. Just what nurses should be. The support staff was great. Even the nutritionist from Food Services visited my room frequently and tried to encourage me to eat. Believe me, I wanted to eat. I just couldn't hold anything down. She went so far as to assure me that if I could think of anything I might possibly be able to eat, she would go to the store, buy the ingredients and have it prepared for me. I was so fortunate to have such a team pulling for me. The doctors, with the notable the exception of the liver doctors, were excellent as well. You wouldn't believe how hard the doctors and residents worked to keep me alive.

Rich was wonderful. I've always said there is nothing worse than a bad marriage and nothing better than a good one. I have been blessed with an incredible husband. We spent our twentieth wedding anniversary in the hospital as well as Christmas. For the New Year, I was at home writhing in pain waiting for my doctors to take my condition seriously. My birthday was celebrated in the hospital with tubes in nearly every orifice as well as in my arms and abdomen.

Rich made it all bearable. On our twentieth anniversary, Rich helped me out of bed and said he wanted to take me for a walk. I was so weak by this time I barely had energy to make it to the bathroom but I agreed to try. He helped me with my robe and guided my IV pole as we shuffled slowly to a large, plate-glass window at the end of the hall. He took me in his arms and began dancing with me very slowly, dragging my IV pole around me as we turned. He sang a silly little song he made up in the first months of our marriage. "I love Danielle…." When the dance was over he kissed me and turned me towards the window. It overlooked a large parking lot. I could see our blue Honda Civic parked on the far side.

"This is our Window of Hope," he whispered in my ear as he supported me from behind. "One day soon we are going to be on the other side of this window looking in."

Rich tried to distract me by making my hospital stay fun and interesting. The only time he left my side was to run down to the cafeteria to eat or to move the Monsters from one boarding facility to another as our reservations expired, or to pick up a change of clothes. He slept in a chair beside my bed for the entire five weeks. I would awaken from a drugged slumber to finding him smiling down at me, a mischievous sparkle in his soft brown eyes.

"We're going on an adventure!"

He had prepared a wheelchair with sheets, blankets and a bottle of water to take with me. Also a pan and some tissues in case I became nauseous. Then we'd go tooling around the hospital. One day he took me to an upper floor where he had discovered a garden, right in the middle of the hospital! It had trees and benches, little bridges and stone paths. It was entirely surrounded by glass. I couldn't go into the garden as it was snowing inside but just to be able to look at something natural and beautiful was such a lift to my spirits.

Another time he surprised me with a room that housed live birds. Then he found a room with an aquarium recessed within its walls and filled with exotic fish. He took me to the children's ward to see the art on the walls, mobiles hanging from the ceilings and bronze statues of children playing. We visited rotating exhibits of local artists on the first floor.

Past the children's ward was a long sloping hall with a ramp. Rich would run, pushing me in my wheelchair as fast as he could. Then he'd release the handles, sending me soaring down the hall, giggling like a child. He sprinted to catch up with me before I crashed into a wall. He began taking me into private areas to visit doctors and technicians we had come to regard as friends. As I began to recover, he made me push my own wheelchair, walking behind it holding onto the handles for support. We had a variety of routes we would travel every day. Always, always, we made our pilgrimage to the Window of Hope.

Finally, I was discharged and it seemed that I was on my way to a full recovery. I looked up at the Window of Hope from within my car in the parking lot. I acknowledged its part in my recovery and believed I would never see it again.

The universe, however, had other plans.

I began to have crushing, acute pain in my upper right quadrant. It would come on suddenly, out of the blue. I could be having a conversation with Rich at a restaurant and suddenly I was doubled over in pain. The pain lasted about 30 seconds and then disappeared completely, as if nothing had ever happened. During the incident, I thought I was about to die. It was as if I were having a heart attack in my side, under my right rib cage. These episodes increased from once or twice a month to every week and increased in intensity and duration each time. The liver surgeon said that it wasn't my liver, that he believed it was something intestinal.

Five or six weeks after leaving the hospital I was on the phone with my brother, Jim. We like to talk every Saturday. I was feeling fine at the beginning of the conversation but somewhere during our usual one hour talk I began feeling a little ill.

"I believe I'm experiencing flu-like symptoms," I said, meaning to be funny.

Jim and I ended our conversation and within fifteen minutes my temperature spiked to 104.7°F. I had a searing pain in my spine. Rich rushed me to the emergency room. I told the emergency room physician about my liver issues and asked him to call my liver doctor. He ignored my request and insisted I had the flu, even though the flu test came back negative. He sent me home with a prescription for Tamiflu. In a few days, I began to recover so I thought the ER doc must have been correct. It happened again five weeks later, though. This time my fever spiked to 104.9°F. Thus began a spiral of liver and bile duct infections that recurred like clockwork every five weeks resulting in high fevers and trips to the emergency room. Each time the liver surgeon repeated what became his mantra, "It's not your liver, it's not your liver." He'd shake his head, "I don't know what it is, I'm stumped." You'd think he would make an effort to become un-stumped but that thought obviously did not occur to him.

My blood became septic and my condition was again life-threatening. I was hospitalized numerous times that first year ranging from a few days to several weeks. It was discovered by other physicians and surgeons that I have recurrent cholangitis, an infection of the liver and bile duct caused, they thought, from the normal buildup of bacteria in the intestines. My new artificial bile duct does not have a valve, as did my original bile duct, to prevent bacteria from migrating up the intestines and infecting my liver. It is also possible I had an obstruction of scar tissue in the new bile duct, where it was attached, which prevented adequate bile flow, as well as causing bile to accumulate around my liver. This caused recurrent and potentially deadly infections. My only option was to take preventive antibiotics, possibly for life. I realized the long-term ramifications of this when my infectious disease doctor compared my treatment to that of an AIDS patient.

I developed an incisional hernia at the site of the two surgeries. The liver surgeon recited a new mantra for this condition, "It's not a hernia, it's not a hernia." He refused to acknowledge it until it became so large it appeared as though I had a seven month pregnancy on my right side, just below my rib cage. Charlie, my plastic surgeon friend, performed the surgery to repair it. He later told me that the tissue was so shredded that he had to reach way underneath my ribcage to find enough healthy tissue that would accept the attachment of a bio-mesh. To this day, nearly six years later, I still have constant pain in this area.

After a year of chronic cholangitis I was sent to a prestigious teaching hospital to see a bile duct specialist. Normally, a scope would be placed down the esophagus to look at the bile duct. Since my anatomy had been changed, that was no longer possible. The bile duct specialist ordered an outpatient procedure, a PTC, a Percutaneous Trans-hepatic Cholangiogram. It is a procedure in which a needle is inserted through skin (percutaneous) through the liver (trans-hepatic) and dye is injected directly into the bile duct. Then a scan (cholangiogram) is done to see if the bile duct is blocked. Apparently, the intern performing the procedure made a mistake and rather than locating the bile duct, she either nicked the portal vein or dug the needle into another vein in the liver, believing it to be the bile duct, thereby causing a massive bleed which she then failed to recognize. She never was able to locate the bile duct and the procedure was aborted.

In the recovery room, I got out of bed to go to the bathroom and began to have horrific referred pain in my right shoulder. It was so severe it took three injections of an extremely potent narcotic, dilaudid, just to stop me from screaming. The bleed wasn't discovered until the next day. I don't remember much of the following week. I had more blood transfusions and ended up with another infection in my liver. I remember waking up in a hospital room on a cooling blanket. I was covered only by my hospital gown. *I must have a high fever,* I thought before losing consciousness again.

Rich and I spent another wedding anniversary, our twenty-first, as well as Christmas in the hospital. I now had a hematoma in my liver the size of a grapefruit that would take a year to resolve. The teaching hospital sent me home with some vague instructions as to follow up care. While Rich was out of the room, I remember a woman from the hospital talking to me, her face inches from my own. I couldn't focus on what she was saying. I just remember how huge her eyes seemed as she mouthed instructions at me. I remember thinking at the time, *Doesn't she know how drugged I am?*

At home I began having fevers again and problems breathing. I had to sleep sitting up because I couldn't breath when I laid down. My stomach started bloating as well. It would swell painfully to the point that I thought it might rupture. It would be relieved by moments of deep, foul, uncontrollable belching. Then it would begin to swell again. Finally, I began violent vomiting that usually lasted an hour. I had intermittent bouts of high fevers and sweats. Rich woke me up one morning and said, "We have to get you to a hospital, Danielle. Your breathing is dangerously shallow." I was dripping in sweat and insisted on taking a bath before we left. Rich said I was confused and incoherent.

I was admitted to the hospital. My veins had been so traumatized by all the procedures at the teaching hospital that it was difficult to even draw blood. I had to have blood drawn from my feet, which was a whole new kind of pain. I had to have a type of ultrasound to even find a vein for an IV. I was told I had plural effusion, which is when fluid collects between the two linings of the lung. A small amount of fluid in the pleural cavity lubricates the membranes covering the lungs and the ribs allowing them to rub together as breathing expands and contracts the lungs.

My pulmonologist said that we don't know whether the injury to my pleural cavity was caused by a sympathetic reaction to the liver injury during the PTC or whether the intern who performed the procedure punctured the pleural wall. Whatever the cause, 1.365 liters of bloody fluid had to be drained from my pleural space in yet another painful procedure. My breathing improved but I was still in a significant amount of pain. I was sent home within a few days with pain medications and antibiotics and was told to follow up with my primary care physician.

Within a week I was hospitalized again with pleural effusion. This time 1.6 liters of fluid were extracted from around my lungs. The fluid continued to replenish so a drain was placed in my pleural cavity. I was told if we could not get the fluid under control we might have to coat my pleural cavity with talc, involving another painful procedure as well as adding foreign material to my already compromised system. My answer to that was a resounding, "NO!"

The days dragged on. I developed high fevers and pneumonia. My body was so exhausted I didn't think I could continue. I didn't want to continue. I could feel the vitality ebbing from me. I just wanted to let go and end all of this medical intervention that had become torture to me. By the concern in the faces of the doctors and nurses who cared for me, I knew I was on death's door. I had been there before but this time I knew it and I no longer had the will to resist. I spoke to my brother Jim over the phone and made him promise he would be there for Rich after I was gone. I knew how much I was asking of him but I couldn't bear the thought of leaving Rich alone. My brother promised he would do as I asked. Afterwards, I talked to Rich.

"I'm ready to go," I said. "I don't want to leave you but I don't want to live like this."

His answer surprised me. "What if I'm not ready for you to go?" He fixed his dark eyes on mine. Usually so gentle, they were now challenging. I noted how tired he looked, the accumulated stress of the past year had taken its toll. His eyes filled with tears and his voice cracked. "If you are not going to fight for yourself, then do it for me!"

Crap! Was he really going to make me live? I didn't see that one coming. He was playing the guilt card big time but I could see he meant it. I promised to try.

It's amazing the role intention plays in our recovery. The instant I made Rich that promise, my health started to turn around. In the ensuing weeks, the drain was removed, my lungs healed and I was sent home. I still have pain whenever I breathe, but at least I'm still breathing.

Over the following months my strength slowly returned, although never to previous levels. It took me about a year to regain my posture. For the longest time I walked stooped over, like a little old lady. I remember going grocery shopping with my friend, author Nora Percival, who was 94 at the time. I had to sit on a bench while Nora did my shopping for me.

Because of the liver hematoma and the hernia operation, I was told not to lift anything heavy for a year or do any exercise beyond walking. The hematoma was finally resorbed by my liver. Rich and I began to increase our physical activity.

I was on long-term antibiotics, blood pressure medication and medication for acid reflux. My gut continued to give me a lot of problems and this continued to worsen. It reached a point where my stomach would swell with gas to the point I thought it would just explode. I would go into bouts of noxious belching; deep, loud, involuntary belches, the kind that would be the envy of any preteen boy. I smelled like a toilet and didn't want to leave the house.

It reached a point where I could expect at least twice a week to have thirteen hours of pain followed by an hour of projectile vomiting. What I was regurgitating was everything that I had eaten since the last episode. Nothing was passing through. It was just sitting in my stomach becoming a concentrated, fetid mush of bile, stomach acid, and old food. No wonder I smelled like a toilet.

The doctors thought I might either have a partial small bowel obstruction or just poor gut motility. After abdominal surgery, the gut doesn't want to work the way it used to. A doctor at the teaching hospital explained it is like a long balloon. Normally, the gut is squeezed on one end and the material inside is pushed out the other end. What often happens after abdominal surgery is the gut becomes confused and both ends are being squeezed simultaneously. The material in the gut has nowhere to go, the contents become concentrated, gas builds up and the result is painful bloating. Another possibility is that the scar tissue that forms after abdominal surgery acts like fingers wrapping around and twisting the intestines, much like a twisting a water hose, until nothing can pass through. I had had three abdominal surgeries in the same spot and my life had become painful and unpleasant. Again I thought, *If this is going to be my life, I don't want it.*

While in the midst of dealing with gastric pain, I learned I had another cancer; a bump on my cheek turned out to be a basal cell carcinoma. An outpatient surgery was performed to remove it, leaving a scar on my cheek that resembled two sides of a triangle about an inch long on each side. I was beginning to feel like the protagonist in Oscar Wilde's novel, "The Picture of Dorian Gray." *Was this never going to end?*

Then I received a call from our friend that would change my life. Tess had just completed a workshop on healthy eating at a well-known health-food grocery store chain. Many of the leading proponents of plant-based nutrition were in attendance. Tess and I have long shared an interest in nutrition. I introduced her to raw foods and green smoothies which she and her husband, Jim, embraced with enthusiasm. Tess introduced me to a book by T. Colin Campbell called *The China Study*. It is about the largest cohort study ever done on nutrition and the effects of animal protein on the human body. It reads like a mystery novel.

Dr. T. Colin Campbell is a Jacob Gould Schurman Professor Emeritus of Nutritional Biochemistry at Cornell University. He grew up on a dairy farm and was raised to believe that animal protein is a necessary nutrient. He was the first of his family to graduate college and received his PhD from Cornell University. He worked at MIT for two and a half years, with two of the most toxic chemicals ever discovered, dioxin and aflatoxin. Later he went to work for Virginia Tech where he provided technical assistance for a project investigating the high rates of liver cancer in Filipino children. This is where the story gets interesting! It was believed these children were not getting enough protein. The project's studies revealed, however, that the children getting the most animal protein in their diet were most likely to get liver cancer! These were not the poor children; these were the children of the wealthy class, who had adopted largely a western diet.[1-1]

Dr. Campbell subsequently read a study by researchers from India performed on rats. They were all fed the deadly carcinogen, aflatoxin. One group of rats was fed 20 percent protein and one group was fed five percent protein. *ALL* of the rats who received 20 percent protein, the amount we typically consume in the US, got cancer. *NONE* of the rats who received five percent protein got cancer. Was this really possible? Campbell duplicated the study and came up with the same results. The correlation between protein and cancer was clear! [1-2]

And not all types protein, only animal protein. The milk protein Casein, he discovered, promotes cancer cell growth. In further rat studies, Campbell was able to literally turn cancer on, off, and on again simply by adjusting the amount of casein he fed to the rats.[1-3] Turning cancer off with diet? I was blown away! Does this mean that I didn't have to have melanoma? Or carcinoma? Does this mean if I stop eating animal protein my chances of recurrence are significantly reduced? Dr. Campbell definitely piqued my curiosity.

This was the tip of the iceberg. Campbell has devoted his life to understanding the correlation between disease and the consumption of animal products. His conclusion in a nutshell is this:

"...people who ate the most animal-based foods got the most chronic diseases. Even relatively small intakes of animal-based food were associated with adverse side effects. People who ate the most plant-based foods were the healthiest and tended to avoid chronic disease."[1-4]

Immediately after reading *The China Study*, Rich and I went through our pantry and fridge got rid of every animal product in our house. Cold-turkey, (pun intended) we adopted a whole foods plant-based diet. I began to see an immediate difference in my health. From day one, I never had another intestinal episode while adhering to this diet! (However, I did go through a couple of weeks of flu-like symptoms as my body was purged of toxins accumulated over a lifetime of poor dietary choices.)

Within three weeks I was off blood pressure medication I had been taking for twelve years. I no longer had gastric reflux. I could eat with impunity foods I could not tolerate before (peppers, onion, garlic and tomatoes). I began to effortlessly lose weight.

All my lab results, which initially indicated cardiovascular disease and poor health, became perfect. My cholesterol and blood pressure were restored to a healthy low. My energy level soared.

The amazing results I was achieving spurred me to explore plant-based nutrition further. I completed Cornell University's certification program in plant-based nutrition, in conjunction with the T. Colin Campbell Foundation, and became a certified wellness coach through Wellness Inventory. The education I received deepened my understanding immeasurably as well as strengthened my commitment to a whole foods plant-based lifestyle.

Through Cornell's program I became familiar with the work some of the pioneers in plant-based nutrition, Doctors Caldwell Esselstyn and John McDougall, and relative newcomers, Dr. Neal Barnard, who is President of Physicians Committee For Responsible Medicine, and Dr. Michael Gregor who has created a blog, www.nutritionfacts.org, which is a valuable resource for information about diet and disease. They've all written important books on restoring various aspects of health by means of a plant-based diet. And there are many more, too many to discuss to within the confines of this book.

Roughly, two and a half years after going plant-based, the prophylactic antibiotics I had been taking for years to keep the bacteria in my gut at bay was reduced to only two pills per week. Finally, my infectious disease doctor and I agreed to try eliminating them altogether. After five weeks and no infection, I thought I was home free. Unfortunately, I wasn't.

It took about three months for another infection to take hold. I was hospitalized again. Resistance to antibiotics was becoming a concern. Over the past few years we tried several different antibiotics and they each came with side effects. One type, Levofloxacin, caused extreme pain in my legs. This eliminated all antibiotics within that category. We tried Amoxicillin/Potassium Clavulanate. This caused me to have extreme intestinal pain. I tolerated Sulfamethoxazole/

Trimethoprim fairly well for several years. After my last infection, though, my dosage had to be increased from one pill, twice a week, to twice daily. I knew if I was developing a resistance to the only antibiotic I could tolerate, I was heading down a dangerous road.

When the infection was under control, my original gastroenterologist, the same excellent physician who initially discovered my severed bile duct, suggested I go to Orlando, Florida to have a new procedure called a double-balloon enteroscopy. A new MRCP (a type of Magnetic Resonance Imaging) showed that the area where the artificial bile duct attaches had formed scar tissue that has been blocking my artificial bile duct and preventing bile from passing through. This backed up bile is what was causing the liver infections. The idea was to put a temporary stent in my bile duct and remove it in a couple of months. We hoped it would stretch out my bile duct and permanently correct the flow of bile from my liver.

Unfortunately, the procedure had to be aborted. There was too much debris in my bile duct for the gastroenterologist in Florida to have an unobstructed view. Proceeding without being able to see what was going on in there was not an option.

The next morning, I was scheduled for another PTC, the same surgical procedure that nearly killed me four years earlier. The thought of going through that again terrified me.

This time the operation was successful. The interventional radiologists at Florida Hospital were excellent. They inserted a tube through my liver and down my bile duct. For weeks I was incapacitated and in pain. In a month, just as I was beginning to feel normal again, they replaced it with a larger tube. This time the procedure wasn't nearly as painful. The PTC allowed increasingly larger tubes, and finally a balloon, to be inserted into my bile duct, which stretched out the scar tissue allowing the bile to pass unimpeded. Ten days after the final tube was removed I was able to discontinue the antibiotics! I've been antibiotic-free nine months at the time of this book's publication, and so far, so good. I'm told that 90 percent of the time, this procedure is a permanent fix. We are keeping our fingers crossed.

Rich and I have been enjoying a plant-based lifestyle for three and a half years as of October, 2014. To date I've lost a total of 65 pounds. It has come off naturally and effortlessly and I've eaten as much as I've wanted.

I haven't been this thin since I married a lovely Italian-American man 26 years ago and began cooking his family's pasta recipes made with fatty ground pork, ground beef, bricks of cheeses, creamy sauces and gallons of olive oil. Not to mention the fried Southern food I grew up with, the rich fare of neighboring New Orleans, as well as other decadent cuisines from around the world I discovered during our years of travel.

Even though I can still stand to lose a few pounds, no one looks at me as a fat woman anymore. When people discover I'm writing a cookbook, several have commented, "You've never been heavy, have you?" *Yeah, right.*

As I mentioned before, I thought I was stuck with this genetic inheritance. Now I know nothing could be further from the truth. We are what we eat. If you eat foods that are fresh and alive, you feel fresh and alive. If you eat foods that are dead and lacking vitality, guess what? That's how you will feel. If you eat foods laden with fat, you may as well bypass the eating process altogether and spread it directly on your thighs because that is where it will remain. Worse, is where it remains invisible to the naked eye, in your arteries.

This book isn't about weight loss, though that is a natural side-effect of eating a whole foods plant-based diet. It's about feeling well, being energetic, and enjoying your life in this body with which you've been entrusted. If you let your body down, if you don't give it what it needs to flourish and thrive, your time on this earth will be diminished in both quality and quantity. Believe me, I've learned this the hard way.

A year after becoming plant-based, one of my doctors was shocked to see how well I looked. She commented on how great my skin looks and how bright my eyes are. She said I glowed with health. The last time she had seen me I had one foot in the grave. I told her about removing animal products from my diet and transitioning to a plant-based lifestyle. She asked me if I could teach her patients to do the same.

The trouble is, people have no idea where to start. They don't realize how delicious vegetarian food can be. It isn't all about tofu and wheatgrass. I eat very little tofu and I never eat wheatgrass. I haven't missed animal products at all. Neither has Rich. We've been introduced to a new world of fresh, clean flavors. I love teasing out wonderful combinations of flavors from a handful of raw ingredients and a few spices.

Discovering wellness through healthy eating has made the difference for me in whether I live my life in pain and discomfort or with energy and vitality. I believe it can be helpful to you as well. It certainly can do no harm.

No diet is going to repair my altered anatomy. I'll have to live with that the rest of my life. But I am daring to believe my bile duct issues are behind me and I never have to take antibiotics again just to stay alive. Time will tell.

I have to admit, I am also very concerned about all the radiation exposure to my vulnerable organs. I had thirteen CT scans at one hospital and at least two at another. Each CT scan is the equivalent of a thousand x-rays, not to mention the actual x-rays, nuclear stress tests and who knows what else I've been exposed to over the years. I sometimes think it will be a miracle if I don't end up with another cancer. Yet, I'm hopeful. One of the amazing things about the simple act of supporting your system with whole foods (fruits, vegetables, grains and legumes) is that much of the damage to our bodies by environmental toxins, and even by radiation, can be mitigated by a healthy diet. I am betting my life on it. I have to, I have no other option. And if you think about it, none of us do!

I am determined to give my body the nutritional support it needs to keep me functioning at the highest level possible. The rest is in the hands of forces outside my control. For now, it is enough to feel well again, to be able to fully live my life, plan for an amazing future with the man I love, and appreciate every day of my life for as long as it lasts.

How much better can it get than that?

# 2

WHAT'S IN OUR FOOD?

There is nothing you can get from animal products that you can't better get from plants. — T. Colin Campbell

There is little argument in the scientific community that eating whole plant foods is the healthiest fuel for humans. So anything you add to a plant-based diet (that is, a diet rich in fruits, grains, legumes, tubers, nuts, seeds and green leafy vegetables) will not improve your health and may very well harm it. Before making a food choice it is important to eat consciously and really think about what you are putting into your body. That choice can make a difference in whether you are sick or well; whether you live a long and vibrant life, or whether you wither away in years of steady decline with pain and suffering as your companions.

When deciding what I want to eat, there are two questions I have asked myself so many times that now my brain summons them forth without a conscious thought. 1-Is this food good for me? 2-Does it taste good? These have become my mantras when it comes to satisfying both my body's need for nutrition and my mind's need for pleasure.

Our SAD Diet

Whether you realize it or not, if you are eating the Standard American Diet (aptly referred to as SAD) you are initiating disease processes in your body. SAD has created a culture of Americans who are sick and fat and getting sicker and fatter by the minute. We now know that nearly every child in North America over the age of three years old is already exhibiting signs of coronary artery disease.[1] Incidents of diabetes in children is increasing at an alarming rate. Obesity in today's youth is epidemic.

We don't eat real food anymore. We eat stuff that looks like food, that we have been taught to think of as food, yet has little or no nutritive value. It is amazing we have lasted this long. Our foods have been degraded by over-processing and by the inclusion of toxic chemicals in the form of preservatives, additives, pesticides and food coloring. We are ingesting unnecessary hormones, antibiotics, antidepressants and other medicines that are fed to livestock and poultry in order to make them grow larger and faster, and survive cramped, diseased and stressful environments. We are being biologically attacked by genetically modified foods created by companies who don't care that their products are turning our guts into pesticide factories and our children into guinea pigs as long as their pockets continue to bulge. The Standard American Diet contributes to problems with circulation, heart disease, MS and other autoimmune diseases, cancer and diabetes, to name only a few. Virtually every organ in our bodies is affected.

It is vital to look at what we are putting into our bodies. The question we have to ask ourselves when we sit down to eat is, is this food helping me or hurting me? Why eat it if it doesn't serve you? *But it tastes so good!* Is that a good enough reason to put your health at risk? Is it worth getting sick over? Is it worth your vitality, your future, your life?

The good news is it is never too late to make a positive change. It doesn't matter how old you are. When you begin a plant-based diet you are moving from a diet that is making you sicker to a diet that is making you better. Results are stunningly rapid.

While shopping at one of the big chain warehouse grocery stores, I met a couple in their sixties, (I'll call them Jack and Jill.) Jack was seated at a blood pressure machine and I noticed Jill was reading a book I had just completed, concerning plant-based nutrition. I was in the midst of the Cornell program on plant-based nutrition at the time. We became involved in a conversation about the health benefits of a plant-base diet. Jill said she was on high-cholesterol medication and her husband was as well. Jack was also on five blood pressure medications. They were both quite overweight.

I talked to them about some of the science I was learning and discussed some of the research findings. I also shared with them some of my own wellness journey. My excitement was contagious. They were intrigued and ready for a change. Together, we decided to give this diet a try. We had all reached a stage in our lives that we knew if we didn't make some significant changes in our lifestyles our futures were destined to become a downward spiral of sickness, incapacity and, potentially, early death. We wanted to see if we could make a difference in our health after five weeks of a wholehearted effort to adhere strictly to a healthy, vegan lifestyle. I was ahead of the game since I had been practicing a plant-based diet for several weeks and I had already seen amazing results.

They returned the fish and the milk they had in their cart back to the refrigerator sections of the store where they had found them. (Weeks later, I laughed when Jack said to his wife, "I'll never forget the day Danielle took away my fish.")

We agreed we would to eat as much food as we wanted. Quantity was not an issue, quality was. We would not eat any animal products, no oil and very little salt. We would eat organic products and fresh produce whenever possible, rather than canned, packaged or frozen.

We agreed to meet at a large health food store in a neighboring town the next morning. I introduced them to grains and beans they had never heard of. Together, we read labels and shopped for healthy items, mostly from the organic produce section. We found organic grains and beans in the bulk section. We replaced milk with almond milk. I introduced them to marvelous whole grain breads. Jill told me she couldn't believe Jack, a meat and potatoes man, would willingly eat this kind of food. Yet, he did. They both followed the program faithfully.

"This is the easiest diet I've ever been on," Jill reported. "You don't count calories. You know what you can eat and what you can't eat. It tastes good. What could be easier!" She was so pleased when she began to shed pounds.

Over the next five weeks, they came to my house frequently and I taught them how to cook delicious plant-based meals. We cooked pizzas, grain dishes, all kinds of Mexican food, sandwiches, curries, bean dishes and gumbos. I fed them delicious desserts and sent them home with leftovers to see them through the coming week. We also spoke during the week to offer additional support to one another. Jack said the only thing he really missed was his cornbread. I emailed him the vegan cornbread recipe I had just created and Jack was in hog heaven!

We kept a daily diary of everything we ate, weighed once a week and checked our blood pressures each day. I approached the diet from a culinary perspective. I do not pretend to be a nutritionist, nor do I have any medical training beyond first aid. However, I am a creative cook and know how to turn the foods we have learned we should eat into tasty meals we could all enjoy.

I insisted that Jack visit his doctor to have his medications re-evaluated. His blood pressure was dropping and I was concerned it would become too low. I was adamant that his doctor be involved. Jack's doctor reduced his medication after three weeks on this diet and at the end of five weeks he took him off all his blood pressure medications completely. Both Jill and Jack were able to discontinue cholesterol medication. All they had to do was to show their doctors the records they were keeping of their food intake, their daily blood pressure readings and their weight. A cholesterol test told the rest of the story. Jack could not believe he no longer had to take pills every day.

Both of them lost weight. Jack's big belly disappeared before my eyes. Neither one of them wanted to tell me their starting weights but the loss was obvious. Jill didn't lose as much, nor as quickly as Jack, but she did report consistent weight loss. She also said the swelling in her ankles she had been experiencing at night completely went away. I lost ten pounds during this period. What a difference five weeks can make!

What Are GMOs? Why Should I Avoid Them?

The creation of GMOs, or genetically modified organisms, is not as many believe simply the practice of breeding strong genetic traits into foods, such as breeding a red tomato with a yellow tomato to create a third tomato of a different color. Nor is it the practice of breeding similar species together to create a third, like breeding a tangerine and a grapefruit to create an orange. What scientists involved in genetic engineering are doing is taking material from an unrelated species and inserting them into the genetic material of plants and animals. For example, inserting salmon genes into tomatoes may make them more tolerant of cold temperatures. This kind of gene manipulation cannot occur in nature.

The health and environmental consequences of this kind of altering of natural genetic expression over the past eighteen years is only now becoming known, as this research has been carefully guarded by the biotech industry and there has been little governmental testing or oversight. Corn, soybeans, canola (also known as rapeseed), sugar beets, alfalfa, and some yellow squash and zucchini are the largest genetically modified crops in the US. Genetically modified salmon is nearing a reality.

GMOs are pervasive in our food supply, present in virtually every processed food on our grocery store shelves. Vermont is the first state in the Union to require the labeling of GMO foods. Vermont is gearing up for a lawsuit over this issue with Monsanto, the leading producer of GMO seed and manufacturer of Roundup, the herbicide glyphosate.

Genetically Modified Foods: Are they safe?

The American Academy of Environmental Medicine (AAEM) doesn't think so. The Academy reported that, "Several animal studies indicate serious health risks associated with GM food," including infertility, immune problems, accelerated aging, faulty insulin regulation, and changes in major organs and the gastrointestinal system. The AAEM asked physicians to advise patients to avoid GM foods.[2]

FDA scientists have adamantly warned that there should be further testing on genetically modified organisms before allowing them into our food supply. Yet, there is little regulatory control. President Obama, who promised fervently to label GMOs in his first presidential campaign, appointed Monsanto's former lawyer and vice president as advisor to the FDA with the obverse title of Food Safety Czar.

Glyphosate, the key ingredient in Monsanto's weedkiller Roundup, is patented as a chelator, herbicide and a powerful antibiotic. Some crops have been genetically modified to resist Roundup, called Roundup-ready crops. Theoretically, when

Roundup is sprayed on a crop, the weeds are killed but the plant is unharmed. Unfortunately, what has arisen from this practice is a new breed of super weeds which have become resistant to Roundup. Another problem is the toxicity of glyphosate to plants and to humans. Glyphosate is now thought to be one of the most toxic chemicals ever created, many times more toxic than DDT. Kidney failure in sugar cane plantation workers of South America and rice farmers in Sri Lanka have been associated with the herbicide, Roundup.[3] Glyphosate is thought to contribute to the rise in gluten intolerance, celiac disease, kidney disease, miscarriage, infertility and a host of other illnesses.[4]

In March of this year, Sri Lanka was the first country to ban the sale and use of Round-up because of its suspected link to kidney cancer, resulting in the deaths of 20,000 Shri Lankan rice paddy farmers from the North Central Province, and spreading to other farm communities.[5]

Unfortunately, the ban was lifted two months later. Sri Lankan's Agriculture Department "…say that a glyphosate ban will affect the tea plantations and also the paddy cultivation drastically as it is the only effective weedicide for paddy and other commercial crops like, tea, coconut and rubber." and claim that "a European glyphosate task force also has concluded that there is no true link to the kidney disease."[6]

GM Watch, an independent watchdog group that monitors and reports on news pertaining to genetically modified foods, responded to this claim, "for the "European glyphosate task force" mentioned in the article, which has 'concluded that there is no true link' between glyphosate herbicide and chronic kidney disease, let's hope the Sri Lankan government recognises that this "task force" is entirely made up of the pesticide companies that make and sell glyphosate herbicide!"[7]

The costs of using GMO seeds on struggling economies in term of human suffering, land viability and economic impact must also be considered.

Over 250,000 Indian farmers who have planted GMO seeds have taken their own lives, creating what is now known as the Suicide Belt in India. Seduced by promises of astounding yields, these farmers borrowed against their lands and planted genetically modified seeds at as much as a thousand times the cost of conventional seeds. When the yields did not occur as promised, these indebted farmers were faced with losing their lands, often the only means of supporting their families. Suicides resulting from failed GMO crops in India have reached as many as 1,000 per month. GMO seeds have to be purchased annually, as these seeds do not replicate. (Andrew Malone, UK, Daily Mail, visited the region and interviewed farmers and their families).[8]

In 1969, MIT, Massachusetts Institute of Technology, began a collaboration between faculty and students, which has since grown into an alliance of over 400,000 citizens and scientists working together to "combine technical analysis and effective advocacy to create innovative, practical solutions for a healthy, safe, and sustainable future." The conclusions and efforts of UCS, Union of Concerned Scientists, are based on scientific evidence, rather than political or corporate considerations.[9]

Does UCS Have a Position On GE?

Yes. We see that the technology [genetic engineering] has potential benefits, but we are critics of its commercial application and regulation to date. GE has proved valuable in some areas (as in the contained use of engineered bacteria in pharmaceutical development), and some GE applications could turn out to play a useful role in food production.

However, its applications in agriculture so far have fallen short of expectations, and in some cases have caused serious problems. Rather than supporting a more sustainable agriculture and food system with broad societal benefits, the technology has been employed in ways that reinforce problematic industrial approaches to agriculture. Policy decisions about the use of GE have too often been driven by biotech industry PR campaigns, rather than by what science tells us about the most cost-effective ways to produce abundant food and preserve the health of our farmland[10].

Dr. Don Huber, professor emeritus of plant pathology at Perdue University, has spent 50 years researching the epidemiology and control of soil born plant pathogens. In a recent interview with Carol Grievé, host of *Food Integrity Now*, he asserts, "When we disrupt the integrity of the genetic code, as we do with genetic engineering, there are literally thousands of changes that occur because we upset the normal regulatory mechanism of gene function."

Dr. Huber speaks out against genetic engineering and the use of glyphosate:

"Samsel and Seneff, in their second paper, concluded that glyphosate is probably the most toxic chemical we have ever had because of its effect on nutrition and the entire biome we rely on for survival. …We've pretty much sacrificed an entire generation of children. The longer we go on, the longer the damage is going to accumulate. So, if you look at the predictions for autism, one of two children being autistic in 2025, and you look at what has happened over the last eighteen years of genetic engineering, and you see how all of those major modern diseases are reaching epidemic proportions now, and all of them have an epidemiological track or curve that only fits genetic engineering and glyphosate.

....and without that safety testing, we are playing Russian Roulette. We are playing with the health of our children and future generations, as long as we remain in this massive experiment we call genetic engineering, without establishing research to determine safety and proper utilization."[11, 12]

How does one avoid GMOs? Since these products do not have to be labeled, our only recourse is to buy only organic or products that are labeled *Certified Non-GMO*. When you shop for produce, there is usually a little sticker on each item. If the sticker begins with the number 9 and has four or five numerals, it indicates that the produce was organically grown. If it begins with a 4, it was conventionally grown and likely contains pesticide residues and/or is genetically modified. (You usually don't have to bother looking for the sticker; grocers selling produce proudly display signs indicating their organic selections. But if there is a question about a particular item, this sticker will come in handy.) This, at least for now, assures that there were no harmful chemicals used in its production, and that the item in question has not been genetically modified. Pressure is being exerted to reduce the integrity of organic produce. Keep an eye on this issue to stay abreast of attempts to lessen organic standards.

You can help to eliminate genetically modified organisms in your food supply by voting with your wallet. If we as a society refuse to purchase genetically engineered products and insist on having the right to know what is in our food and the food of our children, GMOs will disappear from the shelves of our markets very quickly. This strategy worked very well in Europe. Every time you make a purchase, you are making a decision as to the kind world you want to inhabit.

While learning about GMOs and pesticides in our food supply may be overwhelming and seem like I'm trying to scare you into changing your diet, that is the furthest thing from my mind. I feel it is necessary to include this information to give you a more complete picture of what is actually in today's foods. We often think if we just eat like our grandparents ate, we'll live as they did to a ripe old age. The unfortunate reality is that we no longer share the same food supply as our ancestors. It has been changed, possibly irreversibly, and it is vitally important we understand what we are consuming and make informed choices, for our sakes and the sake of our next generation. The take away message here is that limiting conventionally grown produce in favor of organic, and reducing intake of animal protein, will go a long way in keeping your family safe.

Environmental Working Group's 2014 Dirty Dozen™ List

The Environmental Working Group (EWG) is an organization devoted to the protection of consumers against chemicals in products and environmental practices which may cause them harm. According to EWG, The Environmental Protection Agency (EPA) currently allows 82,000 chemicals on the market without proper safety testing. By providing consumers with guidelines to follow in choosing safe produce, cleaning products, cosmetics, etc., The Environmental Working Group helps us to take matters into our own hands to ensure we are not ignorantly exposing ourselves and our vulnerable children to harmful chemicals in our food, our drinking water, and in products we use every day.

The EWG puts out an annual list of commonly consumed produce with both the highest levels of pesticide residue and the lowest levels of pesticide residue. This enables us to make decisions as to what we choose to eat, since we are not informed about the level of toxicity of these pesticides nor the potential harm they may cause. If an item falls in the more toxic range, you may want to consider buying this product only if it is organically grown. If it falls in the least toxic range, you may feel comfortable buying it conventionally grown. EWG also has a guide for pesticide residues of 51 commonly available fruits and vegetables, as well as a guide for avoiding GMOs, which you can find on their website, www.ewg.org. Be sure to check their site for annual updates to pesticide toxicity.

The worst offenders in pesticide residues for 2014, according to EWG, are:

1. Apples (99 percent tested positive for at least 1 pesticide)
2. Strawberries (each testing positive for 13 pesticides)
3. Grapes (each single grape tested positive for 15 pesticides)
4. Celery (each testing positive for 13 pesticides)
5. Peaches
6. Spinach
7. Sweet Bell Peppers
8. Nectarines - Imported (every sample tested positive for at least 1 pesticide)
9. Cucumbers
10. Cherry Tomatoes (each testing positive for 13 pesticides)
11. Snap Peas - Imported (each testing positive for 13 pesticides)
12. Potatoes (The average potato has more pesticides per weight than any other food.)

The Dirty Dozen Plus™

Collards, Kale and Hot Red Peppers!!! There are a few produce items that are so toxic they fall into a category all their own. The Environmental Working Group contends that, while collards, kale, and hot red peppers do not meet the traditional ranking criteria for the Dirty Dozen™ list, they are often contaminated with pesticides toxic to the human nervous system and should be bought organic.[13]

There is a wealth of information and guidance on the pages of the EWG website. I encourage you to check it out and learn what you can do to protect your loved ones from chemical toxins and genetically modified organisms in our food supply.

Facts About Fat

Before my illness I would use gallons of olive oil every year in preparing food. I actually thought I was doing something healthy for my family. I even popped popcorn in olive oil rather than butter. Why not? Isn't olive oil "the good fat" touted by the purveyors of the Mediterranean diet? When I was taking Cornell University's program on plant-based nutrition I learned facts that totally altered my view on processed fats of any kind.

First of all there are our endothelial cells, a single cell layer that lines the interior surface of all the body's blood vessels. This layer is called the endothelium. One of the myriad functions of the endothelium is to emit a gas called nitric oxide. This gas signals the blood vessels to relax, causing them to open more fully and allow more blood to circulate through them.

This process is extremely important to our cardiovascular health. Why is this important to know? Cardiologist Dr. Robert

Vogel of the University of Maryland performed some experiments which demonstrated that a meal that includes saturated fat damages the endothelial cells and impairs their ability to produce nitric oxide. For five minutes he restricted the blood flow to the brachial arteries of ten students with a blood pressure cuff. Then he used an ultrasound to measure the rate of blood flow when the blood pressure cuff was released. The test has since become known as the Brachial Artery Tourniquet Test (BART). After this he took the students to a fast food restaurant where five were given meals with 900 calories and 50 grams of fat while the other five ate meals with 900 calories and no fat.

After two hours, the brachial artery test was repeated. Dr. Vogal found the blood flow of the students who ate the fatty meals had been reduced to nearly half their normal volume! But the arteries of the students who ate no fat had normal blood flow. The test was repeated every hour. What Dr. Vogel learned was that the damaging effect of eating a single meal including dietary fat was evident even four hours after ingestion![14]

What does this mean? If we are eating animal protein containing saturated fat, or are adding processed oil at every meal, we are severely limiting blood flow to our vital organs and tissues. If the effect lasts four hours, we're talking a minimum of twelve hours each day of reduced blood flow.

Still, olive oil, which showed a 31 percent reduction in blood flow, is preferable to butter or canola oil, and is certainly better than bacon grease or other animal fat. The problem with canola oil, which performed somewhat better in another of Vogel's studies, showing a ten percent reduction in blood flow, is that the majority of canola in the US is genetically modified, creating a host of potential health issues, aside from endothelial impairment.[15]

If you do choose to cook with canola oil, make sure it is organic. If you choose to include olive oil in your diet, beware of what you are buying. Don't go by the price! Even some of the pricier olive oils, according to author Tom Mueller's book, *Extra Virginity: The Sublime and Scandalous World of Olive Oil* (published 2012 by W. W. Norton & Company, Inc.), are polluted with canola oil, linseed oil, green dyes and even toxic, cancer-causing chemicals added to prevent them from tasting rancid.

Olive oil, in addition to being a highly processed food, contains nearly fourteen percent saturated fat.[16] If you don't believe that, try putting it in your fridge and see how quickly it becomes a solid. The best thing you can do for yourself is to remove animal protein and processed oils from your diet altogether.

You can rid your diet completely of processed oils by replacing them with oily whole foods, such as nuts, seeds and avocados. This may require some trial and error, but it is possible to eliminate processed oil without sacrificing flavor.

It is never necessary to use oil in sautéing vegetables. They release enough natural juices and sugars to keep them from burning or sticking to a pan; a slight amount of water will aid in this process as well. After a while you'll find food with added oil will just taste greasy and unappetizing.

According to Dr. Cauldwell Esselstyn Jr. (head of preventive cardiology at the Cleveland Clinic and author of *Prevent and Reverse Heart Disease),* if you can keep dietary fat that occurs naturally in vegetables, (having excluded those from meat or processed oils), below 15 percent, you will lose your craving for fat within 12 weeks.[17-1]

Dr. Esselstyn is an ardent proponent of a low-fat plant-based diet. Initially a general surgeon, he became disillusioned with the medical profession's inability to prevent cancers and heart disease and became interested in food as a first line of defense against illness. He is one of the early pioneers in plant-based nutrition. In 1985, he began a 12-year experiment in which he used 24 patients, referred to him by the cardiologists at the Cleveland Clinic, all of whom suffered from advanced heart disease. Most had other debilitating symptoms, such as angina.[17-2] Using a plant-based diet, and in some cases a low-dose cholesterol lowering drug, he was able to reduce all their cholesterol levels to below 150, a level at which he considers a person to be heart-attack proof, based on evidence found in populations in which heart attacks are rare.[17-3]

"All of the participants in my research were severely ill with disease in all three coronary arteries. Most had undergone a previous heart bypass operation or an angioplasty that eventually had failed. Several had failed these procedures twice and several had been told by their cardiologists there was nothing further to be done — that they must prepare for the inevitable progression of their disease."[17-4]

From the early days of the study, it became evident that six of the patients were not going to comply with the study's guidelines. They were returned to their cardiologists for care.[17-5]

At the end of the formal study, 12 years later, only one of the 18 original patients had any further coronary events. More than 20 years later, these patients were still flourishing. The one patient who did not adhere to the study's dietary guidelines had to have another heart bypass operation.[17-6]

In a larger study, 198 cardiac patients were followed for an average of 3.7 years. They were placed on a diet that excluded meat, dairy, eggs, fish and added oil. Twenty-one of the volunteers did not follow the prescribed program, reverting back to the Standard American Diet. Of these, 13 went on to experience at least one adverse cardiac event each, including two deaths, two strokes and a heart transplant, to name only a few. Of the remaining 177 compliant participants, only one had a major cardiac event, a stroke, that was related to disease progression. That is .6 percent adverse events in the plant-based group as compared to 62 percent in the group that had gone back to the standard diet. With results 100 times more favorable, the plant-based diet is clearly the better choice.[18]

☙ 3 ❧

GETTING TO THE TRUTH

In the vast world of conflicting opinion and often downright misinformation, it is difficult to figure out what is healthy and what is not, what is reliable science and what is just another sales pitch. What it comes down to is; who can you trust? I've concluded our best bet is to trust the doctors and scientists doing the research in our areas of concern. I turn to experts in nutrition and science to inform me of what is currently the best information available. So, how do we know what information is reliable?

Following the money is one way to learn if there is bias in science. If you find a study is funded by a special interest group, that would be a good study to take with about a pound of salt. If the egg industry, for example, funds a study showing that eggs are healthy, despite all available evidence to the contrary, I would hesitate to consider that study reliable. If a physician is prescribing tons of supplements which, luckily, you can purchase from him at a bargain price, that's a physician I would avoid. He might be more interested in selling you his miracle cure than actually helping to cure your illness.

Peer-reviewed articles garner a higher level of trust because they go through a higher level of scrutiny from people familiar with the subject matter. It is good to look at all the information out there, but it is necessary to look at it with a critical eye. Who wrote the study, who funded it, what industries are they connected with that could bias their findings? These are questions we have to ask ourselves if we have any hope of getting to the truth of any health claim.

Luckily, for those of us who do not have science backgrounds, there are a host of trustworthy physicians, nutritionists and researchers committed to doing this work for us. I have provided a list of resources at the end of this book.

Adrift In The Murky Waters of Science

It is important to realize that just because a doctor says something is so, doesn't mean it is so. A typical physician has very little education in nutrition. Scandalously, it is not a requirement that doctors study nutrition in medical school. It makes no sense at all to not begin any medical conversation with a concern about what one is putting into one's body.

It is also true that doctors who champion plant-based diets don't always agree with one another. Even within the plant-based community there is room for disagreement. Rich and I attended a seminar in California in which a number of doctors, scientists and nutritionists presented their viewpoints on plant-based nutrition. When you get these experts in a room together, it can be interesting to observe as human bias creeps into what they believe to be truly unbiased perspectives.

Most proponents of plant-based nutrition agree that all animal protein should be eliminated from one's diet, that most processed foods should be eliminated, and that oils, sugars, and salt should be strictly limited. One doctor maintains that a little salt and sugar is fine for most people. Some doctors think a little coconut milk is acceptable, others think it is tantamount to eating lard. One doctor believes that eating fish is beneficial while the rest shake their heads in disagreement. Some think you should limit fruit, others think you should eat more fruit. Some say more starch, some say less starch. One doctor feels that olive oil is ok. I have to say I liked him best. He just shrugged apologetically and admitted with a sheepish grin, "I'm Italian!"

One can easily understand why doctors and scientists get so worked up over these issues. They've devoted most of their lives trying to find answers to our pressing health concerns. And we should be very glad, and grateful, that they have.

My point is that while these experts disagree, perhaps ten to twenty percent of the time, in the big picture they agree far more than they disagree. The science has been done. It is no longer up for debate. If you want to reduce your exposure to disease of all kinds, eating a diet rich in whole, plant-based foods is your best protection from sliding into a life of physical and mental decline to infirmity and early death.

There may be minor differences in opinion as to what is the optimal diet to maintain good health. What's the optimal percentage of protein one should include in one's diet? Is a little fish good? That really isn't the issue. Any change you can make towards a plant-based diet is taking you closer towards health and farther away from disease.

The real question is whether eating a whole foods plant-based diet is healthier than the Standard American Diet. There is no question that a plant-based diet is the healthier option. These little differences are small matters in the big picture. If we continue eating the way we are eating now as a society, we will continue to decline, as individuals and as a nation.

No responsible scientists in the field of nutrition disagree about the fact that you should eat less meat, dairy and processed foods and include more whole foods in your diet. Kaiser Permanente, the largest managed healthcare organization in the United States with 17,000 doctors on their payroll, recommends that doctors prescribe plant-based diets to all their patients.

Healthy eating may be best achieved with a plant-based diet, which we define as a regimen that encourages whole, plant-based foods and discourages meats, dairy products, and eggs as well as all refined and processed foods. ...Research shows that plant-based diets are cost-effective, low-risk interventions that may lower body mass index, blood pressure, HbA1C, and cholesterol levels. They may also reduce the number of medications needed to treat chronic diseases and lower ischemic heart disease mortality rates. Physicians should consider recommending a plant-based diet to all their patients, especially those with high blood pressure, diabetes, cardiovascular disease, or obesity.[1]

This is becoming a global movement. Recently, the country of Australia acknowledged a plant-based diet as a viable option for all of its citizens.[2] With so much at stake, the world at large is beginning to reject the processed foods we've grown up with and is turning to whole foods to recover our health and the health of our planet as well as our dwindling natural resources.

How Do I Get Adequate Protein?

I had to laugh when I came across an image of vegan super middleweight champion boxer Omowale Adewale pummeling his opponent, Nick Olson, in a mixed martial arts fighting event promoted by NYFE, March 15, 2014. The caption on the image read: Ask me where I get my protein, *ONE MORE TIME!*

This is probably the most misunderstood issue and consistent question vegans hear when asked about a plant-based diet. Where do I get my protein? The animals with the largest muscle mass on the earth are herbivores. Where do cows, horses, and elephants get their protein? From plants!

Professional and amateur athletes are awakening to the virtues of fueling their bodies with plants rather than animal protein. Omowale Adewale is an enthusiastic advocate of a vegan diet. He won the Brooklyn Brawl Boxing Championship in 2012 and later created a program called "Going Vegan 2014" in which he offered free personal diet and fitness counseling to anyone in the world wishing to transition to a vegan lifestyle. He continues to spread the message about the benefits of a plant-based lifestyle across the country and has become a prominent speaker at vegetarian festivals and other health venues.

A relative newcomer on the scene, 35 year old triathlete Kate Strong discovered her asthma symptoms were alleviated by eliminating dairy from her diet. Her improved breathing allowed her to contemplate a new life as a triathlete. Over the past year, as her training sessions intensified, she realized she had already been unconsciously reducing her consumption of meat. That's when she made the decision to give up animal protein altogether. On September 21, 2014, in Weihai, Shandong Province, China, Kate Strong not only became World Champion in women's long-distance triathlon, in the most competitive age group (30 to 39), she sailed ahead of her competition with a staggering lead of over 15 minutes! This was her first competition powered solely by plants!

Photo reprinted by permission of William Strong, Photographer

Kate Strong

Kate Strong, more aptly referred to by friends as "Strong Kate," continues her passion for racing and a vegan lifestyle.

"I couldn't be happier with the result, and also that I know one hundred percent that this 'diet' is sustainable and a great building block for my health, happiness and future."

Kate passionately forges ahead, training for the next competition, wowing sponsors with her dedication, energy and a smile that exudes joy and radiant well-being.

"华发股份杯" 2014年威海长距离铁人三项世界锦标赛
'Huafa Cup' 2014 Weihai ITU Long Distance Triathlon World Championships

Photo reprinted by permission of Photographer, William Strong

2014 World Champion Women's Long-Distance Triathlon

KATE STRONG

Virtually every plant we eat has some protein in it. We need far less protein than we are accustomed to eating on the Standard American Diet. Ideally, no more than ten percent of our calories should be in the form of protein. According to T. Colin Campbell's, *The China Study,* we may eat as much as 90 percent protein in our SAD diet. Too much protein overtaxes our organs, particularly the kidneys, which are tasked to eliminate excess protein.

Beans are an excellent source of protein as well as other nutrients. If you are eating a diverse, whole foods plant-based diet you do not need to concern yourself with getting adequate protein. A cup of beans a day will give you all the protein your body needs. It is actually possible to eat too much protein on a plant-based diet. Since beans contain an abundance of protein, no more than a cup of beans per day, in addition to a variety of other vegetables, is recommended.

New information from the largest study ever done on plant-based diets showed that vegans get 70 percent more protein on average than we need. For that matter, it seems that everyone is getting more protein than they need. Protein is a non-issue, as 97 percent of the population gets enough protein. However, 97 percent of Americans are NOT getting the recommended minimum intake of another important nutrient, fiber, which only comes from plants. So the better question is: Are we getting the fiber we need?[3]

WHO WINS THE RACE?

So, who wins the race, the tortoise or the hare? The answer is: it depends. It depends upon you, your personality, your strengths and your weaknesses. Do you jump in with both feet and stop eating all animal products all at once or do you taper off over time until you have animal products completely out of your diet? Again, it depends on what works best for you.

The Hare

Studies show that those who jump in with both feet, going plant-based all at once, have a greater chance of long-term success. This is what I did. My pain and other health issues were great motivators for me. The fact that my gastric issues disappeared in one day was enough proof that this was a positive route for me. That my husband witnessed this was enough proof for him. He sat up too many nights watching helplessly as I writhed in pain.

There is a down side to this, however. Our bodies have accumulated a considerable amount of toxins from ingesting materials we as humans were never intended to consume. It is possible you will go through a detox process which will mimic flu-like symptoms. I felt like I had been run over by a truck for about two weeks. It was worth it to me. Experiencing headaches and body aches was far more acceptable than living with agonizing intestinal pain. On a more positive note, ridding yourself of animal protein all at once allows you to free yourself very quickly of animal dependence. (Animal food dependence, that is. I would never give up my critters!)

If you strictly adhere to a Whole Foods Plant-Based diet (WFPB), in a few weeks cravings usually disappear. After that, you will have developed new habits. The thought of eating meat and other animal products will lose its appeal. After a few months, it will become unthinkable. You have been set free!

After adopting a diet free of animal protein, (low in salt, sugar and fats, and rich in nutrients, fiber and healthy protein), you will find the foods you previously consumed are unacceptably salty, greasy and nauseatingly sweet. They may make you feel sluggish and even a little sick. I don't even see fast food restaurants anymore. I literally don't notice them. If someone were to tell me to meet them at McDonald's, I would have to think carefully to remember just where our local McDonald's is located. Hardy's? Burger King? Kentucky Fried Chicken? I have no clue where they are in my town. Fast food restaurants have become that irrelevant to me. In fact, most restaurants have become irrelevant to me. If they don't serve healthy, plant-based meals, they are simply not on my radar.

As healthy diners become more prevalent in our society, more restaurants are offering the kinds of foods we demand. The smart restauranteurs are learning they are missing out on a growing segment of the population when they ignore plant-based diners. Again, you can help make these changes by voting with your wallets. I've personally seen restaurants start offering vegan options simply by telling them I'll come back when they offer something I can eat. It only takes a few requests of this kind to create a shift in a restaurant owner's thinking. Why shouldn't they take advantage of this growing market of plant-based diners?

The sooner one embraces a whole foods plant-based diet, the sooner one's body will show improvement. With the immediate health benefits I experienced by switching to this diet, nothing will make me go back to the way I was eating before.

The Tortoise

If you think you'd like to go plant-based but are not quite as motivated, you may want to begin in baby steps. To paraphrase the poet, Khalil Gibran, even if you are crawling, you are still moving forward. It's important to look at your goals and consider them when you are making food choices. There are more than 20 years of scientific evidence suggesting animal protein does not belong in the human diet. Some people are slow to believe it. Like me, it takes getting sick to finally see the light. If you really don't want to give up eating animal products entirely, at least consider adding larger portions of fresh fruits, vegetables, grains and legumes to your diet.

Some of us just can't imagine not eating meat. If not meat, then cheese, milk, eggs... Can you imagine eating less meat, less cheese, fewer eggs? Can you consider using almond milk rather than cow's milk? Can you imagine filling most of your plate with fresh colorful vegetables, grains, legumes and starches so that the meat or cheese on you plate is only a small percentage of the total?

If this is your approach, your goals may take longer to achieve but if you persist you'll eventually get there. *What you will discover is the better care you take of your body, the more your body insists that you take care of it!* Once we develop the habit of including healthy foods in our diets, our bodies will begin to reject the foods that do not serve us. You'll find yourself automatically pushing away those dead foods filled with sugar, salt, preservatives and chemicals and will discover you prefer fresh, natural flavors over the junk we've come to think of as food.

The down side is it will take a little longer to see positive changes. You will also have a harder time battling cravings since you haven't given yourself the time to overcome the patterns that haven't served you. You will still find yourself craving meat, cheese, sugar, etc. Don't despair. Even modest changes will show cumulative beneficial results over time. I recently read that one soda a day is enough to add 15 pounds a year to one's weight. A small change like reducing the amount of soda you consume can have astonishing results.

One way to deal with cravings when eating out is to eat only at places that offer plant-based options. For example, Indian restaurants often have a lunch buffet which usually includes at least two vegan options. So, let's say they have an eggplant and potato option, and a spicy chickpea stew. They also have Tandori chicken and maybe even a lamb dish. You taste the eggplant and potato and you find that you like it. You taste the chickpea stew and you like that as well. You taste the Tandori chicken and the lamb and your well-trained pleasure centers in your brain are activated. Your eyes roll back in ecstasy and you realize you LOVE these two dishes.

Ok, that's fair. Your tastebuds have been trained over a long life to love meat dishes. Try filling most of your plate, say 80 percent, with the eggplant and chickpea dishes. Fill the remaining 20 percent with the chicken and lamb. If you go back for seconds, choose only the eggplant and chickpeas. If you can't begin with 80 percent, try 50 percent, or even 20 percent. Begin where it is comfortable for you. Each time you go out to eat, try to lower the amount of the animal portion on your plate until you have the control to not reach for it at all. Before long you'll find your eyes rolling back in ecstasy over the eggplant and chickpeas.

Try the same approach at home. Make the lion's share of your meals healthy beans, grains, starches, colorful fruits and vegetables. Make animal protein a tiny part of your meal, more like a condiment than an equal portion. When you are able, get rid of it altogether. A few weeks of animal abstinence is all it takes. You can have that monkey off your back forever!

Whether you choose to be a tortoise or a hare, expect to have relapses. None of us is perfect. It has taken me a while to learn not to reach for the cookies readily available to us at my writers group meetings. It is like a reformed cigarette smoker suddenly finding a cigarette in his mouth without being conscious of how it got there. I may not be craving a cookie, I might not even like the cookie, but I have years of an engrained habit of reaching for that cookie that I had to consciously overcome. Fortunately, it only took awareness of that habit to break it. Others are not so easy.

Give yourself a break. We are all only human. We can only do the best we can. Be patient with yourself, just as you are with a child. You wouldn't tell a child you hate them if he or she made a mistake. Don't do that to yourself. Just try to correct the behavior and move on. You'll soon find yourself having more successes than failures and a vibrant, energetic body to show for it.

❦ 5 ❦

RITES OF PASSAGE

When first embarking on a whole foods plant-based adventure, you must prepare yourself to encounter travails along the road. Like any worthwhile adventure, there will be obstacles to overcome. Our bodies are trained to be abused. We must retrain them to be protected and nurtured. Some of it is less than pleasant, though it is a small price to pay to for a healthy and energetic life. Let's address these issues right away so we can begin our journey.

A Bit About Beans

Beans, beans. Good for your heart.
The more you eat, the more you fart.
The more you fart, the better you feel
So let's have beans for every meal!
—Anonymous

Beans are a staple of a vegan diet. There are so many varieties of beans that you never run out of options. They also can be prepared in countless ways, taking the boredom out of eating the same old thing. Just the number of ways you can make veggie burgers from beans is a revelation.

Every culture seems to have some kind of bean as a dietary staple; chickpeas and lentils of India, soybeans of Japan, snow peas and mung beans of Thailand, red beans of Mexico, fava and cannellini beans of Italy, flageolet beans of France, long beans of China, black-eyed peas and lentils of Ethiopia... the variety is endless and often overlaps cultures.

When you first begin to embrace a WFPB lifestyle, beans will probably become a part of your daily life. If not every day, most days you should be eating beans. Why? Because they are loaded with nutrients, complex carbohydrates and fiber as well as the much sought after protein. Beans are versatile, filling and satisfying. Combined with a grain, they form a complete protein. They also help prevent constipation, assisting in the easy elimination of waste products and the formation of solid stools. Beans should also be a daily part of our eating regimen. Studies have shown that including beans as a regular part of your diet will significantly lower cholesterol and reduce blood pressure.[1] It isn't as difficult as you think to eat beans every day.

Keeping hummus on hand is an easy way to get your bean fix. You can have it as a snack with fresh raw vegetables or with pita bread, applied liberally as a sandwich spread, or as a sauce on other vegetables.

Delicious bean soups can be starters for any meal or can be the main course. Beans can be added to salads, as stuffing for burritos, and as ingredients in countless dishes.

There is a downside to eating beans, at least in the beginning. As the children's rhyme implies, flatulence is an inescapable part of the bean experience. Most beans contain sugar molecules which create gas as they are digested in the small intestine. Fortunately, these problems can be mitigated by the addition of some herbs and spices which suppress the formation of these gasses. A few of these are anise seeds, basil, cumin, dill, onion, oregano, parsley, pepper, rosemary, sage, savory and thyme. Cooking beans with a pinch of baking soda may help as well. A culinary instructor I know recommends that students add the seaweed kombu (kelp) to beans to aid in digestion. The problem with that is kombu contains an inordinate amount of iodine and should be avoided because of the potential for iodine toxicity.[2]

Fortunately, after two or three weeks of eating beans daily your body will become accustomed to them and flatulence will become a thing of the past. As long as you include beans as a staple in your diet, you will probably never be bothered by this issue again.

Another issue with beans is they contain a lectin, Phytohaemagglutinin, which is a protein thought to be a natural insecticide. Prevalent in raw and undercooked beans, especially concentrated in red beans, these lectins can be deactivated by cooking. *It is important never to eat raw or undercooked beans!* However, cooking beans in a slow cooker can actually increase lectin toxicity. These lectins can damage the epithelial lining of your intestinal tract. Your body will do its best to remove this toxin by ejecting it as quickly as possible by means of diarrhea and vomiting. Some individuals will be more sensitive to lectin toxicity than others.[3]

Do not despair. As an omnivore, or a former omnivore, you know you have to cook poultry thoroughly to remove salmonella toxin, you have to cook beef thoroughly to prevent transfer of mad cow disease and cooking fish and pork destroys parasites. Take the same precautions with beans as you would with other foods.

Soak the beans overnight or all day (at least five hours) and discard the liquid. Rinse and cover with fresh water. Boil the beans a full ten minutes, stirring occasionally, to deactivate the offending lectin toxins. Reduce the heat and simmer until done, usually 30 minutes to one hour, depending on the type and age of the bean. Pressure cooking beans, after the initial ten-minute boil, is another sure-fire way to eliminate lectin toxicity. Beans are safe, healthy and delicious if prepared properly. So, eat and enjoy!

Eliminating Toxins

Our body wants to rid itself of toxins that have accumulated over a lifetime of indulging in the Standard American Diet. When you begin a whole foods plant-based lifestyle, you may find yourself having to endure an unpleasant detox process. If you choose to give up animal products all at once, your body may feel achey and you may experience headaches from mild to severe. My advice is to hang in there. It will last a week or ten days, just like a cold. When you've gotten past it, you will feel so much lighter. Food will taste better and you'll be starting with a clean slate.

Choose a time when you can afford to pamper yourself a little. It may not even be an issue for you. For me it was worth it. I not only gave up toxic animal products but I also lost my cravings for them. That is the reward for allowing your body the time to cleanse.

If you choose to eliminate animal protein from your diet slowly it is unlikely you will encounter this problem or, if you do, the effects will be minimal. You will have a harder time eliminating cravings for animal protein, however, and changing your taste preferences will take longer.

There is a lot of hoopla about detox regimens touted by health practitioners of all kinds. Your liver is a detox organ. If you eat green vegetables your liver will detox naturally. Dr. Michael Gregor talks about this issue succinctly in his short video, http://nutritionfacts.org/video/the-best-detox/. Dr. Gregor's website, http://nutritionfacts.org is a fantastic free resource for well-researched and entertaining information on just about anything you want to know about nutrition.

Cravings

I never thought I could live without meat, fish, and dairy. Everything I ever cooked for the majority of my life involved at least one of these categories. When I first decided to adhere to a whole foods plant-based lifestyle, the rewards were immediate. I was no longer in pain. This made the decision to stay on this diet easy for me. I had been on a cheesecake kick, experimenting until I had created what my neighbors agreed was the best cheesecake they had ever eaten. It was so beautiful. Crowned with a sweet glazed topping of fresh strawberries, it belonged on a magazine cover. It was also decadently delicious. That was the last cheesecake I have ever eaten or will ever eat again.

Do I wish I could have a big, fat slice of it today? Not at all, though I admit there are times I think I might like to have something sweet. When I've been in an uncontrolled environment I've fallen off the wagon a few times, reaching for cookies at a pot-luck or brownies at an annual family gathering. At a meeting of one of the groups I attend, we were served a celebratory cake, made with egg and milk, with buttery, sugary frosting. Yes, I indulged. And I regretted it. My intestinal problems flared up and I was sick and in pain for 24 hours. It was definitely not worth it. That was over a year ago and I haven't transgressed since.

The thought of eating any kind of meat, fish or dairy has become unthinkable to me. Philosophically, Rich and I were not opposed to eating fish in the beginning because we understand the protective benefits of omega-3 fatty acids* found in fish. However, when we found ourselves standing at a fish counter at a local health food store looking at slabs of tuna, salmon and trout, we found we were unable to make ourselves order anything. I realized then, there was no turning back.

I no longer have any desire to eat any kind of animal product, with the occasional exception of raw honey. I have no good reason for this, it has no nutritional benefit over sugar, which has none. I just like the taste of it better.

Honey is not a vegan product. There are different perspectives as to whether or not one should consume it on a plant-based diet. I like to support local honey producers who are raising bees not only for honey but to pollinate crops of surrounding farms. I'm not suggesting you do the same. You have to act in accordance with your own convictions. My opinions on a lot of issues surrounding the vegan movement have changed over time. I no longer buy or wear products that include animal products. I expect my opinion on eating honey may change as well. I just want to be honest as to where I am today in my evolution of adopting a plant-based lifestyle.

Do yourself a favor and give yourself the time it takes to reeducate your tastebuds. Hang in there, you can do this. This will go faster if you abstain from animal products entirely. However, if you are not prepared to go completely plant-based and choose to only add healthier options to your current diet, that's fine. Overwhelm your plate with fresh colorful fruits, veggies, starches and grains and you may discover you don't want to eat as much meat as before. Eating lots of green vegetables with meat has been shown to have some protective benefits that could mitigate some of the damage caused by eating animal protein.

*It turns out in subsequent investigation that the risks of eating fish outweigh the benefits. Also, you can easily get omega-3 fatty acids from ground flaxseeds.

6

WHAT'S THE DIFFERENCE?

Those who abstain from eating meat fall into different categories. These categories seem to be based on the level of adherence one follows in a plant-based diet as well as whether one includes an ethical component having to do with the consumption of other sentient creatures. Religion is sometimes a factor as well. This can be a bit confusing for those embarking on a plant-based diet for the first time.

I find it interesting, if not a little annoying, that I have to say I'm "vegan" when ordering food before the person taking my order understands I don't eat animal products. Vegetarians will typically eat dairy and eggs. Is cheese a vegetable? Are eggs? I suppose, depending upon what you consider acceptable, breaking it down into categories isn't a bad thing. I fall into the WFPB (Whole Foods Plant-Based) category, though it often is easier just to say I'm vegan.

The list I'm providing can be broken down even further. There are numerous sub-categories. Vegetarians who eat eggs but not milk are ovo-vegetarians. Those who eat dairy products but no eggs are lacto-vegetarians, those who eat both are classified as ovo-lacto vegetarians, while a pescatarian will eat fish but no other meat. In terms of this book, these distinctions are irrelevant as science clearly demonstrates that all of these vegetarian categories promote disease and should be avoided.

Vegan

Vegans (pronounced vee-gan) are those who don't eat animal products of any kind, no meat, seafood, poultry, eggs, dairy or honey. Nothing that comes from an animal. They usually abstain from eating animal products for ethical reasons, not wishing to cause harm to other sentient beings. Some people are vegan only in the foods they consume and others extend this to any product from any source made from the exploitation of animals.

Vegans do not necessarily follow a healthy diet. French fries cooked in genetically modified corn oil contain no animal products and can accurately be considered vegan, yet a steady diet of french fries can be detrimental to one's health. Soft drinks made of high-fructose corn syrup and caramel coloring, and with no nutritional value whatsoever, can technically be considered vegan. Vegan web sites are inundated with recipes of decadent sweets dripping in sugar and butter substitutes. While many vegans follow a health-conscious lifestyle, veganism does not in itself equal good health.

Raw Vegan

Raw vegans eat no animal products of any kind and they prefer their food in their natural state, uncooked and whole. They often blend, dehydrate and sun dry foods to make them more interesting and delicious. Nuts are a big part of a raw diet. The theory is that foods in their natural state contain live beneficial enzymes that are destroyed in the process of cooking. This notion is not largely supported by the scientific community which suggests that some foods require cooking to release their nutritional content or become more bioavailable (that is more readily utilized by our bodies) while other foods should be cooked to destroy harmful bacteria and toxins. It is generally believed that a diet of both cooked and raw plant foods is preferable to one or the other.

Vegetarian

Vegetarians do not eat meat. However, depending on the kind of vegetarian they purport to be, they may choose to eat honey, cheese or eggs (or both), and some even include fish. I've even known people who claim to be vegetarian who eat poultry, rationalizing that since it isn't a mammal, it isn't meat.

Certainly becoming vegetarian is better than consuming meat, but because of what we now know about the link between animal protein, including milk protein, and cancer as well as a host of other diseases, it is better to exclude these products from one's diet.

WFPB - Whole Foods Plant-Based

People who fall into this category, WFPB, are primarily concerned with the nutrition and health benefits of food. They do not eat any animal products and they prefer foods in their whole form with little or no processing.

Animal protection is a secondary concern. However, I've discovered in myself, and have seen in others, that it is nearly impossible to become plant-based without awakening to the plight of animals. My observation is that once one has developed an ethical position on preserving the life of other beings with the ability to fear, grieve and experience human emotions, it is impossible to go back to eating animals.

What brought this point home to me was watching a video of shark expert, Valerie Taylor, making friends over a period of years with a spotted eel. Once the eel learned to trust her, she looked forward to her visits, rushing out to greet her like an old friend. She rubbed up against Valerie like a cat, demanding and accepting her caresses. *Wow!* If an eel can form such an intense emotional bond with a human, where do we draw the line on what can feel and express love and what cannot?[1]

Common Concerns

All of these groups are concerned to greater or lesser degrees about the toll raising animals for food takes on the health of our planet. The meat industry is responsible for the majority of the earth's deforestation and contributes massively to global warming from the production of methane gas. Runoff of nitrogen by chemical fertilization of agribusiness and factory farming manure has already created huge dead zones in our oceans which continue to worsen. Our planet is reaching a tipping point of no return. If we do not do something to reverse the damage to our home, our planet Earth, in our lifetime it will be too late. What then, becomes of our children?

Growing numbers of medical doctors and scientists across the globe agree that their is no need for animal protein in our diet. The accumulation of scientific data is clear. The eating of any animal of any kind is harmful to our health and triggers disease processes in our bodies.

Why, then, kill animals for food when the overwhelming body of evidence shows that it doesn't serve us, that it is not in anyone's best interest? It seems to me a just and divine symmetry. We kill the animals for food, and the animals kill us by promoting disease processes in our bodies. When a diet of whole plant-based foods is so health promoting and so delicious, why is this necessary?

7

HOW DO I BEGIN?

As they say, the most difficult part of any journey is taking the first step. It may seem an overwhelming task. How does one begin to make such a radical shift in culinary perspective? First, by understanding it really is just a shift in perspective. You aren't really giving up anything. You are simply changing what you prefer to eat. Tastes change all the time. Our tastes in clothing, hair styles, and in food are constantly in flux. Just look at your high school or college photos to see how much you have changed.

We used to believe that whole milk was the only way to go. Then markets began offering two-percent and skim milk. After becoming used to those, whole milk began to taste as heavy as whipping cream. Once lard and oils containing trans-fats were acceptable food choices. Most of us eventually shifted to cooking with vegetable oils and wouldn't dream of using lard.

There are many foods I once refused to eat, like spinach, I now can't seem to get enough of. I used to love ice cream. Now I wouldn't dream of putting that in my mouth. I've simply made a paradigm shift which doesn't include animal products.

We can get used to just about anything. We can also decide to prefer one thing over another. I remember as a little girl my father convinced me that raw oysters on the half-shell were the most delectable treat on the face of the earth. He made the prospect of swallowing a live, slimy sea creature (that from my child's perspective looked for all the world like a huge bugger) sound irresistible. I scarfed down my first oyster when I was about six years old and have eaten dozens of them in my lifetime. I absolutely loved them.

The same was true of snails. Give them a fancy name like escargot, smother them with a thick dollop of garlic butter on a fancy dish and we line up and pay a small fortune for this delicacy. Yes, I'm guilty of this one too. When I lived in France, escargot was a favorite treat. I wonder who the first person was who looked at this slithering little slug and decided to put it in his mouth.

The hardest part about transitioning to a whole foods plant-based diet is making the decision to go for it. Do it! You have nothing to lose and everything to gain. You may find it the best decision you have ever made.

What If I Just Can't Live Without Meat?

I hear this all the time, "I just can't give up meat. I can't live without milk, eggs, fish, cheese, ice cream... and so forth!" To a lot of people this is simply inconceivable. We were raised on bacon and eggs, steaks and pork chops and pizzas. Give up ice cream? Perish the thought! What pleasure is there in life without these comfort foods of our youth?

I hear you; I've been there too. If my body had not rebelled so forcefully, and I did not know what I now know about the dangers of the Standard American Diet, I probably would never have made the leap myself. I might not have sought the information that propelled me to make a change and my health would still be in ruins. The truth is, animal protein is not oxygen; we can live without it, and live better.

Ok, so you can't give up animal products entirely. Can you cut back on your animal intake? Can you add beans, grains, greens and fresh vegetables to your plate? The more vegetables you can add the better off you are. Even making small changes is better than doing nothing. If you can simply switch to using almond milk on your morning cereal as opposed to cow's milk, you are significantly reducing the animal protein load on your body.

If you can bake your french fries rather than fry them in a vat of oil, you are significantly reducing your daily intake of fat, calories, possibly genetically modified organisms, and harmful cancer-causing toxins created from cooking oils at high temperatures. You also reduce the likelihood that they are being cooked in beef tallow. I learned when reviewing restaurants for *Veggin' Out and About!* that restaurants often deep fry foods in beef tallow, particularly french fries. If you refuse to eat at fast food restaurants you are making a HUGE leap toward healthier eating.

These little things add up to big changes. My brother works with a man who recently lost a lot of weight. When he asked him how he achieved his weight loss the man said simply, "I gave up sodas." That was it. Little changes can make big differences in your bottom line.

Do something now to protect your future self. Even if it is as simple as reducing your animal protein intake even one ounce per day less than your normal portion and replacing that ounce with a one-ounce portion of a fresh vegetable can make a big difference over time. Reversing your animal/vegetable proportions in almost imperceptible increments over time can make a significant difference.

Your doctor may be recommending that you reduce sodium in your diet. There is ample sodium in the plants you will be eating so it isn't necessary to supplement one's diet with salt. This may be one of the hardest things for you to get used to. Just do it and be patient. Some foods will taste bland at first but will reward you before long with an awakening of your taste buds. You will experience subtle flavors your hardened palate had previously failed to recognize. Before long foods will taste too salty. If I forget to tell the wait-staff to eliminate the salt in a dish I've ordered, often I cannot eat it at all as the salt overwhelms my palate.

One way to get the salt and fat monkeys off your back is to go on a juice fast for a couple of days before going plant-based. This gives your olfactory receptors and taste receptors in your tongue a rest. When the fast is over, you'll now enjoy the more interesting flavors of whole foods.[1]

The last chapter of this book includes a sampling of healthy recipes that are low in salt and processed oil, and free of animal protein. If you simply incorporate these recipes into your current diet, you are already in the process of transitioning to a whole foods plant-based lifestyle.

Give Your Tastebuds A Chance

You may be one of those people who know how to throw a steak and a potato wrapped in aluminum foil onto a grill, sprinkle it with some ready-made seasonings and some garlic powder, maybe some butter, and you're all set. You can't go into cooking vegetables with the same expectations or you might be disappointed. You will have to reeducate your palate.

Give yourself a chance to become attuned to the needs of your body and to appreciate new flavors. Your tastes will change over time. Remember, it only takes a few weeks in most cases to change flavor preferences.

When you quit eating salt, for example, everything tastes bland. You will feel like you are eating cardboard. After a few weeks on a bland diet you'll find yourself savoring subtle flavors you never knew you were missing because they were being overpowered by salt. You'll discover a subtle sweetness to many vegetables and a nuttiness to many whole grains. After a month or two without salt, you'll find eating the often over-salted foods in restaurants is enough to ruin the meal.

The same is true of sugar and oil. Pizzas dripping in oily cheese, once an image of gastronomic delight, now looks just like what it is, fat and cholesterol loaded with cancer causing milk protein. I was first introduced to cheese-less pizza in Florence, Italy, long before I considered a plant-based lifestyle. It was the best pizza I'd ever eaten. I could savor the individual ingredients more intimately. The bricks of mozzarella cheese we use to cover our pizzas is an American invention and we have the big butts and bellies to show for it. Have you ever gone into a pizza restaurant and looked around at the patrons dining there? You are not likely to find many trim figures in the room.

Reintroduce yourself to foods you have trained yourself to dislike. I grew up hating brussels sprouts and broccoli. As a child you couldn't force me to eat either one of these foods. Yet I loved collard greens, which are similar in flavor and are in the same plant family as brussels sprouts. In fact, brussels sprouts look exactly like collards growing in the garden, before the long stems appear in the middle of the plant where the sprouts form. I was in my fifties before I tried brussels sprouts again. To my amazement, I loved them! They are now one of my favorite foods. So is broccoli. I can't seem to get enough of these vegetables.

Trying new spices might seem a bit strange at first but as you come to appreciate them, they make wonderful additions to your repertoire of new flavors to enjoy. Anise, with it's mild licorice flavor, is wonderful in breads and stews. Indian spices add a world of flavor to simple vegetables and Ethiopian spices make a plate of ordinary lentils sing.

Aroma is an important factor in enjoying food. The tempering of spices in Indian dishes fills the kitchen with such heavenly aromas you can hardly wait for the cooking to end and the eating to begin. The odd combining of ingredients can produce unexpected and delectable results, such as combining mangos and lentils. Or pineapple and rice, chocolate and chili.

A few weeks of abstinence from all animal products, while limiting or excluding salt and oil, may create changes in you that may very well save your life. Give it a chance to make a difference.

Supplements

T. Colin Campbell succinctly argues in his book, *The China Study*, that taking dietary supplements is not only unnecessary, but can be detrimental to one's health.[2] Unless lab results show a deficiency in a particular vitamin, there is no need to take supplements. We can get nearly everything our body needs from plants. However, there is one vitamin all vegans and vegetarians should take and that is vitamin B12. Vitamin B-12 (methylcobalamin or cyanocobalamin) is not actually a vitamin, it is a bacteria found in soil. In the past we've received ample supplies of this in well water and in vegetables we've grown ourselves, which were not as scrupulously cleaned as in current, more sanitary practices. The tradeoff is we now have fewer soil born illnesses. We also got B-12 from eating animals who have ingested the bacteria while grazing. Since ingesting animal protein is so detrimental to our health and most water has been sanitized to the point that B-12 is no longer present, we should take a B-12 supplement. B-12 deficiency can result in serious maladies, among them; thickening arteries, anemia, nerve damage, neuropsychiatric disorders, and rising levels of homocysteine in the blood.[3] We only need a tiny amount of B-12 so buy the smallest amount available. The benefits of a plant-based diet can not be overstated, but it is important to understand the need for vitamin B-12 and to take it religiously. I prefer to buy the methylcobalamin because it is derived from natural sources rather than cyanocobalamin, which is a synthetic form of B-12. Have your B-12 levels checked annually to be safe.

Before learning this important information, Rich and I discovered in annual lab tests that our B-12 levels were very low. We began taking a 1,000mcg methylcobalamine supplement and within a few months our labs were perfect.

Partner With Your Physician

Make your doctor your partner in this endeavor. When I first told my physician my goal was to get off blood pressure medication she said to me with a condescending smile, "It's good to have goals." Within three weeks I proved to her the difference a whole foods plant-based diet can make. Not only are my blood pressure and cholesterol completely under control, but all my lab tests have improved. Even my liver enzymes are nearly normal. After all the injury to my liver, this is nothing short of amazing.

We can't expect doctors to know everything. Just as we have to be engaged with our food choices, we have to be engaged in our medical care. As illness proliferates within our society, patient loads for doctors increase. A practicing physician often must choose between the immediate demands of his patients and sorting through extensive medical literature to stay current in his field. Because of the number of drugs available, and the number of potential side effects accompanying each of them, staying abreast of new developments becomes an insurmountable task for even the most competent physician.

I am not saying that taking physician prescribed drugs is always a bad thing. I would not be alive today had I not been prescribed a reliable antibiotic. However, when a drug is necessary, we should know what that drug can and cannot do, and what are the potential side effects. The same is true for medical procedures. We must become engaged in our own recovery. Only by understanding the complete picture can we possibly give informed consent.

When I first discovered I had high blood pressure, in 1999, I had been sent to the emergency room on a military base where my husband had been stationed as an Air Force dentist. My ears felt like they were filled with fluids and to me it sounded like I was talking into a drum. My voice echoed in my head. I thought I had an inner ear infection. The nurse took my blood pressure and abruptly left the room. She returned with a physician. My blood pressure was so high I was in imminent danger of having a stroke. The doctor kept me for an hour for observation while I was administered a medication to lower the pressure.

The next week I was sent to a physician on base for a follow-up appointment. He immediately began yelling at me for not taking care of this blood pressure issue sooner. He looked at my chart and said that my blood pressure had been high for five years and had gone untreated. I was astonished! I didn't know I was hypertensive. None of the nurses who had taken my blood pressure nor the physicians who had treated me over the years ever told me my blood pressure was high.

He put me on a blood pressure medication that I was expected to take the rest of my life. I suggested to the doctor it may be better to change my diet rather than take drugs indefinitely. He looked at me like I was crazy. "If you were going to do that, you'd already be doing it," he said.

In retrospect, I should have changed doctors. Your doctor is, or should be, your partner, not your boss. If he or she prefers to write prescriptions to mask symptoms, rather than dealing with the actual root cause of a disease process, you may want to look for another doctor. Most doctors have little training in nutrition and many have little faith in their patients.

I had very little knowledge of nutrition at the time, but I was a perfect candidate for a nutrition-based health care program. Unfortunately, at the time this approach was not widely embraced by the medical community at large, and was clearly not encouraged by my doctor.

Sometimes you have to take matters in you own hands. It is, after all, your body, your health and your life. You can educate a resistant physician by becoming proactive. Make a commitment to change your diet; keep clear and accurate records and present them to your doctor.

NEVER take yourself off medications because you feel you no longer need them!!! Show the record of your progress to your doctor and discuss with your doctor the medical decisions that are crucial to your well-being. Most doctors want to see your health improve, but they also want to see proof that your diet is working the way you believe it is working.

AND they want to know you are committed to this lifestyle before they make any drastic medical changes. This is both a responsible and fair attitude. Give your physician something to work with, something tangible.

Keep a food diary for six weeks. Record your daily weight, your daily blood pressure, and the food you eat each day. Everything. Be honest. Your lab numbers will tell the tale so there is no point in trying to cheat. If there has been a significant change in your blood pressure within three weeks, as is often the case, insist on seeing your doctor immediately to address modifying your medications. It is dangerous to be on blood pressure medications if you are no longer hypertensive.

At the end of six weeks of maintaining a rigid WFPB diet, you may want to have your blood pressure meds evaluated again. Also request a cholesterol test. You might have to pay for this yourself, depending on your insurance policy. Many grocery stores, such as Krogers, will do the test for around $50 at the time of this writing.

Again, and I can't state this too strongly, NEVER TAKE YOURSELF OFF PHYSICIAN PRESCRIBED MEDICATIONS!!! You've worked hard to get where you are. Don't kill yourself trying to play doctor.

SOCIAL SITUATIONS

While the plant-based population is growing, it is likely most of the people with whom you associate are meat-eaters. Many occasions for enjoying the company of friends, family and even business associates involve sharing meals. Whether in a formal or more relaxed environment, navigating social events can be a tricky business. But with some pre-planning and creativity you can have your cake and eat it too, vegan of course!

Family and Friends

Well-meaning family and friends seem to suddenly become experts on what you should eat when you change to a healthier way of life. You don't have to argue, become defensive, or get into long discussions with them when you sit down to a family dinner and they try to pile loads of animal proteins onto your plate. You can stick to your guns without being rude. Just politely decline and bring your own food.

Be considerate and let your host or hostess know in advance that you won't be eating animal products, added oils or salt. That way they don't prepare your former favorite meal only to have you decline it. Just as it isn't fair for them to force their choices on you, it isn't fair to expect other people to cater to your needs. Preparing a special meal, or even side dishes, for you may be more disruptive for your hosts than you may know, and in my opinion is uncalled for. Even asking them to provide a simple baked potato and a salad throws off their whole game plan, especially if other guests are included in the invitation. A baked potato requires time to cook, monopolizing an oven or microwave that might be needed to prepare the main course for other guests. A salad takes additional preparation time when your host may be juggling other tasks. If they have the time, love to cook and want to make something special for you, then of course you may accept their hospitality.

Breaking bread with friends is more about spending time together than about the food that is being served. Often it is more considerate to just bring something you can eat to any occasion where you must interact with omnivores. When I receive a dinner invitation and tell my hosts I'll bring my own food, invariably I see a wave of relief wash over them.

I have a Japanese friend, Sadako Ishizaki, who visits me from Tokyo every couple of years. I have become accustomed to her habit of pulling snacks out of her purse to munch on while we are together. It wasn't until I became plant-based that I realized Sadako was controlling her food environment by providing for herself the items I had not realized she needed. I never even noticed!

Dining Out

Because restaurants use so much oil, and particularly canola and corn oils, it isn't wise to eat out often. I have to qualify this by admitting this is a "do as I say, not as I do" statement. Rich and I write a food blog called *Veggin' Out And About!,* which is a plant-based resource for vegan travelers (www.vegginoutandabout.com). Because it is so difficult to find wholesome food while traveling, we began this service to direct vegans to restaurants we have found where one might stop in for a good plant-based meal along the road. Therefore, we eat out much more than we recommend. Having said that, if I am eating out and really like a dish, I make sure to bring some of it home, or even order another serving to take out. Then, when I get home I experiment with it to see if I can come close to recreating it. The great thing about that is you can make it healthier by taking out the offending oils and salt when you make it yourself. Also, there are often happy accidents, whereby I am not able to recreate that particular dish but in the attempt, I create something completely new that is very, very good. These happy accidents make experimenting with food great fun.

A fabulous way to introduce yourself to new foods is to try ethnic cuisines that have a long history of vegan and vegetarian dining in their culture. They have already done the work of figuring out what spices work with a variety of fruits and vegetables. Ethiopia has a religious culture of fasting days in which no animal products are consumed. The typical Ethiopian will have 180 days of fasting in a year. Because it is encouraged by the church, it is not unusual for some Ethiopians to fast 300 days in a year. Therefore, it is safe to assume you are likely to find reliable vegan food at an Ethiopian restaurant. The same is true for other cultures. Thailand, for example, celebrates a vegetarian festival every year that lasts nearly two weeks. Because of this annual tradition, they know how to prepare inventive and appetizing vegetarian dishes. I've never had a problem finding vegan food at a Thai restaurant.

My husband, Rich, is of Italian decent and was raised in a Catholic tradition of eating no meat on Fridays. He says Fridays were the Catholic's Meatless Mondays! While a number of Catholics substituted fish on Fridays, others would have spaghetti marinara or pasta fagioli. There are numerous pasta dishes that can be made just as tasty and a good deal healthier than spaghetti with meatballs or lasagna laden with artery clogging meat and cheese.

Indian cuisine will usually have numerous vegan choices on their lunch buffets and even more on their a la carte menus. Japan and China, until recent years, have had largely vegetarian diets in general, using meat more as a flavoring agent or a condiment rather than as the main focus of the meal. I tend to steer away from Chinese restaurants due to their use of chemical preservatives and because I have found they still tend to flavor with animal flesh. I continue to search for Chinese restaurants serving fresh, whole foods that are chemical and animal free.

Japanese noodle restaurants are inexpensive, filling and loaded with fresh vegetables. You may have to ask for the vegan versions without fish sauce, however. This is true of all the Asian cuisines. Soy sauce is usually used to replace fish sauce in these recipes. I created a broth made from seaweed that is a great substitute. Vietnamese food is a vegan's mecca of tasty dishes from the vegetable and noodle dishes called Pho to rice paper rolled with fragrant herbs and lettuces and dunked in a spicy dipping sauce. So many options and so little time...!

Eating out at one of these restaurants is a great way to explore new flavors and include new foods into your diet. You reduce the risk of not knowing whether an unfamiliar food tastes as it should when preparing it for the first time at home, having no basis for comparison. The disadvantage is there are a lot of really bad restaurants out there. If your first experience with ethnic food is at a lousy or even mediocre ethnic restaurant it might give you the wrong impression. It is important to find restaurants that use fresh ingredients and cook their foods daily, rather than using yesterday's leftovers.

My first experience with Ethiopian cuisine was awful. The food tasted like old food, many times warmed over. Being an experienced cook, I recognized it for what it was and didn't let that thwart me from trying Ethiopian food again. My next experience was marvelous! I have learned to absolutely adore Ethiopian cuisine and I make it often. We recently stopped by a food court to eat at a Thai restaurant advertised as vegan on a travel website. We ordered Pad Thai. It was the worst Pad Thai ever! If that had been my first experience with Pad Thai, I might have never ordered it again. Fortunately, we had enjoyed excellent Pad Thai in the past so we knew this was no fair judge of Thai food. You may have to take a chance, and then another. It will be worth it. When you discover something wonderful, go home and make it yourself!

Dining In

Your home is your domain and the one place where you have the freedom to live as you like. Obviously you want your guests to feel at home, but that doesn't mean you have to disrupt your life or change your newly formed habits to suit them. Don't make a big deal of food. It isn't necessary to announce that you aren't cooking meat. Just don't cook meat. Chances are no one will even notice.

Recently I had a disaster in my kitchen with a leaking garden window. It had been installed improperly and water was pooling in its base. The support was rotting and ants were marching double-file into my kitchen! A friend recommended a competent contractor who we promptly hired. Tom and his young assistant, Harrison, replaced the window, which entailed replacing exterior siding and repainting as well.

I was taken aback when I first met Tom, who looked for all the world like Robert De Niro in his prime. Tom and Harrison are meat and potatoes kinds of guys. I told Tom that I always feed my workers and that Rich and I are vegan. While we were discussing the building project, I fixed Tom a sandwich of fresh tomatoes on a homemade bun topped with a vegan cream cheese I had made earlier that day. "There's no dairy in this cheese?" he asked, clearly surprised. "It tastes just like cream cheese, even better!"

Tom must not have believed me when I told him I would cook for them because when they arrived the next day, he and Harrison had brought their lunches with them. I had made a huge pasta salad with fresh basil, tomatoes, olives and capers. They tried some of it and loved it. Tom said, "I'm not bringing my lunch tomorrow!" The next day they eagerly wolfed down the vegan calzones I'd prepared for them, stuffed with vegan mozzarella and ricotta cheeses, Tofurkey Italian sausage, mushrooms, onion, garlic, kalamata olives and spicy banana peppers. On the side was a marinara sauce for dunking the calzones. Between bites Tom and Harrison said over and over again, "This is delicious!" Music to my ears! They also had more of the pasta salad and took some home to share with their families.

The next day I took it a step further and instead of cooking something that disguised the vegetables, I made a complete meal of nothing but vegetables. I prepared one my favorite veggie sandwiches with a homemade bun. To this I added sides of steamed kale, oven-"fried" potatoes, barbecued cauliflower florets and roasted yellow squash. Tom took one look at his plate loaded with colorful vegetables, and said, "Wow!" Harrison pronounced repeatedly, "This is delicious, this is delicious!" as he sampled each dish, savoring them one at a time. He said when he first looked at the sandwich he thought what it needed was a big chunk of meat and some cheese. But when he bit into it he realized the meat would have ruined it. "It is so flavorful it doesn't need anything else." Both Tom and Harrison agreed they didn't miss meat at this meal. The third day I made pasta shells stuffed with vegan ricotta cheese and baked in a creamy tomato-dill sauce. Tom said, "I never knew vegetables could taste like this. I mean, I love vegetables, but I never realized you could prepare them in so many ways that taste so good."

This is typical of the reaction we get when we invite omnivores to dinner. Wendy is one of my favorite nurses who took such excellent care of me when I was so ill after the botched liver surgery. We later discovered she had changed jobs and moved to the town where we live, so we invited her over for lunch. I made a vegan pizza with a whole grain crust, pizza sauce and a layer of spinach, then loaded with artichoke hearts, onions, bell peppers, olives, mushrooms and pineapple. Her response was very similar to Harrison's, "It is so flavorful you don't miss the meat or the cheese."

You don't have to change the way you eat to serve food your guests will enjoy. You don't have to contaminate your cooking surfaces with the flesh of dead animals. If your guests can't live without meat while they are visiting you, they can do what you do when you visit them, bring their own food. Or you can elect to go out to eat at a restaurant that will cater to everyone's needs.

Vegan Groups

One easy way to sample good plant-based foods and to further one's education on the subject is to join a local vegan group. Like-minded vegans gather once or twice a month to share a meal that has been prepared without meat, fish, poultry, eggs, dairy or honey. These groups are active throughout the United States. Some are made up of only a few people and some have scores of members.

These groups are usually comprised not just of people concerned about eating well, they are primarily concerned about animal welfare, protecting our planet and living consciously and humanely. In my experience, these are not pushy people. You will be accepted at whatever level you are at present.

I belong to several of these groups. I attend one group, that I consider my base group, more regularly than the others. They are fantastic resources for plant-based restaurants, educational events, social gatherings and even animal rights activism if one is so inclined. They also offer support and encouragement to one another in our attempts to transition to a plant-based lifestyle.

Once a month, each group puts on a pot-luck lunch or dinner where everyone brings an animal-free entree or dessert, enough to feed six to eight people. Usually, we bring our own dinner plates and utensils as well. Sometimes there is a small fee, around $3 per person, to pay for the facility if the group has to rent a place. Most of the time the cost of admission is simply your plant-based contribution to the meal.

Additionally, and this is the great part for beginner plant-based cooks, everyone also brings the recipe for their dish. In this way, you can quickly accumulate a wide variety of recipes that contain no animal products at all. You will have already tasted the dish, so you will know if you like it and what it is supposed to taste like. It's a no brainer!

I have met many lovely people at these events and have always been welcomed and made to feel at home. You can usually google the name of the city where you live, a mileage range and "vegan group," "veg group," or "vegan meet-up". Dozens of groups are likely to pop up on your computer screen. I just googled the tiny little town where I grew up in rural south Mississippi and a vegan group appeared only 30 minutes away from my mother's front door. It's easy as that!

COOK YOUR OWN FOOD!

Cooking And The Art Of Self-Defense

I learned to cook in self-defense. As were many of the parents of my generation, mine were clueless as to nutrition. They also, bless their hearts, were very poor cooks. My father had an adventurous palate and he thought he knew something about cooking. As it turns out, he didn't know much. Most of my early culinary skills I learned from him. It wasn't until after I was a young woman out in the world that I learned most of what he taught me was just plain wrong. I didn't even know how to cut an onion properly! While there are many ways to cut and onion, his method was without question the least efficient and most impractical. He did share with me his enthusiasm for food and his willingness to experiment. I learned I was cheating myself if I didn't at least try everything.

My mother was a horrid cook, by anyone's definition. She never enjoyed cooking. Trying to raise eleven children while working full time as a nurse was more than she could manage. The only thing I remember her cooking well were scalloped potatoes with ham, chicken and dumplings, and beef stew, things I would not in a million years eat now. She also did a fair job of biscuits and bread, though she invariably walked away from the oven during the last five minutes of baking and burned the bottoms. Every single time. That was her entire repertoire of palatable fare.

She was also dangerous in the kitchen. She had a habit of walking out of the kitchen "for a few seconds" to attend to something in another part of the house only to return to a stove that was on fire. She has burned cabinets, curtains, and destroyed numerous stoves over her lifetime, not to mention pots and pans. I always worried that she would burn down the house one day. My response to living with a pyromaniac was to learn to cook myself. I have a friend whose experience with her mother was very similar. Her response was to fear cooking.

Now that my mother has passed away and I've turned 60, I am mortified at how much like her I have become. I, too, have left food simmering on the stove only to return to find my dinner ruined and my pot no longer functional. It drives me crazy how easily distracted I am. Rich follows behind me making sure all the knobs on the stove are turned off, and I do the same for him. Though he'd never admit it, Rich is nearly as bad as I am.

I once repeated an old expression to him in an attempt to justify my inattention to the stove, "A watched pot never boils!"

To which he responded, "Danielle, a watched pot never boils *OVER!*"

Another thing I inherited from my family is how to cook for large groups. As the fifth child of eleven siblings, I became accustomed early to cooking for at least thirteen people at each meal. If we had visitors, as we often did since each of my ten brothers and sisters frequently brought their friends home with them, I learned to improvise. When Rich and I were married, he was astonished that I wanted to cook our wedding dinner. "No problem," I assured him, "I'll just double the recipe!"

In our increasingly frenetic lives of eating on the run, fast food and restaurant dining have replaced good home cooking. If it doesn't come in a can or a box or can't be handed to us from a drive-through window, it simply isn't going to make it into our bodies.

More of us are discovering the perils of this kind of eating. Our habits and addictions are catching up with us. Our bodies are not receiving the nutrition we need in order to sustain health, fight off disease, and avoid premature aging. We are consuming unsupportable quantities of artificial ingredients, genetically modified foods, and food-like substances which do not support our bodies with the nutrition required to sustain us. Instead, toxins from these fake foods build up in our systems causing damage to our genes, creating disease processes and an environment for them to flourish. We are a fat, sick society and it is only getting worse.

What can we do about it? Take control of our eating! When you shop for your own groceries and cook your own food, you know exactly what is going into it. If you enjoy gardening, you can increase this certainty by growing your own vegetables or herbs.

If you have simple tastes and are happy with the same six or eight meals over and over again, this lifestyle will be a piece of cake for you. Once you've figured out what plant-based foods you like and have learned to cook enough recipes to satisfy you, you are good to go. There is certainly nothing wrong with this approach. This is the way most people eat. They cook the same dishes most of the time and occasionally treat themselves to something special.

If you are easily bored with food, as I am, you'll have a more difficult time of it in the beginning. Your desire for variety will motivate you to expand your horizons and you will find yourself spending more time in the kitchen learning how to create flavors and textures that will please your fussy palate. Rich's transition to whole foods was easy because of my need to constantly seek new culinary experiences. He doesn't have a chance to become bored.

Whether you are comfortable with a limited menu or need to explore the entire range of plant-based options, meals you prepare yourself from whole plant-based foods are your best defense against the onslaught of chemicals and unsafe farming practices overwhelming our food supply and threatening our health.

Why Learn To Cook?

We, as a society, have come to think of cooking as some kind of drudgery, an unpleasant, time consuming task better left to someone else. This does not have to be the case.

First of all, it is generally unwise to entrust someone else with something as important as what is fueling our bodies, much less the developing bodies and brains of our vulnerable children. I spent many of my young adult years working in a variety of restaurants. Some of the acts I've witnessed restaurant management and staff perform on food being served to their customers have been appalling, if not downright disgusting.

Generally speaking, restaurants use the cheapest ingredients they can find and alarming amounts of oil, sugar and salt to make their food taste good. While reviewing restaurants for *Veggin' Out and About!*, I have discovered a few restaurants who are responsible guardians of their customers health, but the vast majority are just trying to make a profit in an extremely competitive environment, cutting corners wherever they can. It is best to save restaurant dining for special occasions and prepare most of your food at home.

Secondly, studies show that people who cook their own food live longer and healthier than people who do not, no matter what kind of food they are preparing![1] The reason for this is that when you buy your own food and prepare it at home, you are more conscious about what goes into it and how it's cooked. You automatically make healthier choices. Even if you continue to eat animal products, when you cook for yourself you are more likely to make better food decisions.

Most pre-prepared, convenience foods are loaded with preservatives, high-fructose corn syrup and other unhealthy sweeteners, salt, chemical additives and genetically modified organisms, which do not have to be disclosed in labeling. The word "natural" has come to mean anything but natural. It is best to do your shopping in the produce isles and bypass the packaged and canned products altogether. Generally speaking, if it comes in a can, bag or box, avoid it. If there is a commercial for it on TV, avoid it like the plague!

If you can afford it, buy organic as much as possible. Fresh produce labeled "conventional" are likely contaminated with poisons such as high levels of toxic pesticides and herbicides. I sometimes feel that the label "natural" should include a picture of a skull and crossbones, designating it as a poison.

If you are lucky enough to have a good farmers' market in your area, get your produce there. I buy most of what I need in season from my local farmers market. When you buy locally, you infuse capital into your own community, reduce the impact on the environment of transporting foods from other countries, and personally get to know who is growing your food. You can look them in the eye and ask them about their growing practices. Usually, there is a local governing body who oversees these practices so you'll know if they are telling you the truth.

You are likely to find bugs and/or blemishes on much of the produce you buy organically. That's a good thing. Bugs cannot survive on foods sprayed with toxic pesticides, or have had pesticides inserted into their genes through genetic manipulation. I'm very suspicious of the "perfect" produce I see in grocery stores, lined up in immaculate rows without a blemish in sight. They look too good to be true, and they are. They may look perfect but their flavors and nutrition pale in comparison to freshly picked organic produce. I witnessed a conversation between a vendor at our local farmers' market and one of her customers who was surprised to see a worm on the corn she had just purchased. The vendor responded, "That's how you know it's organic!"

There is something sublimely intimate about shaking the hand of the person who grows your food. Plus, fresh organic produce just tastes better. I do not buy produce labeled "conventionally grown," regardless of where it is grown. Just because someone is spraying poisons on locally grown produce, doesn't make them any less toxic.

We live in an age where the art of preparing healthy and delicious food has been lost. There is a skill to the combining of certain ingredients to emphasize some flavors and subdue others. Cooking is an art, and should be a pleasure, not a chore. Chopping raw vegetables crunching with freshness and bursting with pungent and sweet aromas piques our imaginations to create something new. The mundane task of cutting fresh vegetables becomes something of a zen-like experience, at once soothing and life affirming. Preparing a meal can be a transcendent experience. It really depends on the attitude you bring to the task.

Like a child whose first attempts at creating art begins with mud pies, crayons and finger-painting, begin with the primal impulse to express yourself in a way that is both original and fun. Start with something simple and build from there. Learn one skill at a time and before you know it you'll be creating dishes that will not only surprise you, but will delight your family and dinner guests. Exploring exotic foods handed down from many cultures and many generations will open up new worlds that will excite all your senses.

Are you one of the millions of Americans who eat their meals at fast food restaurants and are beginning to feel the effects of this lifestyle on your health? A lot of people share this reality.

Are you a young adult, newly out into the world, and have no experience in the kitchen? Do you feel your life is just too busy for the additional chore of cooking your own meals? Or do you find learning new kitchen skills just too intimidating? If your answer is yes to any of these questions, I hope the simple recipes in this book will guide you painlessly through the process of learning to enjoy cooking and becoming a healthier individual as a result.

10

WHAT'S HOLDING
YOU BACK?

At no time in history have so few people learned to cook, yet more cookbooks are sold now than at any other time. People love food. We are fascinated by cooking shows and colorful pictures of delicious looking recipes in cooking magazines and cookbooks. It is often referred to as "Food Porn," we are that into it. We build designer kitchens we rarely use. What's that all about?

We all make excuses as to why we don't have time to cook, and many of them are valid. Eating out, however, isn't the answer. You have no idea what is going into your food when you eat in even the best restaurants. The reality is, if you want to eat a healthy diet and you can't afford to hire someone to cook appetizing, nutritious meals for you, you really should make an effort to learn to cook. As in most things, if it is important to you, you'll find a way to do it. I hope you have come to understand just how important it is to eat well to give your body the nutritional support it needs to thrive.

Let's address some of the reasons we choose not to cook.

I Don't Have Time To Cook

This is a reality for many of us. We rush from one activity to the next and hardly have time to come up for air. We must treat the fueling of our bodies and the bodies of our loved ones as a priority and carve out time in our busy schedules for preparing healthy meals. When our bodies aren't functioning at an optimal level, we can't do anything well.

Time

There is no question that it takes time to put a good meal on the table. It also takes time to shop for grocery items and to clean up the messes we make in our pristine kitchens. There's no getting around it.

Thinking about what you want to cook and making a shopping list before going to the grocery store will save time in the long run and will also reduce waste. When you buy impulsively, just because you want to try cooking with a particular vegetable but haven't made a plan, the vegetable in question is likely to end up in the compost bin before you get around to preparing it. Always make a plan and a shopping list. This will make the task of buying groceries quick and painless and you won't find yourself loading up on unnecessary items. The more organized you become, the easier time you'll have of it.

One way to deal with time constraints is to cook while we are attending to other necessary tasks, such as doing laundry. If you are stuck at home doing laundry for the coming work week, writing a report or even watching a movie, you may as well put on a pot of pasta sauce, or a pot of beans on the stove, or a casserole in the oven to cook while you are working. Batch cooking is an excellent way to have healthy foods on hand at all times. (Be sure you keep a timer with you so you don't forget about the food on the stove or in the oven and burn it.)

Putting aside time to cook large quantities of food is a great way to stockpile food in your freezer, freeing up time for other activities later. Spending a day or two cooking can give you weeks and even months of free time to attend to other pursuits you may prefer.

When Rich was stationed in Germany and I was about to begin an art program in France, I arrived a few weeks early to find a place for him to live and to receive our household items which were being shipped to us from Japan. By the time Rich arrived, I was already in France immersed in my studies. Raymonde, the wife of one of his colleagues, asked Rich if she could prepare some meals for him to tide him over until he had a chance to shop and get settled. "No, thanks," Rich replied, "Danielle stocked the freezer for me before she left."

Raymonde was astonished. "How did Danielle have time to cook?" She knew very well how much work was involved in unpacking household items and organizing a new home, especially in the short amount of time I had. Then the lightbulb went on. "Oh, she made it a *priority!*"

If you make preparing healthy foods a priority, you can accomplish much more than you might imagine. Sure, I had a lot of work to accomplish before leaving for France. But since I was stuck in the house anyway, I was able to cook sauces, pots of beans, casseroles and stews and freeze them in single serving portions for Rich to pull out of the freezer whenever he was hungry. I was able to stock a three months supply of meals in an average-sized freezer.

Freeze meals in the appropriate serving sizes for your family, in glass containers with BPA-free lids. You have only to pull one out and defrost it in your microwave or pop it into the oven when you are in need of a quick healthy meal. This also works well with large batches of burger buns or scones. Freeze in ziplock bags what you don't need within a day or two. Then you can pull out what you need from your freezer as you need it.

Cleaning Up

Wouldn't it be nice if we could wave a magic wand and the kitchen, with all our prep-work mess, would just clean itself? Since that's never going to happen, keeping your work organized is again the key to making life easier.

My husband swears I can get sauce on the ceiling. It helps if there are two people working together. I gave Rich the title, "Sous Chef," which he interprets as "Kitchen Slave." He's also my taste tester, an activity at which he rarely balks. We have many of our life discussions in the kitchen while I'm preparing food. He sometimes reads novels aloud to me as I work. Working together and cleaning up dishes we are finished with as we go makes the experience less daunting and more enjoyable for both of us.

I Can't Afford To Cook

If you eat the majority of your meals in fast food restaurants, you can't afford not to learn to cook. While these foods may be cheap and filling, it is only a matter of time before your health and the health of your family members will begin to suffer. Fast food is made to be addictive and is loaded with ingredients that are simply not good for you. The up front costs may be less, but your costs in lost wages from missed work days due to illness, as well as in medical expenses, will more than make up the difference. Plus, by avoiding fast foods, you will just feel better.

There are many plant-based foods that are inexpensive to prepare. At today's prices, you can buy a pound of the most expensive organic beans available at my local health food store and a pound of the most expensive organic brown rice for $6.68. With these two items and a few herbs and spices, you can feed a family of ten a nutritious, satisfying meal. Or you can feed one person an artery clogging, disease promoting, Double Quarter Pounder with Cheese, french fries and a coke for $6.45.

You will have to invest in some up front items like pots and pans, some cooking utensils, herbs and spices and possibly some specialty items. You can buy these items as you need them and before long you'll have a fully functional kitchen with all the accoutrements you need to prepare a host of delicious foods. Some of the items I have in my kitchen took me years to accumulate. Just buy what you need when you need it and begin with simple foods and simple goals.

I Don't Know How To Cook

Fear of cooking is the most likely reason more people haven't learned to cook. It can seem an insurmountable task when faced with odd gadgets, unfamiliar spices, and new terms, like learning computer language to those of us born when telephones had dials. Like anything worthwhile, there is a learning curve to cooking. Start with something simple and build your skills one at a time. Rome wasn't built in a day. Give yourself permission to fail. After all, every attempt at cooking is just an experiment. If one experiment fails, try another. That's how we learn.

Watching cooking shows is a good way to learn some techniques, and there are many books on the subject. If there is a local course in basic cooking techniques, why not try it? It could be great fun and you will meet some people in the same boat as you. All of us were beginners at one point.

Many of the recipes in the back of this book are simple and will reward you with delicious flavors and a few new cooking skills. Each of my subsequent books will have tips on cooking and will help you achieve a new level of competence.

Even if you never learn to enjoy cooking, it is important to develop some skill in the kitchen, if only to maintain a certain level of independence. Teaching your children to cook is one of the most valuable gifts you'll ever give them.

Cooking can and should be a joyful, creative, comforting experience. Nothing is sexier than a man who will cook for a woman. I fell in love with Rich the evening he cooked for me the most delicious pasta sauce I had ever eaten. Twenty-seven years later we are still cooking together.

Cooking is a labor of love that can bind families together. Many of our most cherished memories of lost loved ones have taken place at kitchen tables throughout the world over hot beverages and home cooked meals. These are memories our children might have of us when we are gone.

❧ 11 ❧

EXCITING NEW INGREDIENTS

TO EXPLORE

There are lots of exciting options in the world of plant-based cuisine. Some of it you may embrace with open arms. Other aspects you may not care for at all. It's all good, there are plenty of options for everyone.

You may be the adventurous type who wants to try every mushroom on the planet, experimenting with the various flavors and textures. The old standby, the white button mushroom, found in the chiller of nearly every grocery story in the country may be all you'll ever want or need. Both approaches are perfectly fine. It is your food and your tastes are all you have to cater to.

In this chapter, I'll introduce you to some of the products available to the plant-based cook. This list is only a pittance compared to what is actually available in markets today. I'm discovering new grains, beans, fruits and vegetables regularly. I want to try them all, knowing full well I'll never get around to all of them.

Included later in this book is a list of herbs and spices. Don't feel pressured to go out and buy them all. Some may taste strange to you and others you will never learn to like. Still others may help you to create dishes you'll adore and you'll wonder how you ever lived without them.

The options are endless and yours to explore to the extent you care to. Make your plant-based experience uniquely yours.

Soy, Seitan and Other Meat Substitutes

When I was a young woman in college and soy burgers were first introduced to our university cafeteria, we students referred to them suspiciously as "mystery meat." These meat-like products now include seitan and tofu, TVP or TSP, and tempeh. Some of the newer products are more palatable than earlier versions. Made from peas and grains and other truly natural ingredients, as well as the aforementioned items, they are also healthier. While I still prefer foods in their whole state, these faux meat and cheese products allow you to continue to eat your old favorites without compromising your health.

Seitan

If you are intolerant of gluten, you should know that seitan (pronounced say-tan) is nothing but wheat gluten. It is quite literally the glutenous protein of wheat, the part that makes bread dough stretchy. It is made from washing wheat dough until all of the starch is dissolved and only the stretchy gluten remains. This process results in a lot of wasted water. When this gluten is cooked it resembles meat.

You can buy powdered wheat gluten in a box. It is mixed with water until it becomes a stretchy dough. It can then be sliced into cutlets. Next, boil it in vegetable stock or water (without stirring) for about 20 minutes. It will roughly double in size. At this point, it can be treated like any meat. It will make a facsimile of meat but it is highly processed and has little nutritional value. It does contain about 18 percent protein and no fat to speak of.

Seitan is relatively flavorless and has no ability to absorb flavor. However, it can be slathered with a marinade or sauce and grilled, fried or baked, and it can be combined with other, more nutritious ingredients. It can also be ground up to look and feel like hamburger, molded into substances that look like steaks, meatballs, strips of meat, or mixed with tofu to make hot dogs and sausages. It has its place, especially when you are trying to convince your carnivorous significant other to try something plant-based, or if you are having trouble transitioning to a whole foods, plant-based diet yourself.

Tofu

Tofu is a soy product. It is 47 percent fat, is highly processed and has virtually no flavor. Tofu does contain a significant amount of protein and is a good source of some minerals. To make tofu, soybeans are cooked in a vat of water. They are then pureed, along with their water, and strained through a porous cloth to make soy milk. The soybeans, which remain in the cloth, are discarded. Then, a coagulant is added which causes the milk to curdle. The curds are poured into a sturdy box lined with another porous cloth. A heavy weight is placed on the top to compact the curds into what will become a brick of tofu.

The fiber is often thrown away in its production. Tofu does not, as purported, really take on the flavor of what it is cooked with. We can add seasonings to it or coat it with a marinade but it is nonabsorbent. It can be fried, crumbled, pureed, or frozen to create a texture similar to ground beef, baked, steamed, grilled and smoked. Tofu can be used to create facsimiles of meat and cheese products and can be used to make delicious sauces and gravies.

Although it is high in fat, there is some research that suggests that soy blocks fat cells from storing fat.[1] Plant estrogens in soy have been shown to reduce breast cancer risks and menstrual symptoms. Studies show men eating soy have less prostate cancer and better prostate cancer survival while not effecting fertility or sexuality.[2] Soybeans are also rich in omega-3 fatty acids. It is best to eat soy in the least processed manner possible. Boiled edamame, or soybeans, are delicious as a snack.

Soy is also a plant that has been genetically modified to an alarming extent. It is reported that up to 90 percent of the soy crop in the United States is genetically modified. The same is true of corn, canola, and sugar beets. I will no longer touch corn products* or soy* unless they have been certified to be organic. Canola oil* is harder to avoid. When eating out, most restaurants use copious amounts of canola oil and/or corn oil. Genetically modified vegetable oil is pervasive in the food industry.

*Be sure to look for the Certified Non-GMO label when buying these products.

Textured Vegetable Protein

Textured vegetable protein or textured soy protein (TVP or TSP) is a meat substitute made from soybeans by processing it to the point that it resembles meat and retains a good deal of protein. It also no long resembles anything close to the soy bean's natural state. Many manufacturers of TVP use hexane (a solvent also used in gasoline) to extract the oils from the soybean. Trace amounts are left in the TVP after it is processed. Whether this is harmful remains to be seen. I, personally, do not eat it.

Tempeh

Tempeh, like tofu, is made from soybeans. Unlike tofu, it is a whole food that has been cultured and fermented to bind soybeans into a cake form. It is used often as a meat substitute. It is nutritious, retaining not only its protein but also its dietary fiber and vitamins. Still, it is soy, which means it is likely to have been genetically modified. Eat this only if it is certified organically grown.

A number of vegan and vegetarian restaurants offer some kind of soy product, usually tofu, as a substitute to meat. Unless it is certified organic, you may want to skip the tofu and have extra vegetables instead. I've never had a restaurant refuse this request. Also, note that soy sauces found in restaurants are rarely organic as this product is cost-prohibitive to most restaurants.

Commercially prepared vegan cheeses and imitation meats are really a kind of old school vegan, in my opinion. There is a lot of fat and salt in soy cheeses. As these foods are highly processed, there is nothing whole about them. They only resemble meat and cheese in a superficial way. They have become widely popular and are convenient in offering a meat-like option to consumers. As a transitioning tool they do have their place. They are certainly better than eating actual meat and cheese. They should not, in my opinion, be thought of as the final stage of your plant-based journey but rather as a step in your transition to a plant-based lifestyle.

I have incorporated a limited amount of these ingredients in my cookbooks as a nod to those who feel they need these foods in order to adhere to a WFPB diet, at least in the beginning. I rarely cook them for myself and eat them only occasionally, usually when dining out with friends. The restaurants that serve these kinds of foods are certainly places where you can eat once in a while, when you would simply like a change of pace or satisfy a craving for a particular treat. They are especially nice to find when you are traveling, when restaurants offering whole foods are few and far between. Restaurants such as these usually will also offer some fresh whole foods options as well.

You can make your own cheeses from organic tofu or nuts that are both tasty and healthy since you can control the amount of salt you use and reduce or eliminate it by substituting lemon, dill, citric acid, etc.

In my view, it is better to learn to like new things rather than trying to make plant-based whole foods into something they are not. In the end it is more satisfying and much healthier. Whole foods in their natural state with minimal processing, that's the real deal!

Miso and Other Fermented Products

I used to prepare and eat lots of fermented vegetables as they have been widely touted as being highly beneficial in promoting "good" gut flora. These vegetables, pickled in brine, are staples of Asian cultures, particularly in Korea, Japan and China. However, new studies suggest a strong link between fermented vegetables (such as kimchi and sauerkraut) and certain cancers, particularly intestinal, breast and prostate.[3, 4, 5] They are also high in salt, which is not appreciated by our arteries. Still, I use a limited amount of these products in cooking; sometimes only a drop or two of a fermented brine can make a difference in taste and it is a far cry from the quantities consumed in these cultures. If you feel uncomfortable using them you can certainly eliminate these products with only a subtle sacrifice of flavor.

Miso
Miso is a paste made from soybeans, barley, brown rice, soy or other ingredients. I first discovered miso during the years Rich and I lived in Japan. It is rich in vitamins and minerals and high in protein and has long been a dietary staple in Japan where miso soup is a starter for most meals. I occasionally use garbanzo bean miso in cooking as it imparts little flavor but adds a creaminess to broths, gravies and sauces. There are numerous varieties, the lighter colored misos are the

mildest and the darker more savory and robust. They are both salty and sweet and can even be used in preparing desserts.

Tamari

Tamari, true tamari, is a brine by-product of making miso. It is a brown liquid, similar to soy-sauce and is fantastic for adding just a pinch of flavor to sauces and soups. Don't overdo it! Tamari can easily overpower a dish, but by adding just a little you can create an extra dimension of flavor without anyone recognizing the source. Since it is a brine, it also adds salt so consider that when adding it to your food. Tamari has become so popular in the United States it is now being produced as a product in and of itself and is often separate from the miso making process. It will frequently contain wheat, so if you are allergic to gluten, avoid this product. It is best to purchase tamari from a reputable organic dealer.

Umeboshi Vinegar

Umeboshi vinegar is another product I use occasionally in cooking. It is a by-product of pickling plums. Using only a few drops will add a sparkle to many dishes without changing the principle character of the dish. It is usually sold as a vinegar but it is, in fact, a brine.

Condiments

Mustard

Whole grain Dijon mustard is available nearly everywhere and is a wonderful condiment to use in making sauces with tofu and cashew cream. You can also easily prepare your own.

Rice Wine

Mirin is a versatile, sweet Japanese rice wine. I like Mitoku brand. This is lovely sprinkled on greens, added to sauces for a little sparkle, making vegetarian sushi, and for many other uses. Use sparingly as the flavor is distinctive.

Chipotle Peppers in Adobo Sauce

While you may have to shop around to find this little gem of southwestern flavoring, it is worth keeping on hand. It is one of the few canned items I buy. You might find it a bit ungainly to use; you will never need more than a smidgen in most recipes as this pepper is seriously hot. Chipotles are smoked jalapeños and adobo is a type of Spanish marinade. I find pureeing the entire can and keeping it in a sealed glass container in my fridge makes this much easier to use. The brand I prefer is San Marcos. Don't overdo this seasoning; a little goes a very long way!

Capers

These little buds of the caper bush can be found in jars pickled in brine. They are fantastic additions to pasta salads, many kinds of sauces, and in green salads. They are often paired with olives to create an exciting layer of flavor undertones.

Olives

Keeping a jar of Kalamata olives on hand is never a bad idea. They last a long time in your fridge. You can buy them by the pound in open olive bars in some grocery stores, pitted or whole. They are great in pasta salads, tomato sauces, green salads, on pizzas, and much more. Mixed olives are delicious appetizers, raw, roasted, or baked with lots of roasted garlic.

Vegan Mayonaise

Veganaise is a brand name for an organic vegan mayonnaise. It is a processed oil but contains no animal protein. It comes in handy in a pinch, but it is healthier to make your own. Use sparingly.

Butter Substitute

Earth Balance is a butter substitute that can be used in any application calling for butter. It is a processed fat and is not a product that could reasonably be considered healthy, but it is better than using butter or margarine. Use sparingly.

Sriracha Sauce

Sriracha is a pepper sauce commonly seen in Asian restaurants. It has gained popularity in the United States and is now readily available. Sky Valley by Organicville is a flavorful brand that I like to use. If you can't find sriracha, you can substitute Tabasco sauce. The flavor and texture are quite different but will not greatly alter the recipe. You can also omit it altogether or substitute a little cayenne or red chili pepper.

Note: If you or one of your guests love spicy food but are in the minority at the dinner table, adding some sriracha to only your servings is often a perfect remedy.

Mushrooms

White Button Mushrooms

The most common mushrooms, white buttons are available almost anywhere. Interestingly, as it turns out they are one of the most healthy. White button mushrooms are extremely protective against breast cancer and should be eaten often.[6] They can be put into sauces, stuffed, broiled, braised, grilled and smoked.

Portobello Mushrooms

Large, meaty mushrooms, portobellos are usually about four-inches in diameter. These mushrooms are often grilled and used as a substitute for meat in veggie burgers as they give the chewy mouthfeel of eating meat. They can be sliced for use in sandwiches, stuffed and baked, or broiled, sliced, chopped, marinated and stewed. There are many ways to enjoy this hearty mushroom.

Baby Bella Mushrooms

Baby Bellas are just what their name implies. They are baby portobellos and can be prepared in exactly the same ways button mushrooms can be prepared.

Shiitake Mushrooms

Possessing a unique, smokey, savory flavor, fresh shiitakes have a much more subtle flavor than dried. These mushrooms can be found in Asian markets. It takes about 30 minutes to rehydrate the dried shiitake. They are often used in Asian soups. Their chewy texture makes them a great substitute for clams.

Enoki Mushrooms

These odd straw-like mushrooms are commercially grown together in clumps, like long white pins packed together on a pin cushion. They are typically used in soups and stews but are great in stir fries and other dishes. You can buy them canned, though if you are lucky enough to live near a good Asian grocer you can find them fresh.

Oyster Mushrooms

Fresh oyster mushrooms are delicate and very nice with light sauces. When rolled in corn or potato starch and fried or broiled, they resemble fried shrimp. While I don't recommend fried foods, broiling this mushroom is a real treat.

Straw Mushrooms

Straw mushrooms can be found canned or dried. I've never found fresh ones. Straw mushrooms are a common ingredient in Thai cuisine.

Maitake Mushrooms

Maitake mushrooms are common to Japanese cuisine. They can be found dried in Asian markets.

Morel Mushrooms

I have never tried this widely prized wild mushroom. Wild mushrooms are a tricky business. When I was in college, I had a botany teacher who was mourning the death of a colleague and friend. His colleague had been an expert in mushrooms, yet he managed to poison himself foraging and eating wild mushrooms. That cured me of any desire to experience morels or wild mushrooms of any kind. Local foragers brag that they've eaten hundreds of wild mushrooms with no ill effects. While that may be true, it only takes one mistake to end your life. It's not worth it to me.

Dairy Substitutes

Cow's milk is not necessary for humans. Its only true purpose is to feed and nurture suckling calves. If you are not a suckling calf, you have no need of milk from a cow. There are several plant-based options that are delicious and are better sources of calcium than cow's milk and are better utilized by the human body. Soy, almond, rice and coconut milks are low in calories and can be used in hot chocolate, on breakfast cereals, in cooking and in any application where cow's milk might be employed. Be sure to buy certified non-GMO if you are buying soy milk.

Coconut milk used in Thai and Indian dishes is not the same as the type bought in the dairy department of your grocery store. These will be found in cans where Asian goods are found.

There are also numerous vegan cheeses, yogurts and ice cream substitutes available in most grocery stores. They do not contain animal protein, though they are often loaded with comparable fat, sugars, and salt. Limit your use of these items.

Another ingredient you may find even in organic products is a food additive called carrageenan, an extract of red seaweed widely used in dairy products and baby food as a thickener. It has no nutritional value and is believed to cause intestinal problems, such as bloating, abdominal pain and prolonged gastrointestinal inflammation. Carrageenan is such a powerful inflammatory agent it is often used in laboratory animals to induce inflammation in order to test anti-inflammatory drugs. Carrageenan must be disclosed on the nutritional label of these foods. If you see it is in a food you are thinking of purchasing, you may wish to look for another product that doesn't contain this ingredient.[7]

≈ 12 ≈

STOCKING YOUR KITCHEN

You don't need a lot of specialized equipment to cook well. When Rich and I were building our barn/house, we spent four years living in a nineteen-by-eight feet, thirty-year-old travel trailer, with a cat and two dogs, cooking on two burners. We had a mini-fridge with six inches of freezer space, a tiny oven, a chopping board, a few dull knives, a strainer, measuring cups and spoons, and an immersion blender. Everything else was boxed up in a storage unit for lack of kitchen space. Beyond a few pots and pans, a large spoon, a whisk, and a spatula, that was about it. We made great meals in that little kitchen.

The above mentioned items are essential. You may also want a citrus juicer, a vegetable grater, a rolling pin, an assortment of mixing bowls, a pair of oven mitts or potholders, and a few other items I might have failed to mention. You can pick most of them up very cheaply at discount stores. A sharp citrus zester (used to remove thin strips of the flavorful, oily outer layer of the peel of lemons and oranges) is nice to have, though you can zest citrus peels without it using a sharp paring knife. You may also want a good, sturdy handheld potato masher. One with connecting S-curves (not squares or holes punched in the base) is fine for mashing potatoes or any other root vegetable. I don't like the potato mashers with the squares or holes because the holes clog, making the option of leaving on the skins more difficult. The S-curve masher doesn't clog.

If you can afford to, invest in a good sharp knife and a sharpener to keep it that way. Cooking is so much more pleasurable when you don't have to wrestle with a dull knife. An eight-inch chef's knife, a paring knife and a good bread knife are all you really need. I use these three knives almost exclusively in my kitchen.

While it is convenient to own kitchen gadgets, you can certainly live without them. Having said that, I must admit I am a gadget junkie and I've collected lots of shiny new toys for my kitchen. I did not acquire them in a day, a month, or even a year. I have collected them over a lifetime of cooking. Many of them I use frequently, while others are now collecting dust in my basement. I can share with you the pieces I find valuable and the pieces I rarely use. Your needs may be different. I only address the products with which I have personal experience. You may have others you like just as well and you may have favorites I can't appreciate. Fortunately, there is much to choose from. Buy what suits you and your needs.

Kitchen Equipment

What you really need, what you might like to have, and what is just taking up space in your kitchen.

Baking Stone

I enjoy using a baking stone for baking flat breads and pizzas. I keep it in the oven most of the time as it helps to keep the temperature of the oven constant, even when the door has been opened. It makes the bottoms of my pizzas crisp when cooking vegetable toppings, which tend to release moisture when heated, making crusts soggy. This is a serviceable item to have but another one you can live without. They range in price and size. I have several I use for different purposes. My favorite is a round, deep dish pizza stone made by a beloved Appalachian potter Debbie Grim, who creates unique, lovely utilitarian pottery. (www.grimpottery.snappages.com) Your pizza stone will stain with use and eventually turn very dark. That's when you'll know you've arrived as a baker!

Ball Jars

Ball Jars are the greatest organizational tool of all time. They are made primarily for canning fruits and vegetables, but their uses are endless and they last forever. If the lids become lost or broken, unlike specialty glass jars, they are easy to replace. They are fairly inexpensive and make organizing one's pantry a breeze. Here are a few ideas that you may find helpful.

Half gallon Ball jars are great for storing bulk grains, flours, nuts, and pastas. You can write the name of the product and the date you purchased it on the glass with a permanent marker, so you will know when it is time to use it or toss it out. The ink will come off with a nylon scrubber and a little soap so you can relabel it and fill it with a new item. You have the option of buying white plastic caps that keep them looking neat.

Quart jars are good for many things — smaller amounts of beans, remnants of shaped pastas, flaxseeds, chia seeds, small amounts of grains, nutritional yeast, potato starch, couscous, date sugar, etc.

Pint size jars are best for items you are buying in small quantities. They are also the perfect size for canned tomatoes. I store herbs and spices I buy in bulk in these jars, after first filling the small spice jars I use on a daily basis.

Four ounce jars are perfect for all the spices and dried herbs I use regularly. I write their names on the lids and line them up alphabetically in a large shallow drawer. That way, I can find the spice I need at a glance. The mouths are wide enough to insert any size measuring spoon and they are easy to refill. This has been a great organizational system I wish I had thought of 30 years ago.

Blender, High-Powered

A Vitamix blender has eventually found its way into the home of nearly every vegan and vegetarian I know. This high-powered blender can be a great time saver. They are very expensive; mine cost nearly as much as I paid for my range. When I bought it seven years ago, I was experimenting with raw foods and I made green smoothies several times a day. It will grind up fruits and veggies, allowing them to be served as a drink, while retaining the fiber. A regular blender will burn up performing the same task. I make wonderfully creamy sauces in record time with this machine, as well as banana ice creams and fruit sorbets. A traditional household blender cannot do this. If you want to make vegan cream cheese, a high-powered blender makes this task much easier. You can accomplish this with a food processor and a blender, but you won't be able to get the authentic creamy texture of traditional cream cheese. I use this machine regularly. It will blend anything quickly and smoothly. While I can certainly cook without it, it is a nice tool to have in the kitchen. The brand I have is a Vitamix, though I'm told there are other good brands available. The Vitamix company is very customer oriented and the one time I had a repair issue, they replaced the part in record time, with no cost or hassle to me. The machine comes with a very nice, seven-year warranty. Use earplugs with this product as it is a little loud.

Another thing I use my blender for is composting vegetable scraps. We keep a compost pile near our garden which consists of mostly chopped up leaves. In the winter, when our area is covered with snow, veggie scraps tend to just freeze. We got the brilliant idea to grind up our scraps in a high-powered blender and dump the liquid onto the leaves. It soaked in and in the spring, we had the most amazing, healthy compost we'd ever had, with earthworms in abundance.

If you aren't making smoothies, nut cheeses, ice cream or composting vegetables, a regular blender will meet most of your needs. An immersion blender works for many cooking tasks, and will work for most of them if you are persistent and patient.

Coffee Grinder

I consider this a must have in my kitchen. I use my coffee grinder to grind spices, though the manufacturer says not to use it for this purpose. It is inexpensive and does a great job of grinding flaxseeds daily and many of my spices. It has its limitations, though. It will not grind nutmeg, cloves or pink peppercorns. It's a little difficult to clean. I usually wipe it out with a damp paper towel. A good spice grinder is on my wish list.

Cookware

I'm not an expert on the materials that go into creating cookware. You'll have to look at your budget and buy the best you can afford. All Clad is an excellent brand, but expensive. A good set of All Clad is definitely on my wish list. I use stainless steel cookware with a copper exterior. Copper allows for more even temperatures and I've been pleased with my set. I purchased the pieces individually over time. Be sure to pay particular attention to the handles. If the handles are hollow, like a long tube, the heat from the pan is funneled into the handle making them very hot and likely to cause you significant burns. You will also have to use pot holders every time you touch the handles. I have learned this the hard way. The best handle I've found divides into a fork where it attaches to the pot and then becomes solid as it moves away from the pan. These handles remain cool and are less likely to cause you to be seriously burned.

It is helpful to have these items:

9- or 10-quart stock pot
2-quart saucepan
3-quart saucepan
8-inch skillet
12-inch sauté pan, or skillet

Get lids with everything you can. In many sets, most of the lids serve more than one pan. However, it is best to have a lid for each individual pan. These are the most practical items in a cookware set, in my view. Some will include a small wok, or extra fry pans, a double boiler, and/or a steamer basket. They are all good to have but these five items, with lids, would be my first choices.

It is also helpful to have on hand a couple of cookie sheets for baked goods and roasting vegetables. I also recommend at least one nine-inch cake pan and a glass pie plate. You may also want a casserole pan for vegetarian lasagnas and other casserole type dishes.

Cookware, Non-Stick

A good, seasoned cast-iron skillet is nice to have. Lodge is an old reliable brand and is carried in many discount stores. It comes pre-seasoned, but you'll have to cook with it several times before your food truly stops sticking to the pan. I recently bought a 14-inch flat cast iron griddle for making South Indian and Ethiopian pancakes and crêpes. This cast-iron griddle seems to be the best bet so far. It works well now that the seasoning process is behind me and I have come to really like this product. I prefer it over non-stick pans. Before each use, coating the surface with a little oil on a paper towel is enough to keep this stick-free. I have tried expensive ceramic pans with a white coating that worked well for a couple of days, but rapidly lost their non-stick properties. The one that works best for me is the most inexpensive. It is a gray ceramic pan that looks a lot like Teflon that I picked up at Sam's for about $15. I'm still searching for a reliable non-stick product that is safe.

Dehydrator

A dehydrator is something I don't use often, but when I do, nothing will replace it. It is ideal for drying tomatoes, apples, herbs and spices, kale and corn chips, and much more. A nine-tray Excalibur allows plenty of space to work with. It takes up a lot of space, a 15-inch cube on your countertop, but if you have things you want to dry at low temperatures, you can't beat it. One of the great advantages a dehydrator has over heating food at low temperatures in the oven, is that you can leave it overnight or longer and you never have to worry about over-drying your food. When oven drying, a minute of inattention can ruin all your hard work. The Excalibur is relatively expensive, considering it is just a plastic box with tray frames, a fan and a small heating element. The silicone sheets sold separately are pricy too and they don't last forever. I bought my Excalibur at the same time I purchased my Vitamix, seven years ago, and it still serves me well, but I rarely use it.

Alternatively, you can dry most things at low temperatures in your oven. I don't find it works as well for making things like kale or corn chips, but you can have success with oven drying if you pay attention to your timing and keep an eye on your work.

Earplugs

Many appliances are louder than I believe is safe. Once your hearing is gone, it's gone, so be safe rather than sorry. I keep two pairs of labeled ear plugs with their own cases for both Rich and me in a kitchen drawer and we use them faithfully every time I turn on a loud appliance.

Flame Tamer

A flame tamer is worth its weight in gold. It is an inexpensive, flat, aluminum disk that looks much like a pingpong paddle. When placed underneath a pot, it disperses the heat from the burner so you can cook delicate sauces without the need of a double boiler or constant stirring. Whenever you are cooking anything that will simmer for hours, a flame tamer is a great asset. It comes with a wooden handle that will burn off after your first or second use. Don't let that concern you. I don't know why they even put the handle on the flame tamer. You don't need it and it just gets in the way. Let it char, twist it off and toss it. You'll have a little point of metal left that once fit into the handle, which is more than adequate. Just don't handle it while it is hot, or if you do, use a pair of tongs.

Food Processor

I would hate to think of life without my food processor. It makes prep work so easy. If I were allowed to keep only one appliance, it would be a toss up between this and my Vitamix. A food processor makes quick work of so many tasks. It has a fantastic grating attachment for large projects. It allows me to prepare dips and spreads in no time. It chops nuts, grates coconuts, and makes patty mixtures for veggie burgers. I am always finding new, time-saving uses for this machine. I use this so often I bought one for each of my residences and another for my niece. The brand I have is a Cuisinart. My first was a seven-cup version. I upgraded to the eleven-cup model. I like them both, though the eleven-cup version gives me more flexibility.

If you can't afford or don't want to buy a food processor, you can do all of these tasks by hand with a hand grater, a chopping board and a knife, and a potato masher. I worked with these items most of my life before breaking down and opting for the convenience of a food processor.

Grain Mill

A good grain mill will provide frustration-free grain every time with perfect results. Wear earplugs, it can be very loud. This is another luxury product that is nice to have, but not an essential kitchen item. Fresh grains are healthier, since the pre-ground flour one buys at grocery stores are likely to become rancid quickly. Plus, freshly ground grain just tastes better. I've only had my Nutrimill a few months and I have to say I really like this machine. It comes with a two-year warranty. There are other grain mills available with good reputations. I found the Nutrimill to be a good price and it performs well. Do your research and decide for yourself if you need one and, if so, which product suits your needs.

Juicer

If you love fresh juice, you may want a juicer. I prefer to eat foods in their whole state. When you juice, you are throwing away the fiber that is so beneficial to the functioning of your gut and for slowing down the absorption of sugars into your bloodstream. However, if owning a juicer is going to help you consume more fruits and vegetables, by all means, buy a juicer! I have a Jack LaLane juicer. I think it was a reasonable price and does an excellent job, but is a little difficult to clean. It is almost painful to me to throw out all that good pulp when the juicing is done. Despite what the brochures say, unless you are making endless carrot cakes, there is just no viable use for the pulp. I use a juicer only when a recipe calls for fresh juice with no pulp, such as my rosemary-grapefruit sorbet. Most of the time, my juicer stays in the basement. Though, I have to say, it was a great transitioning machine that introduced me to the health benefits and fantastic flavors of fresh fruits and vegetables.

When I do need fresh lemon, lime or orange juice for preparing food, I use an inexpensive handheld juicer, which is a wooden grooved pinecone-shaped tool with a handle, or a little glass juicer with a saucer for catching the juice.

Kitchen Scale

While you can get along fine without it, an accurate kitchen scale will make cooking results more consistent. A cup of flour measured by volume can vary from cup to cup, depending upon how densely it is packed. But when measured by weight it will always be the same. A scale is a very useful kitchen tool.

Mortar and Pestle

A mortar and pestle to grind spices is a handy thing to have in one's kitchen. I have a large granite mortar and pestle I found at TJ Max for a steal. It allows me to crush garlic into a paste, grind difficult spices, roasted seeds and spices, and more. It is heavy and, therefore, cumbersome to wash. It was more expensive, even at the bargain price I paid for it, than the coffee grinder, and I use the coffee grinder more often. But it is a handy tool to have for crushing difficult spices like cloves.

Pressure Cooker

This is one of my favorite kitchen tools. Once you get the hang of cooking with a pressure cooker, you won't want to be without one. It cooks in less time and is handy for cooking many kinds of foods from root vegetables, to grains, to stews, and then some. I first bought a small 3.3 liter Prestige Deluxe stainless steel pressure cooker. It is inexpensive, works well, is good looking, and is fine for cooking for two people. As much as I cook, I finally upgraded to a German made WMF Perfect Plus 6 1/2 quart stainless steel pressure cooker with a steamer basket. I just love it. While there is nothing you can't cook with your basic set of pots and pans, this is another luxury item I do not want to be without.

Salad Spinner

A salad spinner is an item I never knew I couldn't live without, until I bought one. You can wash your green leafy vegetables in it and then spin them dry in only a minute or two. These can be bought very inexpensively at a discount store, or you can pay a premium for a higher quality product. Don't get the kind with a pull-string, like the old lawnmower pull cords; the string will quickly fray and break. Get the kind that has a push pump on top. (You push it and the basket inside spins.)

Seedling Mat

I came up with this idea one spring after planting my garden. I had been frustrated by the consistently cool temperatures in my house, which makes it a pleasant place to be but makes cooking quick yeast breads virtually impossible. I couldn't even get a good starter going; my house just wasn't warm enough. At night, we reduce the temperature to 55-60°F in the winter, and this interferes with the rising time of my dough. A seedling mat produces a small amount of heat, 15-20°F above the room's ambient temperature. This allows enough heat for the seeds to germinate but not enough to damage the plant.

While cleaning off my seedling mat, it struck me that its constant temperature would be perfect for proofing bread. It worked! It gives off enough heat to create a nice rising action in the dough but not so much that it causes a crust to form. Now for anything I that needs leavening, such as sourdough, yeast dough, Indian dosas, Ethiopian injera, etc., I use my seedling mat. It has made baking much more predictable. If your home temperature isn't an issue for you or you simply don't wish to invest in this product, you can place your dough in the oven with the oven light on. This works fairly well but my seedling mat gives more consistent results.

Silicone Baking Sheets

Silicone baking sheets allow you to bake things like scones, yeast breads, roasted vegetables and the like without placing food directly on an aluminum or Teflon surface. Because it is a non-stick surface, it also lets you omit or limit the amount of oil you use in baking. The best, and most expensive, silicone baking sheet is the French Silpat. It fits perfectly inside a typical half sheet pan and provides a barrier between the aluminum and the food you are preparing. There are others on the market that don't fit quite as well but are adequate. A cheaper alternative is to simply use parchment paper.

Slow Cookers (Crock Pots)

Slow Cookers, or crockpots, are very convenient for entertaining. I find they are less useful for cooking than as a warming unit. Cooking beans in them can be dangerous if they have not been properly soaked and boiled ten minutes prior to placing in the crock pot (see A Bit About Beans). I don't care for slow cooking vegetables in these machines as I find I can't control the level of doneness of each particular vegetable. I have an old crockpot that Rich actually had before we married over 25 years ago. It still works great, though the design is dated. I also have a set of three crockpots within one metal unit. It was inexpensive and has proved to be of great benefit when entertaining larger groups. These are luxury items that spend most of the time in my basement. But when I the occasion calls for them, they are quite useful.

Spiral Vegetable Slicer

If you choose to go the raw foodie route, your spiral slicer will get a lot of use. It cuts very thin slices of potatoes, zucchini, yellow squash, etc, for chips, salads and fancy garnishes. It will also allow you to make spaghetti out of zucchini and other vegetables. I know lots of raw vegans who love this contraption.

I rarely use mine and so it has spent most of its life in the basement gathering dust. I find that while the slices are thin, their accordion shape makes them difficult to spread out for even baking. A spiral slicer is good for spaghetti zucchini, but I don't prepare it often enough to keep the slicer out, and it's too much trouble to pull it out of its box on the rare occasion I may want to use it. I can see it might be useful for decorative garnishes for large parties.

Stand Mixer

I wanted one of these from the earliest days of my married life. I had hoped to receive one as a wedding gift. I finally bought a Kitchen Aide a few years back and I'm sorry to say it is now collecting dust on a basement shelf. If you make a lot of confections, I'm sure it is a great investment. (Though even vegan confections are normally not healthy options.) As a health conscious plant-based cook, I have little need for it. It can be very serviceable for making bread dough, but where is the fun in that? For me, kneading my own dough, experiencing the art of perfecting an excellent loaf, is what bread baking is all about. But, if you don't like to get your hands dirty a stand mixer can be a great time saver.

Toaster

A wide-slice toaster is fantastic for heating up homemade hamburger buns and other homemade breads in a jiffy. Because we do not use preservatives in our baking, our breads do not have the shelf-life that store bought breads often have. When baking, cut off what you will use in the next two or three days and freeze the rest. Take it out the night before to defrost or zap it in your microwave for 30 seconds. Then pop it into your toaster for sandwiches or super delicious toast. A wide-slice toaster allows for the non-uniform shapes of homemade breads. Shop around. Toasters have become ridiculously expensive and they work no better than they ever have. This is also a convenience item. You can accomplish the same results using the top rack of your oven on the broil setting. You just have to pay closer attention while you are toasting your bread to prevent it from burning.

Wok

While you don't necessarily need a wok, a sauté pan works fine, these are good to have for making stir fry dishes, popular with plant-based diners. Carbon steel seems to be the most venerated but I could not keep it seasoned to suit me. Flecks of the charred seasoning ended up in my food. I finally gave up and bought a stainless steel wok that works for me.

What To Stock In Your Fridge

The following are items I think every cook should have in their refrigerator. Some cooks never refrigerate onions and garlic; I do it all the time and I don't feel the foods I prepare suffer as a result. They last longer in the fridge and the juices from onions do not cause tearing when they are refrigerated. Do what you think is best; there are no hard and fast rules here.

Obviously, there is an entire world of fruits and vegetables from which to choose. The following are the most commonly used. I encourage you to experiment with any others you find interesting and appealing.

Refrigerated Staples

Some items I keep on hand are items I don't use very often but they keep well, which saves me trips to the grocery store when I do need them. These are common sense items like organic tofu, dijon mustard, mizos, and all my condiments, including vinegars, once they've been opened — unless the package instructions indicate they do not require refrigeration. I use almond milk every day and keep a supply in my refrigerator door.

Items To Have Readily At Hand

Garlic

Considered the number one cancer-fighting food on the planet, garlic should go into nearly everything we cook. Each year I grow at least 200 bulbs of garlic in my garden and by the next summer I am picking through the last withered bulbs as I eagerly anticipate my June harvest.

Keep plenty of organic garlic on hand. It is important to crush garlic before cooking, then allow it to rest for ten minutes. An enzymatic process takes place when the garlic is crushed, which converts alliin (a compound in garlic) to the potent phytonutrient allicin. If you cook garlic before the enzyme alliinase has had an opportunity to complete the conversion, the enzymes will likely be killed and allicin can't be created. Once the conversion has taken place, however, the resulting phytonutrient is resistant to heat; now the garlic can be cooked without losing its beneficial properties.[1] Also, from a culinary perspective crushing garlic releases the oils in the cloves. This imparts a more complex flavor to the food to which you add it.

If you want to add raw garlic to your diet, (like in pesto or salsa) crushing and resting garlic makes it milder, more digestible and less likely to cause heartburn. If you can't handle raw garlic, it is perfectly fine to cook it a little. Cooked garlic is usually no problem for those of us with sensitive stomachs. Remember to crush it and let it rest for at least ten minutes before cooking so you receive the maximum nutritional benefits of this superfood.

It isn't always possible to crush garlic before cooking, as in dishes requiring baked garlic. But keep in mind garlic's health benefits and be sure you get enough of the beneficial allicin in your diet.

Ginger

Ginger is a spicy, fragrant root that goes hand in hand with garlic in many dishes, usually in equal proportions. It is easy to grow if you have a long growing season, and it has an attractive bamboo-like appearance. This herb is used in most cuisines throughout the world. Ginger also makes a very soothing tea which aids digestion and helps relieve nausea. It keeps well in the fridge. You may find yourself using this root every day.

Onions

Red, yellow, white and Vidalia onions are all good to cook with. Red and Vidalia are sweeter and are preferable for salads or any occasion that calls for raw onion. Some Ethiopian and Indian chefs I know cook only with red onions. I use them interchangeably most of the time, using whatever is in my fridge. Sometimes my choice depends on how it will affect the appearance of the finished dish. Onions are necessary for good vegetable stocks. Keep a variety of sizes on hand. Once an onion is cut it loses flavor. For your cooking project, try to use the size that will utilize the entire onion.

Celery

Always have celery on hand for when a last-minute stock is needed. It is excellent in bean dishes, soups and stews, potato and pasta salads, and in smoothies. There is no end to the uses for celery. Celery is on the EWG's Dirty Dozen list of highest pesticide residues so buy organic if you can.

Carrots

This is another must-have item in your fridge. They appear often in recipes and complete the basic ingredients for stocks. You can grate them into salads. They can be roasted, steamed, boiled, chopped, grated, diced, julienned, and pureed. Carrots lend themselves to infinite methods of preparation and cooking. They do not compete with other flavors so you can easily slip them into many standard recipes for additional nutrition, texture, flavor and color.

Potatoes

Always keep a few potatoes in your crisper drawer. They keep well and when you are hungry they are a filling and satisfying comfort food. Potatoes can be cooked in innumerable ways in very little time. Make sure the skins have no green tint when you purchase them, nor eyes that are beginning to sprout. The green color shows concentrations of toxic compounds, called glycoalkaloids, which are thought to be natural pesticides. When potatoes are exposed to light, they will begin to turn green as well. It is best never to buy pre-bagged potatoes, as the wrappers often conceal their condition. When you open the bag under your lighting at home, more often than not you will find the contents are green. Potatoes come in varieties of white, yellow, red and purple shades. The darker the color, the more nutritious is the potato.

Sweet Potatoes

These are another superfood. One of the foods the longest living societies on earth have in common is the sweet potato. They are wonderful in soups and stews, and may be baked, grilled, broiled, steamed, and microwaved. You can slice them for veggie sandwiches, puree them for soups, or eat them right out of their skins. They offer natural sweetness to many dishes; their flesh is rich and satisfying. They don't last in the fridge as long as the white potato, so don't buy more than you'll use in a week or so.

Tomatoes

Conventionally grown tomatoes contain residues of lots of toxic pesticides which can cause infertility and birth defects, so only buy organic ones. Tomatoes are good to have on hand for slicing as a garnish, for salads, roasting for a side dish, and as a major ingredient. They perish in a few days so buy only what you'll use. Organic tomatoes are one of the few canned items in my pantry. At the peak of harvest, I buy baskets of ripe tomatoes from my farmers market and prepare some for sauces and some for home canning. They may cost more than store-bought canned tomatoes but the flavor is far superior.

I like to keep Roma tomatoes and cherry tomatoes in my fridge. Cherry tomatoes have a lot of flavor and are tasty complements to many kinds of salads and stir fries. Romas are excellent for baking and roasting, and for sauces since they are a meatier tomato.

Something to keep in mind when cooking with tomatoes is that they should be added to a dish *after* the onions and garlic have been cooked, unless the dish is expected to simmer for several hours. This is true of rice and bean dishes and with other vegetables, such as eggplants, as well. Tomatoes will slow down the cooking process and prevent these vegetables from softening as expected, significantly increasing their cooking times.

Peppers

Green and red bell peppers are versatile and colorful and enhance many recipes as decorative items, while serving as the major ingredient in many others. They are delicious in salads, and as a crunchy topping for bean dishes, along with tomatoes, celery, and red onions. They have a shelf life of a few days, so buy just what you think you will use. Jalapeño peppers are a handy item to have in the fridge. If you want a dish with a kick, leave some of the seeds with the pepper. For a milder flavor, with little or no heat, remove all the seeds. Buy organic, as peppers are on the EWG's Dirty Dozen List of toxic residue from pesticides. There are many varieties of peppers. I love to cook with spicy, long green banana peppers, and there are many varieties suitable for stuffing. Experiment and learn what types you prefer. I consider peppers to be a semi-perishable item.

Perishable Vegetables And Herbs

When I was a student in Germany, I marveled at how women shopped for food every day. Fresh breads and produce were purchased at local markets, often within walking distance from their homes. The reality, however, is that in modern society we don't have time for daily trips to the market.

Buy the freshest produce you can find, preferably organically grown. There are ways to extend the life of greens by putting them in plastic bags and squeezing out all the air. This will give them an extra couple of days. There are also green bags you can buy that extend the shelf life of greens and other vegetables.

To avoid waste, think about what you need for the week. Plan a menu and a shopping list. It is heartbreaking to throw out produce you simply could not get around to cooking. You'll find you need less than you think. Consider how many meals you can make from leftovers, what you can freeze for later and how many people you have to feed when calculating your produce needs. At today's prices, you don't want your hard earned money going into the compost pile.

Greens

These are such an important part of a plant-based diet and should play a vital role in every diet for their antioxidant, anti-mutagenic and anti-tumor properties; and they are also high in fiber, vitamins and other nutrients. They only stay fresh two or three days in the fridge and begin losing potency from the moment they are harvested. Greens can be consumed raw, braised, stir fried, steamed, in soups and stews, and in bean and grain dishes. Collards, many varieties of kale, spinach, romaine, mustard greens and Swiss chard are all excellent sources of vitamin K. Most of them can be blended into smoothies. Kale can be made into chips that are crisp, delicious and far healthier than commercial chips.

Broccoli

Broccoli can be eaten raw, broiled, baked, roasted, braised, and steamed. It is delicious in stir fries, casseroles, rice dishes, salads, and stands up well on its own.

Brussels Sprouts

The brussels sprout is like a tiny cabbage with a slightly bitter, more robust flavor. It is delicious seared or roasted, in stews or in vegetable medleys as well as served raw in fresh salads.

Green Beans

Fresh green beans are a pleasure to cook and to eat. I love buying them just picked from the farmers' market. They come in many varieties, shapes and sizes, from the exquisite French haricot verts, to the flat Italian green beans, to the delicate Asian snow peas, to American favorites. These can be added to soups and stews, sautéed, baked in casseroles, cooked with potatoes, and seasoned with spices from around the world to give these foods a regional flare.

Cauliflower

This plant is very much in vogue today. If you are avoiding starchy foods, cauliflower can be mashed it to create a convincing facsimile of mashed potatoes. It is often used this way in high-end restaurants as a base for food architecture, in which complementary foods are stacked together to form a beautiful finished dish. It can be blended to make a creamy sauce for a vegan version of Fettuccine Alfredo, as well as creamy soups, and pasta casseroles. It can also be coated with various herbs and spices and roasted whole or in florets. Cauliflower can be slow roasted or dehydrated to make a delicious treat similar to popcorn, but healthier. It can be grated as a rice substitute and pulverized to create a grain-like texture. Cauliflower is so versatile, it has become the new kale in plant-based cuisine.

Beets

I never ate beets growing up. It was not something I was introduced to until my late twenties when a boy I was dating piled them on his plate in a pizza restaurant salad bar. They obviously came from a can, but still I liked them. It never occurred to me to buy a fresh beet and cook it. Loaded with antioxidants, they now are among my favorite foods. I eat beets every week and I often go through periods of time where I'll eat beets every day. You can steam, boil, pressure cook, and roast beets. You can use them in salads, sandwiches, as a side dish, or puree them in smoothies. They are fantastic secret ingredients in cakes and salsas, giving a red coloring to foods without having to resort to toxic chemical dyes.

Celeriac

Celeriac is a big, warty root with a mild celery flavor. It is excellent combined with mashed potatoes or in soups and stews.

Turnips

Turnips are a common root vegetable with a distinct radishy flavor. They are excellent baked or roasted, or as ingredients in soups and stews.

Parsnips

Parsnips are sweet root vegetables that can be roasted, steamed, sautéed, or as ingredients in soups and stews.

Daikon

Daikon is a very long root, over a foot long. Its tastes like a mild radish. It is very good grated on salads and makes a nice pickled vegetable, or as a raw ingredient in vegetarian sushi.

Green Onions

A complement to numerous dishes; stir fries, rice and potato dishes, soups and stews, salads and more, this is a versatile, colorful and delicious addition to many meals.

Parsley

A versatile herb, parsley is delicious in just about anything. Its flavor is non-obtrusive and it adds color and nutrients to many dishes. It's always a good idea to keep fresh parsley in your fridge. It lasts a few days and will last a bit longer if you trim the stems and keep it in a small jar with water, just like flowers. Parsley smoothies are my very favorite.

Cilantro

Cilantro has a strong flavor and a more limited use than parsley, but it is a very healthy and delicious herb you'll want to use often. It is a favorite in Mexican dishes, Indian dishes and in dishes we consider standard American fare. It is wonderful in rice, soups and stews, sauces, grain dishes, salsas and more. Cilantro also makes great smoothies if you like a stronger flavor. Like parsley, if you put it in a jar of water in the fridge, it will last longer.

Dill

Dill is a wonderful herb that keeps well in the fridge. It is fantastic in potato salad, soups, sauces, marinades, condiments and more. It requires no special attention. Just wrap it tightly in a plastic bag and it will stay fresh for days.

Fruit

Everyone knows it is important to eat lots of fruit for their antioxidants and other health promoting qualities. In my home we've almost completely replaced dessert with fresh fruit. Even when entertaining, after dinner when coffee or tea is being served, I often bring out a large bowl of grapes, tangerine wedges, sliced bananas or other fresh fruit for guests to help themselves. People are initially surprised, then delighted with this substitution for a heavy, sugary dessert. I've never had a negative response. If you want to make it a little fancier, you can combine chopped fruit with a few nuts to make a fruit salad.

Keeping fresh, organic fruit on hand for breakfast cereals and snacks is a wonderful way to get loads of nutrition with minimal effort. Don't wash berries until just before using so they'll last longer in your fridge.

Apples

We eat apples nearly every day in our house and I often cook with them. I keep a variety of them in my crisper drawer. They keep well and are delicious snacks at night when you want a little something to munch without the heaviness of a meal.

Berries

Strawberries and blueberries are breakfast staples in our home, and we eat wild blackberries and raspberries seasonally. They are all great on cereal and on pancakes, or just in a bowl on the side.

Grapefruit

Grapefruit is wonderful for making sorbets and to eat as a snack anytime. In season, grapefruits are my TV snack.

Grapes

These are my summer TV snack, replacing winter's grapefruits. Grapes must be purchased organic. One individual grape may contain residues of as many as 15 toxic pesticides.

Oranges, Mandarine Oranges and Tangerines

Orange juice and its pulp are irreplaceable in marinades and sweet sauces. Of course, these fruits are always delightful raw, cut up into salads or served in wedges on the side of your plate. Tangerines and mandarin oranges are colorful garnishes and offer a delicious zesty bite to a plain green salad. The juices have a slightly more tangy flavor than oranges and can be used interchangeably. If purchased organically, zesting the peels adds a lot of flavor to many dishes.

Lemons and Limes

These two fruits are indispensable in any kind of cooking. They can be beaten into salad dressings and marinades, added to sauces and condiments or to add another dimension of flavor to many dishes. Keep plenty of them in your fridge. The more you use them, the more you'll not want to be without them. Limes are especially important in southwestern cuisine and pair beautifully with cilantro.

Pineapple

Pineapple adds a delicious sweet accent to stir fries, pizzas, fruit salads, salsas, green salads, and more. Store it frond side down in a pitcher or bowl until you cut it. The sweetest part of the pineapple is at the bottom, so storing it upside down allows some of the sweetness of the bottom to migrate through the entire pineapple. Once cut, store it cut side down on a sandwich plate in the fridge. Pineapples also freeze well, so if you have more than you think you'll use, cut it up and store it in a plastic bag in the freezer. Once you fill the bag, press out all the excess air and flatten the bag as thin as possible. When you need pineapple, break off the amount you need and thaw. Pineapples do not continue to ripen once they are cut, so make sure you don't buy it too green. Nor should you buy it too brown as it is past its expiration date. If it is easier to use canned, buy the kind without additional sweetener or additives.

Mangos

I don't know how I ever made it to adulthood before I discovered mangos. OMG! Mangos are so good and can be prepared in so many creative ways. Delicious on salads, in smoothies, in bean and grain dishes, dairy-free ice creams...

The uses are endless for this yummy treat. Their huge seed makes them a little tricky to peel, but it goes very quickly once you get the hang of it.

Figuring out when they are ripe is also a little tricky, and the technique for knowing when to cut a mango depends upon its variety. With the larger varieties, like Haden mangos, you must rely on your nose because if you wait until they are soft it's often too late. Haden mangos are green, gold and red, or green and rust colored, and range in size from five to six inches with a slightly oblong, curved shape. Cut them when they have a ripe and yummy smell. The smaller mangos, which come from India, the Philippines, Mexico and other regions, are usually golden in color and become brighter as they mature. They are around four inches in length and look much like a chubby apostrophe. You know when these are ready to eat when their skin begins to wrinkle.

All varieties are delicious; I never met a mango I didn't love. You can buy them in season, cut them up and freeze in portions most useful to you.

Some people are severely allergic to mangos so it is wise to ask about that before serving them to guests.

Medjool Dates

When in season, you can often buy medjool dates in bulk at very good prices. They will keep a long time in your fridge. Medjools are considered the queen of dates as they are extraordinarily large and sweet. These are excellent for replacing sugar as they are a whole food replete with fiber and healthy nutrients. They can be ground with nuts to form pie crusts for fruit pies, combined with oats nuts, and seeds to create energy bars, pureed to create sweet sauces, and stuffed to create delicious snacks. Remove the seed, stuff the date with pecans, and you'll have a delicious snack that tastes remarkably like pecan pie! I like to keep a few of these pecan-stuffed dates in a baggie in my purse for food emergencies.

Freezer Items

Sweet Corn & Green Peas
Organically grown sweet corn is a useful item to have in your freezer, as are green peas. They can be added to soups and stews as an accent color and for additional nutrition.

Greens
Large bags of flash frozen collards and kale are nice to have when you don't have time to shop for fresh. They can be tossed into soups and stews and the bags resealed.

Fruit
Fruits, especially berries, are convenient to keep in the freezer for fruit tarts, quick sauces and fruit smoothies. When organic cranberries are in season, I like to throw a couple of bags in my freezer for use in the coming months when they are no longer available.

Grains And Flours
Grains and flours will last much longer in your freezer than in your pantry. If you grind your own flour, frozen grain minimizes heat exposure during the milling process.

Nuts and Seeds
Nuts and seeds contain a lot of oil and can become rancid very quickly. They store well in the freezer and do not require defrosting before use. So if you find a deal on freshly shelled pecans, walnuts or any other nut or seed, freezing them will allow you to take advantage of bulk bargains.

13

PANTRY STAPLES

A well-stocked pantry is a thing of beauty. It makes preparing meals so much easier. Nothing is more frustrating than finding yourself in the middle of a cooking project and discovering that you are missing an important ingredient. Having your major ingredients on hand is time-saving and makes food preparation more efficient.

It's important to become familiar with grains, flours and spices, and so forth, so you learn how long they will remain fresh and when you should replace them. They should be stored in air-tight glass containers to slow down oxidation that can cause your grains to become rancid. This will also prevent grain moths from feeding on your grains, seeds, dried fruits and nuts. Grain moths, also called pantry moths, are insidious little devils that can wreak havoc in your pantry supplies. Regardless of how clean you keep your kitchen, grain moths will find their way into unprotected pantry items. Adding a couple of large bay leaves to each of your staples will keep these critters out and your grains safe. (You can buy bulk quantities of large bay leaves inexpensively at most Indian markets.) A powdery residue at the bottom of your rice or whole grains indicates you may have an infestation. If so, the grains should be thrown out, the glass container thoroughly washed, and the grain replaced. This is another good reason to store your grains in a clear glass container, so you can inspect them periodically.

Organization is key in all pantry matters. Label your containers with the item name and the date purchased. Use last purchased items first. Buy only what you will use in a reasonable amount of time; within weeks or months, not years.

The ingredients in this chapter are only a sample of what's available to you, and you certainly do not need to run out and buy them all and once. Some of them you may never want to buy. Try them in the smallest quantities available and see how you feel about them. If you like something in particular and think you will eat it often, then you can buy a larger supply to have on hand. You may go through phases of eating one thing, then switch to something else for a while. Keep this in mind when stocking up. Unless it is a hard to find item, buying fresh foods more often is a better idea than keeping stockpiles that will degrade over time.

It is helpful to keep a list of your pantry items in a drawer or on your refrigerator. As you run out of an item, add it to your shopping list so you won't find yourself without it when you need it most.

Whole Grains And Flours

Grains

The grains in this chapter are the most commonly used in a plant-based diet, though there are certainly others you may wish to try. I have listed them in the order I most often reach for them. You may wish to rearrange this according to your tastes. Again, don't feel you have to go out and purchase all of these. Buy them when you have a recipe that calls for a particular grain and in the smallest quantity available. Then, decide for yourself whether it is something you want to add to your pantry staples.

Whole grains contain oils that may make them go rancid, so it is not a good idea to store them for long periods of time. Whole grains last much longer than ground flours, so keep that in mind when stocking up. Buy only the whole grains you'll use within a few months' time, and only the flours you'll use within a few weeks. If you have a grain mill, all the better. Freshly ground grains are healthier and more delicious than the grain you buy already milled, especially since we have no way of knowing when the packaged flours were milled. Grains and flours can be stored in airtight containers in the refrigerator to preserve freshness, if you have room for them. They may also be frozen. Most grain flavors can be intensified by roasting and made more digestible and nutritious by sprouting. Roasting amaranth, quinoa and millet may cause these grains to pop like popcorn.

Rice

Rice is a staple of a plant-based diet. It can be found in long or short grains and in white, brown, red, purple, and black varieties. White rice has had the husk, bran and germ removed and has been polished to give it a longer shelf life. It has almost no nutritional value nor fiber and should be avoided. It also has poor flavor compared to the wonderful nutty rices of the colorful varieties. The darker the color of rice, the more nutritious.

Experiment with the different rices, which are available in large health food chains and in Asian markets. No meal in Asia is complete without a side of rice, eaten with chopsticks. Rice can be used in countless ways — as a porridge, ground into flour for baking breads, crackers, flatbreads and pastas, whole in soups and stews, in stir fries, mixed with vegetables in a pilaf, and as a complete side dish on its own with or without a gravy or sauce. It is often used as confections in Asian cultures, pounded into cakes stuffed with a sweet bean in Japan, and as desserts, as in Thailand's famous Sticky Rice.

Recent concerns about rice contaminated with arsenic, and possible radiation from Japan (washing to other shores in ocean currents), make rice consumption less appealing than in the past. However, with proper testing practices, it is possible to find plenty of clean rice available.

Oat Groats, Steel Cut Oats, and Rolled Oats

Oats are known for their cholesterol lowering properties. Oats can be found steamed and rolled (rolled oats), chopped into pieces (steel cut oats), ground into flour, sold as a bran, or as whole oat groats. They can be used to bind veggie burger patties, and as ingredients in scones, pancakes, muffins and other baked goods. Rolled oats can be used to make homemade granola and muesli, cooked as a porridge, and are also good in cereal with fruit and a milk substitute. Oats can be gluten free, depending on how they are processed.

Spelt

Spelt is an ancient grain, closely related to wheat; it does contain gluten. Some people who have gluten sensitivities can nevertheless tolerate spelt. It has a pleasing nutty sweet flavor. It is very good for baking; makes wonderful, fragrant breads, flatbreads, crackers, pancakes, and pastas. It usually has to be mixed with another flour to produce good baking results.

Quinoa

Quinoa (pronounced keen-wa) is 17 percent protein. It is high in essential amino acids and is a good source for dietary fiber and minerals, particularly calcium. It can be used in many dishes: as a hot cereal, in baked goods, as a whole grain in soups and stews, as a main ingredient in veggie burgers, and tossed with vegetables as a main course. Quinoa can be purchased in bulk sections of large health foods stores or prepackaged in most large grocery store chains. It comes in red, white (or golden) and black.

Teff

Teff is arguably the smallest grain in the world and is possibly the most nutrient-dense. The grains are either white or brown. Teff hails from Ethiopia and is an essential ingredient in making Injera, an Ethiopian flatbread served at every Ethiopian meal. Injera's consistency is somewhere between a crepe and a pancake. Most large health food stores carry packages of teff, though it can be found more cheaply at on-line Ethiopian markets. I've yet to find an organic source for teff.

Wheat Groats

Wheat groats, also known as hard winter wheat groats, are the hulled whole wheat kernel, that still contains all of its original nutritional properties: the starchy endosperm, the germ and the bran of the wheat. This is the essential ingredient of whole wheat bread. Wheat groats can also be soaked and used whole in breads, just like nuts. Ground, it is the flour used in baking whole wheat breads. Because it makes the loaves heavy and dense, it is often mixed with other flours, such as white wheat or all-purpose; this makes a lighter loaf.

White Wheat Groats

White wheat is a softer grain than whole wheat. It is ground for use in making pastry or cake flours. Again, the whole grain retains all of its original nutritional properties.

Buckwheat

Buckwheat is a gluten-free grain with ancient roots, used most notably in Japanese noodles called soba noodles, and buckwheat pancakes. Buckwheat groats, a triangular shaped grain which is green or tan, can be used as a delicious cooked gain, or as a thickener in gravies and sauces. Roasted buckwheat groats can also be used to make a delicious breakfast porridge.

Millet

Millet is a small round gluten-free grain, usually a light golden color. It can be used in baking, especially flat breads and crackers, and as a substantive addition to soups and stews and as a cooked breakfast cereal. It is good dietary source for B vitamins and several minerals.

Amaranth

Amaranth is a tiny grain that can be used as a cereal or added to whole grain breads in small amounts. I keep a little of this in my pantry. While I don't use it often, it is a nice grain to have for variety. Amaranth grows in tall fronds and is beautiful in a garden and in floral arrangements. Some amaranth leaves are edible. Don't confuse it with pigweed, which is an inedible type of amaranth that can be invasive in your landscape.

Barley

Barley has been around longer than any known grain and has been used to feed both humans and livestock. Hulled barley is considered a whole grain as only the outer husk has been removed, leaving the bran intact. Pearled barley is the most common type of food barley available. It has had its husk and bran removed, which makes it more chewable than whole barley but less nutritious. Pearled barley is used extensively in soups and stews.

Farro

Farro can be found pearled (with the husk and bran removed), semi-pearled or as a whole grain. Like barley, it is used extensively in soups and stews.

Rye

Rye can be steamed and rolled (like oats) and used in breakfast cereals, or it can be combined with other rolled grains to make muesli. It is perhaps best known as an ingredient in rye breads, or pumpernickel breads, and can also be use to make crackers.

Corn

Corn, or maize, is a favorite grain in southwestern cuisines for making corn chips, tortillas, taco shells, tamales and the like. In the southern states of the US, cornbread, a battered bread, is a culinary staple, as are fried hushpuppies, made with cornmeal, onions and peppers. Grits is another southern US dish of coarsely ground corn, similar to polenta, and is eaten as a breakfast cereal or as a side dish.

Unfortunately, corn flour has become one of the most highly contaminated genetically modified products, so processed corn and corn products should be avoided unless they are certified organically grown. According to the Environmental Working Group's 2014 guidelines, fresh, sweet corn on the cob sold in farmers' markets and in supermarkets is unlikely to be genetically modified. Organic popcorn is readily available and can easily be ground into flours, polenta and corn flour with a food mill. Soaking corn in a solution of slaked lime softens the kernels and makes its nutrients more readily available for use by our bodies.

Kamut

Kamut is an ancient wheat that can be used in baking breads, pancakes and cereals. It has a more nutritious profile than modern wheat with more protein, amino acids and minerals. It is also higher in gluten.

Flours

Whole Wheat Flour

Whole wheat flour is ground hard wheat groats and retains all the nutritional qualities of the whole grain. It does contain gluten and should not be eaten by the gluten intolerant.

Whole Wheat Bread Flour

Whole wheat bread flour is a whole grain flour with a higher percentage of protein; it makes excellent yeast breads.

Whole White Wheat Flour

Whole white wheat flour is a different grain than hard winter wheat. It is often sold as soft wheat groats and is a whole grain retaining all of its nutritional properties. Ground into flour, it produces a less dense loaf. It is most commonly used for making pastry and cake flour.

All Purpose Flour

All purpose flour is made from a blend of hard and soft wheats that have had all the nutritional elements of the grain stripped from them. It is nevertheless useful to lighten the consistency of whole grain breads when combined (usually at a 1:1 ratio) with the whole grain. Always buy this flour unbleached and organic, if possible. It is readily available in bulk in large health food market chains.

White Bread Flour

White bread flour is similar to all purpose flour, but contains additional protein and gluten strength for use in yeast breads.

Buckwheat Flour

Buckwheat flour is gluten free and nutritious; it can be added to other flours for higher nutrition and flavor. It has a nutty flavor and is delicious in pancakes.

Chickpea Flour

Chickpea flour is a nutritious flour used extensively in Middle Eastern cuisine, and is becoming more popular in western cooking. It is simply ground up chickpeas and is a nutritious addition to your flour pantry items. It can be found in Indian markets under the name besan.

Lentil Flour

Flour can be made from lentils to make crusts for cooking tofu. It is added to veggie burger recipes and to fermented batters for Indian pancakes and crepes.

Semolina Flour

Semolina is a byproduct of milling wheat. It is used to make pasta and couscous and can be added to baking flours to achieve different consistencies. It is an ingredient in Indian flatbreads and some dessert breads. I keep a little of it on hand but do not use it often.

Rice Flour

Rice flour, which can be brown or white, can be used in place of wheat flour by people with gluten sensitivities. I don't often cook with it, but in baking I use it to line my proofing baskets, in which the dough has its final rise before it goes into the cooking vessel. Rice flour creates a slippery coating, allowing the dough to slip easily from the basket into a hot clay baker. This slippery quality is also beneficial for cleaning my grain mill. Grinding a small batch of rice will keep it in top form for my next milling of an oilier grain. While I don't cook much with rice flour, many Asian chefs do. I often use Asian products made from rice flour, such as rice noodles and summer roll wrappers.

Wheat Bran

Wheat bran is the hard outer layer of wheat and is a byproduct of the milling process. It is nutritious and high in fiber. It is often used in making bran muffins and is sometimes added to bread and to pancakes. Another use I've found for wheat bran is to sprinkle on dough proofing baskets to prevent sticking, similar to rice flour. I find I even prefer it to rice flour for this purpose.

Beans

Beans are an integral part of the plant-based diet. They provide loads of nutrients, fiber and protein. Become familiar with beans and discover the world of flavors and textures that await you. Beans are such a versatile plant, you'll be amazed at how many different ways you can prepare them. You can make veggie burgers, create creamy flavorful dips for chips, flat-breads and vegetables, puree them into wonderful fragrant and tasty soups, use them in hearty stews, and bake them in luscious casseroles and pâtés. They even make surprisingly delicious desserts and cakes. If you can find fresh beans at the farmers' market, snatch them up. Freshly picked beans are a real treat.

The following list are of beans I keep in my pantry. The first ten varieties are the varieties I use most often. The others are beans I like and use periodically to introduce novelty into my diet. You may have others you prefer. This list will give you a good introduction to one of the most delicious and health promoting resources Mother Earth provides.

Chickpeas (also called garbanzo beans)

This versatile bean makes wonderful hummus; chickpea flour can be used in a batter for making Indian pakora and falafels. Chickpeas can be used in soups and stews, baked dishes, served cold in salads, and much more. This is one of my favorite beans and the one I use most. I cook them in large batches and freeze them in three-cup containers so they're available when I want to whip up a meal in a hurry.

Red Kidney Beans

Care must be taken in cooking this bean as it contains higher concentrations of the toxic lectin Phytohaemagglutinin (see A Bit About Beans). Cajun red beans and rice is an all-time favorite in my family. Red beans are also very good for making veggie burgers, southwestern chile, and refried beans.

Pinto Beans

A southern favorite (particularly in East Tennessee, where I spend a good deal of time) pinto beans are often cooked with onions and served in a bowl with a side of cornbread. I use them in southwestern chile, and in soups and stews.

Black Beans

Fabulous for veggie burgers, black beans make delicious soups on their own, or added as an ingredient to many soups and stews. They are also an ingredient in southwestern chile and can be used for refried beans.

Black-eyed Peas

These beans (sometimes called black-eyed beans) are delicious served over rice or crumbled cornbread. They are used to create New Orlean's famous "Hoppin' John" dish, which is served for good luck on New Year's Day, along with collard greens. It is also a favorite in Ethiopian cuisine. This is a versatile bean that can be made into veggie burgers, soups, stews or any occasion calling for a bean.

Navy Beans

Often cooked with molasses and other ingredients to make Boston baked beans, Navy beans also are delicious in soups and stews.

Lima Beans

I love this delicate bean, especially when I can find it fresh. I especially enjoy them piled onto cornbread for a satisfying southern experience. Lima beans make delicious side dishes and can go into soups and stews.

French, Green, Black & Red Lentils

All the lentils make delicious soups. Depending on how you choose to season them, they can reflect the culture of many regions, particularly Ethiopian, Indian, and Mediterranean. Lentils are the only beans that don't require soaking, and they cook quickly. Red lentils cook particularly quickly and absorb a lot of water. These are favorites in my pantry and I used them constantly.

Split Yellow, Green and Pigeon Peas

These peas are cut in half for quicker cooking. Wonderful in split pea soups, they are a favorite of India and Ethiopia for hearty stews. Do not try to cook them in a pressure cooker as they create an inordinate amount of foam and could block steam from escaping, creating a potentially hazardous situation.

Flageolets

A little difficult to find in the US, flageolets can be found everywhere in France. They make a wonderful hearty soup, which is popular in France, particularly in the south. You can purchase them on-line with little difficulty.

Fava Beans

The tough, outer shell of this unusual bean has to be removed before eating. This bean is popular in Europe and the Mediterranean. It makes a wonderful dip.

Painted Pony Beans

Used as a snap bean or shelled to add to soups and stews, this bean has an interesting color, about half cream colored and half a rust color.

Cranberry Beans

Cranberry, also known as October beans, are a cream colored bean with a cranberry stripe around it. It has a similar shape to pinto beans, though the flavors are not the same. They are wonderful when cooked fresh. When it seems nearly every vendor at the farmers' market is carrying them, you can buy them cheaply. They are super-easy to remove from their shells. You can either freeze them for later or allow them to dry.

Adzuki Beans

A small red bean commonly found in Japan, adzuki beans are used in many ways that would seem strange to westerners. I cook it like most beans. While I don't have this often, it has a good flavor and is a nice change of pace.

Mung Beans (split and whole)
I'm not crazy about this bean for cooking but it is great for making bean sprouts. Try them, if you are curious, and see how you feel about them.

There are inexhaustible varieties of beans and I find myself trying new ones all the time. Recently, I purchased several I had never heard of; Corona Runners, which are sweet white beans, Scarlet Runner Beans, Christmas Lima Beans, and a very interesting looking variety called, Rice Beans, for their rice-like shape. I can't wait to try them!

Nuts And Seeds

Nuts

Nuts are an integral part of the plant-based diet. They are rich in essential amino acids and are a rich source of vitamins. They also contain a lot of fat, though studies have shown that people who eat nuts regularly do not gain weight, or increase body mass or waist size.[1] People who consume the most nuts live significantly longer than those who do not. Those who eat nuts daily have been shown to have fewer cancer deaths, heart disease deaths and fewer deaths from respiratory disease.[2]

Using nuts and nut butters is preferable to using processed oils (like olive oil, canola, sesame seed and nut oils) because nuts are whole foods with all their fiber and nutritional components intact. Nuts can be used in making salad dressings, pestos, and sauces for grains. They can be included in breads, muffins and scones, added to fruit salads and green salads, sprinkled atop and inside soups, and included in vegetable, bean and grain dishes. Nuts can be easily added to many recipes. Cashew nuts are particularly practical to keep on hand because their mild, unobtrusive flavor and their thickening capacity makes them a perfect vehicle for creating vegan cheeses, cream sauces, cheesecakes, dessert toppings, and fruit stuffings. Nuts can be combined with dates to make pie crusts and with cauliflower or mushrooms to make a hamburger substitute. They can be roasted, soaked and pureed, chopped, sliced and slivered.

Cashews, pecans, walnuts, peanuts (which are actually a legume), almonds and black walnuts are the nuts I use most often. Hazelnuts, pistachios and pine nuts I use less frequently. You may have others you prefer.

Seeds

Seeds are nutritional work horses worth incorporating into one's diet.

Flaxseeds

Flaxseeds contain omega-3 fatty acids, are high in fiber and have other beneficial nutritional properties. They come either golden or brown. A daily tablespoon of ground flaxseeds is recommended by most experts as part of vegan diet because of their omega-3 fatty acid content. They have a long shelf life while whole, but become rancid very quickly once they are ground. We grind ours daily in a coffee grinder dedicated to that purpose and add them to our breakfast cereal. They can be used in baking and in smoothies, though usually they are ground and sprinkled as a topping purely for their nutritional properties. To create a replacement for eggs in baking, flaxseeds can be soaked in warm water, then blended.

Chia Seeds

Chia seeds are tiny little black seeds which contain omega-3 fatty acids, protein and minerals. They can be used as a thickener to make oil-free salad dressings and puddings. I use them often as toppings for bread and burger buns. They are also good in smoothies and eaten raw.

Sesame Seeds (white and black)

Sesame seeds are a lot like chia seeds in nutritional profile and in the way they are used. I like to sprinkle veggie-burger buns with sesame seeds, half with white and half with black, before popping them into the oven. Sesame seeds can be roasted as well and sesame butter (called tahini) is fantastic in making hummus, baba ghanoush, sauces for grains and in numerous other cooking applications.

Sunflower Seeds

These seeds can be eaten plain, roasted, sprouted, and made into butter. They can also be used as a garnish, cooked in breads as well as sprinkled on top, and added to a variety of dishes to add flavor and crunch.

Pumpkin Seeds

Pumpkin seeds can be used in much the same way as sunflower seeds. They are superior in nutrition and particularly high in protein and minerals.

Herbs And Spices

Whether a dish is sweet, sour, salty, bitter, savory or pungent depends on the types of ingredients you combine together and how they react with the taste receptors on your tongue.

The mixture of herbs or spices you use in a dish can make all the difference in the world in how a set of ingredients will taste. Using the same ingredients with different herbs and spices will produce distinctly unique results. A lentil soup with ginger, cardamom, cinnamon, and cloves will have a much different flavor than the same lentil soup seasoned with garlic, cumin, coriander and hot chili peppers. Some herbs and spices complement one another naturally; others, not so much.

The good news is that much of this flavor combining has been figured out by different cultures who have long histories of cooking with particular spices. Some of these spice traditions overlap. This is often because historically they have been part of the same trade routes between Asia, North Africa and Europe. No doubt this is why India and Ethiopia share a lot of the same spices, though with important cultural variations. Nevertheless, they are compatible cuisines. Indian dishes work very well in Ethiopian cuisine and I often combine the two for variety.

Unless I'm hosting an authentic Ethiopian dinner party, I really don't care whether the dish I'm cooking is authentic. What I care about comes back to those two important questions: Is it healthy? And, does it taste good?

Spice Blends

To save yourself time and money, at least in the short term, you may want to buy spice blends. These are regional or cultural spice blends that are already combined with the most common spices used, and in the right proportions for a particular dish. Later, as you learn more about a particular cuisine, you may want to experiment with your own spice blends, adding a little more of this and a little less of that. Avoid blends that contain salt. I don't advise buying

Mediterranean, Italian, or Cajun seasoning blends. They are made with such common, inexpensive spices, it is more cost effective to make them yourself. Also, many of them contain too much salt, for which you are paying a premium.

Note that the word "curry" simply means a blend of spices. Indian curry is different from Thai Curry, which is still different from the curries of Singapore, Shri Lanka, Nepal or Indonesia. There is not one type that fits all curry blends. Curries are distinctly regional, though when you buy a blend labeled simply as "Curry Powder" it is referring to a general Indian curry.

Following is a list of common spice blends, also called seasoning blends, some of which you may want to have on hand. Again, don't feel you have to buy all of these at once. You may never want to buy some of them. Buy them when a recipe calls for them, and in the quantity you think you will use within a few months time. There are many other spice blends available. Try them if they interest you. Remember, every time you turn on your stove, you are performing an experiment. Have fun with it. If you find that you like a particular blend and use it a lot, then you can buy in greater quantities.

Berbere Spice (Ethiopian)
Chile Powder (Southwestern/Mexican)
Chinese Five Spice Powder
Curry Powder (General Indian spice blend)
Garam Masala (Indian)
Herbs of Province (French)
Hot Madras Curry Powder (Indian)
Jamaican Seasoning Blend
Poultry Seasoning (Wonderful for grain dishes)
Sambar Powder (Indian)
Thai Seasoning Blend or Thai Curry Powder

Note: If you opening a fresh jar of a spice blend that contains hot peppers, such as Indian chilies or cayenne pepper, reduce the amount of additional hot pepper in the dish until you know how spicy the blend is. Freshly opened spices are stronger than those that have been opened for even a few days.

Individual Spices

The first seven spices in my list are items you'll most want to have in your spice drawer. They are called for frequently in the cooking we do in this country as well as in Europe and the Mediterranean.

Basil
Bay Leaf (Mediterranean Bay Leaf)
Black pepper
Oregano
Rosemary
Sage
Thyme

Some additional spices and dried herbs common to numerous cultures:

Allspice (whole and ground)
Asofeotida (A flavor enhancer found in Indian markets, this smells like dirty socks in the jar but when cooked it imparts a flavor similar to leeks.)
Black Cardamom (found in Indian and Ethiopian markets)
Green Cardamom (whole and ground, most often used in recipes calling for cardamom)
Ceylon Cinnamon, preferable to Cassia (sticks and ground)
Cloves (whole and ground)
Coriander (seeds and ground)

Cumin (seeds and ground)
Fennel Seeds (has a licorice flavor)
Fenugreek (seeds and ground, used in Indian cooking)
Fenugreek Leaves (Methi - found in Indian markets, used as a finishing flavor added just before serving many Indian dishes)
Filé (ground sassafras leaves used in making gumbo)
Ginger (ground or fresh)
Hungarian Paprika (mild and/or hot)
Dried Mint
Whole Mustard seeds (black for cooking, yellow and brown for making mustard)
Mustard (ground)
Nutmeg (whole and ground)
Paprika (ground)
Black Peppercorns (whole)
Crushed Red Pepper
Cayenne Pepper (ground)
Hot Chili Powder (ground)
Salt* (I prefer pink Himalayan salt or sea salt)
Turmeric** (ground or fresh)

*Iodized salt is depleted of its natural minerals and can contain additives such as anti-caking compounds and iodine, a necessary nutrient that can also be found in seaweeds.

**Turmeric deserves special attention as it is another superfood we should consider eating often. It is thought to be effective in preventing Alzheimer's disease, is an anti-inflammatory and is thought to be heart-protective as well. India's low incidence of Alzheimer's is attributed to this spice. Historically, turmeric has been used to treat diseases ranging from rashes to liver ailments. It is very easy to grow if you have a long growing season, producing a plant with decorative elephant-ear leaves. The root, which looks a lot like ginger, is harvested, dried and ground into a powder. It is a brilliant orange color and adds marvelous flavor and color to many dishes. A pinch of turmeric in crumbled tofu will create a tasty replacement for scrambled eggs. Always add a little black pepper when cooking with turmeric as it increases its bioavailability 2,000 percent![3, 4]

Fresh Herbs

If you have a sunny deck, some garden space or a balcony where you can have planters, it is a good idea to keep some fresh herbs growing. If not, these are herbs you can usually buy at your local farmers market or grocery store. You'll pay a premium for them but there is no substitute for fresh herbs when it comes to flavor. (Generally, it is best to add fresh herbs near the end of the cooking process.)

If you are purchasing fresh herbs, buy them as you need them because they don't keep long once harvested. The following herbs are far from a complete list but they are in my opinion are the most frequently called for: basil, Thai basil, chives, dill, garlic, lemon grass (found in Asian markets), marjoram, oregano, rosemary, sage, thyme.

I think dill deserves a special mention. It is a delicious herb and excellent for creating cheese replacements, as its fusion with other flavors in these dishes creates something that really tastes a lot like cheese, especially cream and cottage cheeses.

Note: Basil is the least cold-tolerant of all the herbs. Buy it as you need it or pick it fresh. It will brown very quickly in the fridge. Also, when buying basil in one of the plastic cartons in which growers tend to sell them, be sure to look carefully at the back of the carton. Open it if you can get away with it. If you see any leaves turning brown, look for another package. I routinely find whole sections of ruined basil in grocery coolers. Never buy basil on sale. "Reduced" is a huge warning sign for ruined basil.

Additional Items You May Want For Your Pantry

Nut Butters

Try to buy these freshly ground and with no additives. I recently bought some cashew butter that I discovered was blended with canola oil. Another reason to check the label! It never occurred to me that an organic nut butter might be mixed with another oil. Yuk!

Peanut butter, almond butter, and tahini (ground sesame seeds), roasted or plain, are common choices.

Sweeteners

Organic raisins
Organic Molasses
Brown Rice Syrup
Pomegranate Molasses
Barley Malt
Organic Turbinado sugar
Agave Nectar - I don't really care for this product. It is highly processed and no better nutritionally than sugar. I added it to the list because it is popular with vegans.

Flavor Enhancers

Rose water
Orange blossom water
Vinegars
Apple Cider
Balsamic
White Balsamic
Red Wine Vinegar
Brown Rice Vinegar
Sweet Rice Vinegar

Sauces

Organic Worcestershire Sauce
Sriracha sauce - a spicy pepper-based Thai dipping sauce
Ponzu sauce - a Japanese citrus-based sauce. The original
contains fish so look for a vegan version.

Miscellaneous Specialty Ingredients

Nutritional Yeast (Not to be confused with brewer's yeast
or bread yeast) - deactivated yeast flakes make an excellent
replacement for parmesan cheese (Bob's Red Mill, Red
Star and Braggs are all good brands.)
Canned Coconut milk
Organic Salt-Free Tomatoes
Organic Tomato Paste
Dried Coconut
Tamarind paste - a tart pulp used in Asian cooking
Wasabi powder
Thai curry paste (red, green, yellow)

Chipotle peppers (San Marcos brand)
Pineapple juice
Unsweetened Pineapple Chunks
Asian Pastas (buckwheat noodles, couscous, rice noodles, rice wrappers)
Italian Pastas* (orzo, penne, linguini, fettuccine, vermicelli, large shells, lasagna noodles)
Seaweeds** (such as wakame and/or dulse, are used to add a fishy flavor to vegan dishes, act as flavor enhancers and sources of iodine, minerals and omega-3 fatty acids. Nori sheets are sheets of dried seaweed used in making sushi.)

*Much is made of cooking with whole wheat pasta vs white pasta. There is little evidence that one is significantly better for you than the other. Pastas differ from bread in the way they are absorbed. Pasta is so compact it takes longer to break down in the digestive tract. Bread is airy and full of holes, which makes it break down faster and, therefore, more easily converts to sugar. White pasta has less nutritional value than whole grain, but it gives a far better result in cooking and it tastes better. When you complete the dish with additional nutritious and high-fiber foods, I feel it all evens out.

**Never buy kelp, also called kombu, (see page 62) which contains too much iodine, nor hijiki (which acts like a sponge for arsenic in the ocean and passes its concentrated form on to you.)[5]

Pickled Items

Capers
Green Olives
Artichoke hearts
Pickled Ginger

Baking Items

Potato Starch
Arrow Root Starch
Kuzu Root Starch
Organic Corn Starch
Organic Ultra Gel
Egg Replacer (I like Bob's Mill brand.)
Non-aluminum Baking Powder (I like Rumford.)
Non-aluminum baking soda (Bob's Red Mill)
Eno - labeled as a fruit salt, Eno is a combination of baking soda (60 percent) and citric acid (40 percent) found at Indian grocers.
Active Dry Yeast (These come in packages of three.)

14

TIPS TO SAVE TIME AND REDUCE WASTE

Batch Cooking

There are lots of ways to save time in the kitchen, and save money. As I mentioned earlier, with batch cooking, you do it once, and eat several times from the single effort of preparing only one meal. Then divide your goodies into portions sized for your family and freeze them. Don't forget to label them with freezer tape! Many foods look the same in freezer containers.

It doesn't take much longer to cook enough beans to feed ten people than it does to feed one person. It may take a few more minutes to cut up extra onions and celery, or add a few more spices, but the reward far exceeds these small inconveniences. That being said, there are some foods that are more amenable to freezing than others. Never re-freeze food once it has been thawed.

Southwestern Chile (or Chili)

Making large batches of chile entails cutting up a few more peppers and onions, measuring out larger quantities of seasonings and opening up a few more cans of tomatoes. But the cooking time is the same. Chile freezes very well and may even improve over time.

Beans (In General)

Beans are another type of food that freezes well. If you cook them in water or vegetable stock, with no herbs or spices, you can season them however you like when you are ready to use them. They will be a blank canvas for use in whatever type of cuisine you choose. The older beans are, the longer they take to cook. Cooking beans in a pressure cooker will cook them a little faster and provide a better texture regardless of the age of the bean.

Sauces

Spaghetti sauces are fantastic to stock in the freezer for quick satisfying meals. Onion and tomato sauces for Indian cuisine are wonderful time savers. Make a quart at a time and freeze them in one cup containers. Homemade barbecue sauces can be frozen in any size containers, depending on how many people you plan to serve. Creamy sauces do not freeze well, so I limit those I do freeze to tomato-based and some bean-based sauces.

Pasta

Lasagna, stuffed pasta shells, cannelloni and manicotti are all dishes you can prepare in large quantities and freeze in smaller portions to eat when you are ready.

Soups

Some soups lend themselves to freezing and others do not. Bean soups freeze well. Clear soups that are more like a broth are excellent for freezing. You can also make seasoned soup bases to which you only need to add the cut-up fresh vegetables when you are ready to eat them. This cuts cooking time in half. Soups with a creamy base (this includes tofu and nut creams) do not freeze as well.

Vegetable Stock

Keeping vegetable stock in your freezer is always a good idea as many foods are improved by using stock as instead of water. Save the bottoms of your celery, and random pieces of onion (not the skins, as it will make your stock bitter). Store them in your freezer until you've accumulated enough.

You can vary your stocks by the kinds of ingredients you add. The addition of fennel will give a slightly licorice flavor that adds depth to soups and stews. Bell pepper, turnips, parsley can all be added to give additional flavor and nutrition. Saving your kitchen scraps can go a long way to adding more flavor and nutrition to your food. Don't worry about throwing away the veggies when you've finished your stock. They've done their job. Their nutrition and flavor is now in the stock and what remains are flavorless shells ready for composting.

Freeze these in three-cup containers. When you need stock, just pull out as many containers as your recipe calls for. Another way to freeze stock is by pouring it into ice cube trays after it's cooled. Once frozen, break the cubes out of the trays and transfer them to ziplock bags for easy storage.

Rice

Rice can be prepared in large batches and divided into individual portions for freezing. This comes in handy when you are making soups, stews, stir fries or any dish in which rice is required. It will thaw quickly on a countertop or in a microwave or you can simply drop it frozen into a soup.

Roasted Red Bell Peppers

Red peppers are astronomically expensive to buy when they are not in season. In late summer they are plentiful and much cheaper at local farmers' markets. You can buy them in bulk and roast them in your oven. Once cooled, remove the skins, seeds, and stems, wrap them individually, and freeze them in freezer bags. Now they are ready for you to pull one out whenever you need them.

Tomatoes

Frozen tomatoes are preferable to canned, and home-preserved are always better than store-bought. I spend two Saturdays in the summer canning and freezing tomatoes, which gives me enough of the tangy goodness for the entire winter. You can buy bushel baskets of fresh tomatoes at the farmers' markets when they are at their cheapest. Cook them down to the consistency you prefer and freeze them in three-cup Pyrex rectangular dishes for easy stacking or preserve them in pint sized jars, just the right size to replace store-bought canned tomatoes.

Fruit

Cut up and freeze mangos in season for sauces and smoothies. Keeping freezer bags of freshly picked blackberries and blueberries gives you the option of baking cobblers in the dead of winter. Bananas can be cut into quarters or smaller, and frozen for making delicious frozen desserts. (You'll need a Vitamix or other high-powered blender for this.)

Ginger and Garlic

When you know you are going to be making a lot of dishes that call for garlic or ginger, toss them separately into a food processor (standard or mini), and make quick work of grinding them to an almost paste-like consistency. Let them rest for ten minutes, then put the garlic or ginger into separate quart-sized freezer bags about half-filled. Flatten each bag on a baking pan or cookie sheet that will fit into your freezer until it is the same thickness throughout, about 1/4-inch. Then, with the back of a dinner knife draw lines over the top of the bag making an indention about 1/8-inch deep. This should not cut the bags!

The scored lines should form a one-inch grid. This makes it easier to break off a piece when you need it for a recipe. Place the baking pan in the freezer until the pastes have set. Then remove the pan and stack the bags.

Breads

Doubling the recipe makes sense when baking breads. Whether you are cooking loaves, rolls, buns, biscuits, scones, or muffins, it takes only a little more time to add extra flour, water, salt, and yeast. The rising time will be the same and you only have to bring the oven to the needed temperature once, thereby saving electricity or gas. Once your bread has cooled, store the rest in freezer bags or bread bags and pop them in your freezer to be pulled out whenever you want. You can cut loaves into smaller portions or slices, rather than freezing a whole loaf.

It is also possible to freeze dough. You can double or even triple your bread recipe, divide it and let it rise in separate bowls. Then, punch down the dough and divide it into balls sized according to what you plan to use right away and what you would like to freeze for later. Then transfer them to freezer bags. A quart-sized zip-lock bag works well for my needs. If you are baking for a larger family you can go with half-gallon or gallon-sized freezer bags. Don't fill them to the top. Leave about one-third of the bag empty for expansion. When ready to use, thaw for a of couple hours on a countertop or transfer from the freezer to the fridge the night before. (Don't leave the dough sitting out unattended for too long. It will resume rising and might burst the bag. Refrigerated dough rises much more slowly, but if left too long it will also burst out of its bag.) Shape the dough into loaves or buns and allow it to rise a second time before baking. If making pizzas or flat-breads, a second rise is not necessary.

Potatoes, green bell peppers, mushrooms, and most winter squashes do not fare well in the freezer. They are best eaten fresh. Eggplants freeze well as part of a sauce but not on their own.

Advance Prep-Work

If you know you have a time-consuming menu planned for tomorrow, doesn't it make sense to get some of the preparation work accomplished the night before? Celery, onions, peppers, green onions, and mushrooms can easily be cut up in advance, saving time when you are putting the dish together. Toss washed and discarded pieces into a pot to make vegetable stock, or freeze in a bag to make stock at a later date.

Root vegetables and hard squashes will discolor quickly and should be cooked as soon after cutting as possible. You can delay discoloration by covering with water and placing a weight (like a bowl of water) on top to keep the vegetables submerged. Nuts can also be chopped in advanced and roasted if the recipe calls for it. Rice can be cooked the day before and reheated before serving, so can stocks and some sauces. Beans and cashews can be soaked overnight or put on to soak in the morning before heading off to work. It makes life much easier when you reduce your workload to manageable segments, especially when you are just beginning or you are short on time.

Waste Not, Want Not

My eyes are often bigger than my stomach when it comes to buying produce, and I find myself buying more than I can possibly cook before it all goes bad. I admit, I am distracted by colorful objects, especially at my local Farmers' Market. And who wouldn't be when surrounded by purple eggplants, red cabbages, yellow summer squashes, green artichokes, fronds of multi-colored Swiss chard, juicy tomatoes so ripe you can almost taste them, and — oh, fresh herbs... I want to use them all, right away! I've found that making a shopping list for exactly what I need for the next few days helps to keep my attention focused on the tasks at hand.

When you do arrive home with your prized produce, rearrange your fridge so the older produce is in the front, to be used first. Those that no longer make the cut, move to your compost bin. I keep a covered enamel pot on my kitchen counter for this purpose. Trim off dead parts of your produce and toss them into the compost pot. Move the fresh stuff to the rear of your fridge. (But don't forget they are there!) Rotate your fruits and vegetables, using the last-purchased first.

The better you become at shopping frugally, the less waste you'll have. If tomatoes have become overripe, it is a good time to make a quick pasta sauce. If you've accumulated more vegetables than you have meals planned, make a soup or a stock. You can usually freeze these for later and lose the guilt over having wasted perfectly good vegetables, and the money you paid for them.

❧ 15 ❧

LET'S START COOKING!

Cooking is like love. It should be entered into with abandon or not at all. — Harriet Van Horne

We know what food is good for us. We know how we should be eating. The real issue, then, is how to incorporate fruits, vegetables, legumes and grains into our diets in a way that is satisfying and more rewarding in terms of taste and nutrition than animal products. The recipes in this book should move you closer to that goal. They are relatively easy to prepare, satisfying and delicious, and cover a range of cooking techniques. In preparing them you will learn some simple skills that will pave the way for greater experimentation in future culinary endeavors.

As Co-founder and Editor of *Veggin' Out and About!*, I regularly visit restaurants and interview cooks from a range of cuisines. Some of these restaurant chefs share recipes with me and have even allowed Rich and me to make video recordings of them demonstrating how to cook a particular food. In order to adequately describe the recipes, I always go home and make the dish myself. Often I become engaged with the chef throughout the process. He or she answers my questions and guides me through the procedure so I can pass this information on to my readers. In this way, I have gained a hands-on understanding of how these chefs arrive at the marvelous flavors we enjoy in their restaurants.

These experiences have given me the great fortune to learn from chefs of many cultures. Talented cooks from India, Ethiopia, Thailand, Shri Lanka, Vietnam, Japan, and the United States have shared their secrets with me and have given me permission to share them with you!

I first learned about Italian food through my husband's family, learning to make recipes handed down through generations. I discovered the cuisines of Europe from the years I spent in Germany and France. Living in Japan for four years gave me a yen for Japanese cuisine. I was taught how to make authentic hummus, baba ghanoush, and tabbouleh from Saddam Hussein's personal chef, a Christian who fled to the United States during the Iraqi war to escape religious persecution. He now owns a popular Middle Eastern restaurant near my home.

Often I make changes to the recipes to meet the requirements of our healthy diet. Most restaurants use more oil and salt than one may reasonably consider healthy. While this might be fine on occasion, we ought to control the meals we cook at home so they are both delicious and guilt free. Remember our mantra! The first thing we should ask ourselves when preparing a meal is: Is it helping me or harming me? The second is: Does it taste good? These are the foods we want on our plates and in our bodies.

Cooking, however, doesn't just magically happen. The tips I offer presuppose you know nothing at all about cooking. If you are an experienced cook, you can just skip over the basic instructions. These recipes may require more steps than you expect and the ingredient list may seem daunting. Take it one step at a time and you'll find preparing delicious food is not as difficult as it might seem at first glance. If you have confusion about cooking terms or techniques suggested within the recipes, you can refer the relevant sections at the end of this chapter for answers.

As you become more proficient, combining steps can make the process go more quickly. Often, some steps can be prepared a day in advance, making the process even easier. Nuts and beans can be soaked overnight. Vegetable stocks and rice can be prepared in advance. Like any skill worth having, the more you practice, the better you will become.

If you want to prepare meals that are as creamy, flavorful and satisfying as the meals you are currently accustomed to eating, you must realize that preparing good food takes time. It gets easier as it goes and before long you'll wonder what all the fuss was about.

Not every meal has to be gourmet. Most of the time people like to eat simply. I keep a roasted sweet potato and marinated beets in the fridge, and some veggies I can quickly grill so I can throw together a veggie sandwich at a moment's notice. All I have to do is put a bun in the toaster and assemble a sandwich. This is my "go to" meal when I don't feel like cooking. My friend Tess, always keeps beans and rice on hand. She tops them with fresh chopped veggies and that is her "go to" meal. You may want to eat this way a good deal of the time. However, when you want something delicious and comforting, it is worth a little time at the stove preparing a dinner that will satisfy your soul's desire.

Relax. Have fun and give yourself permission to make mistakes. You are taking the first steps of an odyssey that will last a lifetime. Savor the journey!

A Note About Knives

I became intimately acquainted with the hazard of knives when I was a small child. My mother had left a large cardboard box in the living room, which was obviously begging to be transformed into a child's playhouse. I could see I would need to cut holes for windows. My mother was on the telephone, paying little attention to me, so I helped myself to a large knife from her knife drawer and proceeded to cut up the box.

I don't remember cutting myself but I do remember going to my mother, who was still on the phone, and the expression on her face as I opened my hand, blood spewing everywhere. She snatched me up and rushed me to our doctor's office, where my wounds were promptly stitched. I nearly lost three fingers and have telling scars as reminders to this day. The moral of this story: keep a watchful eye on your kids and treat your knives with respect!

It is important to take care of your knives. Buy the best quality you can afford and keep them clean and sharp. This will prevent injury and will save you effort and frustration. A good knife is worth its weight in gold.

As plant-based cooks, our needs are limited. I find I can accomplish every task with three knives; a paring knife for

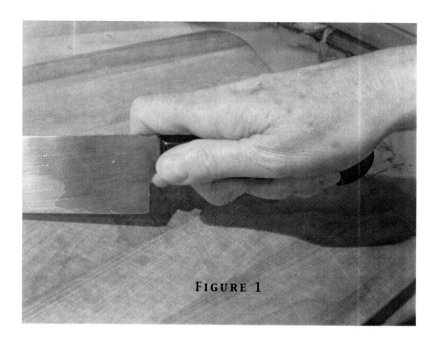

FIGURE 1

peeling vegetables and for small work, an eight-inch chef's knife for most jobs, and a good bread knife. I like my Wusthof and Henkel knives but there are many good brands available. In both, the Classic series seem to be the best quality.

Around the Christmas holidays, I often see four-star Henkel knives offered as a set of three for less than $100 and the Classic Wustof set of two knives for around $125. I recommend buying the sharpener as well to keep your blades in top form. If you can only afford one knife, the eight-inch chef's knife will serve you best.

Hold your knife in your dominant hand with your fingers

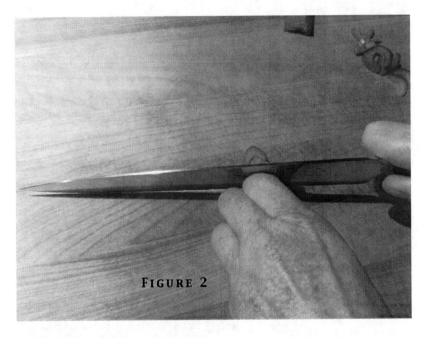

FIGURE 2

wrapped around the grip (Fig. 1).

When you are making slices, cut across a vegetable at the bottom one-third of the knife, nearest the grip (Fig 2).

Grasp the item you are cutting with your non-dominant hand, tucking your fingers underneath. The blade should

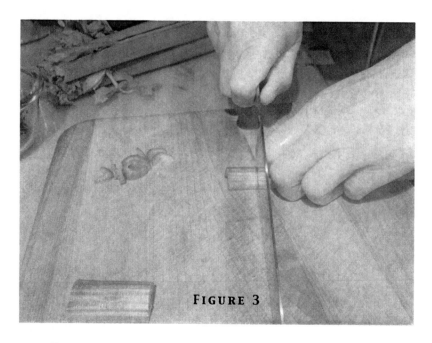

FIGURE 3

actually slide against your knuckles when you make each cut, always making contact with your knuckles (Fig 3).

FIGURE 4

The tip end of the blade never leaves the cutting surface. The blade should work in a rocking motion, all the while sliding against your knuckles in a downward forward motion. As you cut the vegetable or herb, your fingers should push the item your are cutting toward the blade in a firm constant pressure, while your knuckles remain stationary. While this might seem counterintuitive, this is actually the safest way to cut vegetables.

It is advisable to practice this many times until it becomes second nature. Chopping celery is an excellent way to gain practice with least opportunity for injury.

When chopping delicate herbs, such as parsley, dill or cilantro, hold the tip of the blade down against the chopping board (Fig. 4). Then, wrapping your hand around the handle, chop the herbs in a rocking motion, always holding the tip on the board's surface. As you chop, move the knife from one side of the pile of herbs to the other, in an arc, going back and forth until you've reached the desired result.

Kitchen Cut-Ups

Bell Peppers

The easiest way to cut a bell pepper is to lay it on its side and slice off both ends. Remove the stem end and the bottom end. Twist off and discard the stem and cut strips of the remaining end pieces to the desired width, rotating as you complete each side. If you want julienned strips, leave them as they are. To dice, gather the strips and cut across them to the desired sized.

Next, remove and discard the mass of seeds from the body of the fruit. Make one slice down the side of the bell pepper. This will allow you to open the pepper and lay it flat on your chopping board in a long rectangular panel. Gently remove the fibrous ribs with your knife.

To julienne, cut the end of the bell pepper into strips of the desired width.

To dice, gather strips and cut across into preferred size.

To mince, make all your cuts very thin, julienned and diced.

Broccoli

Broccoli has a very tough stem that is quite edible when you remove the outer skin. Slice off the toughest portion and slip the blade of your knife underneath the outer layer of the skin. Anchor it to your knife with your thumb and pull upwards towards the head of the broccoli. Continue in this way until all of the tender stem is exposed. Remove stem and cut into desired shapes.

Remove the florets where their branches attach to the stem. You can divide them into smaller pieces by cutting off smaller florets within the larger group. Cut remaining stem to suit your purpose.

Carrots

Carrots are often grated, julienned, diced or minced. While the majority of nutrients are found in the peel of most vegetables, the peel of carrots is a little bitter and not to everyone's liking. To clean a carrot you can simply scrub it with a nylon scrub pad to remove the outer material.

You can also use a vegetable peeler. Today's vegetable peelers usually have two blades on a swivel rocker, which allow for cutting both on the downward and upward strokes saving time. Another easy way to peel a carrot is to hold it at a 45-degree angle, resting it against a kitchen sink and scrap it, moving the knife away from your body. Turn the carrot with each scrape. Then remove the stem and the tip and rinse.

Carrots should be peeled just before use or covered with water immediately, as they tend to discolor very quickly.

Cauliflower

Turn the cauliflower over to expose the stem. Slice off the stem, cutting away as many of the leaves as possible, until it is even with the first branches of the florets. With a paring knife, gently cut around the stem to get rid of the remaining leaves.

Following the contour of the stem, cut away each branch with a floret. Set in a colander for a second wash. When all of the florets are removed, retain the stem for another use. It is quite edible and can be grated to add to other dishes like Lentil-Cauliflower Sloppy Joes, or added to stock ingredients.

Another easy way to cut cauliflower is simply to cut it down the middle and remove the branches that are clearly visible. This will destroy the shape of some of your prettiest florets, however, so if you want to keep them whole use the first method.

To create cauliflower steaks, turn over and trim the stem,. Make one long, careful cut from the very outside of the stem to the top of the cauliflower, leaving the stem intact to hold the cauliflower steak together. Make another cut down the center of the stem and still another down the remaining edge. This will produce two steaks perfect for grilling. Save the leftover material for another purpose. To divide the florets into smaller pieces, simply cut through the bottom of their branches into the flower.

Celeriac

Celeriac is an ugly tuber with a lovely flavor. It has a mild celery taste and is wonderful in Dutch Stamppot, soups and stews, or roasted. This vegetable does need to be peeled. Peel it like you would a potato, cutting off the warty nodules and the stem. Then treat it like you would any root vegetable.

Chiffonade

Chiffonade is a technique used to create thin ribbons from pliable leafy green herbs. Simply stack the leaves one on top of another. Beginning at the side of the stack, curl them into a cigar-shaped roll. Cut slices across the roll, like cutting off the tip of a cigar. Continue until all the leaves are cut, then separate with your fingers into thin ribbons. This is typically done with herbs like mint or basil, but you can also cut kale, collards, and other flexible leafy vegetables using the same technique, but with wider cross-cuts. This makes them more manageable for cooking and for preparing salads. It is best to first remove their stems and pull or cut the larger leaves in half, lengthwise, along the stem. Then roll lengthwise into a long cigar-shape and cut across to make ribbons of desired thickness. I use this technique for kale when preparing massaged kale salads.

Chopping

Chopping is a rougher form of cutting up or dicing vegetables. For the purpose of this text, chopping refers to cutting herbs into very small feathery pieces or cutting larger vegetables into smaller, irregular shapes, while dicing refers to cutting vegetables into small cubes or various sizes.

Chopping Fresh Herbs

Chopping fresh herbs releases their flavors, infusing them into the foods you are preparing while filling the kitchen with intoxicating aromas. To chop leafy herbs, first stack leaves and then roll them into a cigar-shape. Cut across into a very thin slices to create a chiffonade and separate with your fingers.

To chop herbs with delicate fronds, such as dill, remove the feathery fronds from the stem and stack in a pile on your chopping board. Cut across them in tiny slices, moving your fingers away from the blade as you cut. Turn and cut across the other direction. Repeat until you receive the desired result.

Cuts For Cabbage

To get thin ribbons of cabbage, first cut the stem off at the base of the cabbage. This will give you a stable flat surface to rest on the chopping board. Cut the cabbage in half from top to stem. Lay the halves on a chopping board cut side down and cut them from top to stem. You will now have four quarters.

Turn the quarters over and you will see the hard stem in the middle of each. Rest one quarter on its stem end, holding it firmly at the top. With your knife, cut away the hard center, following its contour to get all of it. Repeat with the other three pieces. Set the hard pieces aside for use in stock, or discard.

Now, lay each piece, one at a time, on its side; cut across to form thin ribbons. Separate with your fingers.

For larger pieces, cut the slices wider and then cut across to make bite-sized rectangles.

Cuts For Green Leafy Vegetables

For green leafy vegetables, remove the long stems by tearing them apart or by cutting along the stem. Tear or cut into the desired size. Interestingly, some chefs believe that greens taste better when they are torn rather than cut, especially in salads.

To dice celery, cut off ends and set aside for stock or discard. Cut the celery lengthwise into three or four even strips. Cut crosswise to create whatever size dice you require. Celery adds a lot of flavor to foods. Many people prefer the flavor to the texture. I personally, enjoy the crunch it can add to a dish. But if this bothers you, cut celery into very thin pieces before sautéing and its texture won't be a problem.

Another way to make celery easier to eat is to remove its strings. To do this, simply cut off the root end and discard or save for stock. Slip your knife blade just underneath the celery's skin. Hold the skin against the blade with your thumb and pull along the length of the stalk. The strings will easily lift off.

Cuts For Root Vegetables and Tomatoes

These cuts can be applied to most firm vegetables, primarily root vegetables like carrots, potatoes, daikon, radishes, turnips, beets, and so forth. Tomatoes can also be sliced, diced, and quartered using these methods.

To slice vegetables to make potato chip cuts, simply cut a thin slice from the side of the vegetable, just enough to create a flat surface so that it will sit on a chopping board without rolling. Cut *across* the vegetable to desired thickness.

For french fries, cut 1/4-inch slices *down the length* of the root. Remove the rounded sides and set aside. Stack the slices and cut, *again lengthwise*, into 1/4-inch strips. Lay the two rounded ends on the chopping board, flat side down, and cut the same way, one at a time. (French fried cuts are the same as julienne cuts, only larger.)

To dice, turn the vegetable and cut again *crosswise*, into 1/4-inch strips, creating 1/4-inch cubes. You can cut the cubes to any size you desire.

To quarter, lay the vegetable down and cut lengthwise down the middle to divide in half. Place each half cut-side down and cut across the center. This should give you four equal quarters. You can alternatively make four lengthwise cuts, depending on the shape you want.

Some vegetables, like carrots, and celery, look more appealing cut on a diagonal rather than in straight cuts across in potato-chip fashion. Firmly hold the carrot or other vegetable in your non-dominant hand on a chopping board. Hold the knife in your dominant hand, at a 45-degree angle to the carrot. Slice repeatedly across the vegetable at this angle in equal segments.

Cutting Corn Off The Cob

Pull off the husks and break off the stem of the corn. Remove the silky threads and rinse under running water. With a chef's knife, slice off the tip of the ear, especially if there is worm damage, making a flat surface. Turn it cut side down onto a chopping board while holding the stem end firmly in your non-dominant hand. Beginning at the middle of the cob with your knife angled, cut away the kernels following the contour of the cob. Don't cut too close to the cob or you'll also cut away hard undigestible pieces of the corn. The kernels will fall onto the chopping board, leaving bare cob where you just finished cutting.

Turn the corn and do another strip, repeating until the bottom half of the ear is bare. Scrape the kernels into a bowl and set aside. Turn over and repeat with the other half. This will yield about a cup of corn kernels.

Garlic

If you need your garlic to remain whole, cut off the root end with a paring knife and with the edge of your blade, lift the skin and secure it with your thumb, then pull it off.

To slice garlic, cut off a small slice on one side for stability. Slice across the clove to desired thickness.

To make thin slivers, stack the slices and cut lengthwise to make thin sticks.

Most of the time you'll want your garlic minced. Lay a clove on a chopping board, on a countertop. (You'll need a stable surface.) Place a large chef's knife on its side, resting on top of the garlic clove, with the blade turned away from you. With your open palm whack the side of the blade right at the point where it sits atop the garlic clove. This should crush the garlic and separate it from its peel; discard the peel.

To mince, crush the garlic. Make thin cuts repeatedly across the length of the garlic and then again across its width.

Grate

If you have a food processor with a grating attachment, this job will go very quickly. Be sure to remove the chopping blade before grating any vegetable. If you have a manual hand-held grater, you are in good company. I used mine exclusively for many years. The type that looks like a pyramid is perhaps easiest to use. Place the grater on a chopping board or plate. Hold the grater firmly in your non-dominant hand while holding the vegetable at a 45-degree angle with the other hand. Push the vegetable in a sliding motion onto the widest holes of the grater. (The smaller holes are for mincing ginger and grating nutmeg. They can also be used to "rice" cauliflower.) With a grater that looks more like a flat board, hold the grater at a 45-degree angle while pushing the vegetable onto its largest holes.

Be very careful that you stop grating before the apparatus nicks your knuckles or takes off a fingernail!

Green Onions

Green onions are delicious cooked or raw. Trim ends and pull off any wilted or brown pieces, all the way to the root. Lay onions flat on a chopping board. Cut across in 1/8-inch slices. I include the bulb in everything calling for green onions. Some people only prefer the green part. It's your choice.

Ginger

The easiest way to peel ginger is with a spoon. I like to use a stainless steel tablespoon measuring spoon for this task, but any spoon will do. Break off a piece of ginger, the size you intend to use. Using the wide end of a spoon, scrape the ginger peel off. To slice, cut a small piece off the side of the ginger to give you a flat stable surface. Cut across or lengthwise to the desired thickness. To julienne, stack slices and cut lengthwise. To mince, cut across julienned slices.

Julienne

Julienne is a term that describes cutting vegetables into small sticks, usually about 1/8- to 1/4-inch wide and up to two inches long. For onions, cut peeled onion in half and lay on chopping board cut side down. Beginning on one side, cut lengthwise, angling your blade toward the center of the onion, making thin wedges or strips as you cut. Separate with your fingers. Repeat with other half.

For root vegetables, slice off a small amount from the side of the vegetable, just enough so it will sit flat on a chopping board without rolling. Cut lengthwise slices the desired thickness of your vegetable sticks. Remove rounded ends and set aside. Stack slices and cut lengthwise again to desired width. Turn and cut across the vegetable to desired length. Lay the two rounded ends on the chopping board, flat side down, and cut the same way, one at a time.

For celery, trim ends off celery and discard or set aside for making stock. Cut each rib of celery lengthwise to the desired width. Cut across to desired length.

Lemons

Citruses, and lemons in particular, are indispensable in cooking no matter the cuisine. Adding a splash of lemon juice finishes off a dish with a brightness you can get from nothing else. Become friends with this fruit and you'll be glad you did.

To juice a lemon, cut it in half and insert a cone-shaped lemon juicer into the cut side of the fruit. Squeeze and twist over a bowl. Remove seeds. If you have a stationary juicer, firmly push cut side of the lemon down onto the cone, while twisting it from side to side. If you don't have a juicer of any kind, cut the lemon in half and squeeze over a bowl, rotating the fruit as you squeeze, working from cut end to stem to get every drop. Remove seeds.

Mashed and Smashed Potatoes

Smashed potatoes are mashed potatoes with the skins on. Using a potato masher, press repeatedly into hot cooked potatoes until desired consistency is reached. Add a little non-dairy milk, cashew cream, cashew cream cheese, or even a little Fettuccini Alfredo sauce to make it creamier. If you feel you can't live without butter, try a little Earth Balance spread.

Mince

To mince is to cut up a vegetable, herb or spice into a tiny dice, nearly a pulp.

Onions

To peel, cut off the root end of the onion. With a paring knife, pull off the first one or two outside layers until the tough brown or silver outer skin has been removed and only the tender shiny onion is visible. Remove the stem end.

To dice, cut the onion in half, from stem to root. Lay one half at a time, cut side down, on a chopping board. Cut across the onion, in 1/8-inch half-rings, holding the onion together as you cut. Next, turn it and cut lengthwise into 1/8-inch wedges. This will give you a nice diced onion. You can adjust the size of the cuts as needed.

For onion rings, hold peeled onion firmly against the chopping board. Cut across the width of the onion to form rings. Separate with your fingers.

To quarter an onion, peel then slice down the middle from stem to root. Lay cut side down on chopping board and cut lengthwise down the middle. Repeat with other side.

To julienne onion, see julienne.

Squash, Hard Winter

Many hard squashes, like acorn, butternut, and pumpkin, usually do not need peeling, as they are cooked it their shells, usually stuffed. One only needs to remove the seeds. Cut the squash in half, from stem to pointed tip. With a spoon, scrape out all the seeds and seed pulp until there is a clean hollow where the seeds had been.

For many dishes, however, you do need to peel the squash. Most squashes, even hard winter squashes, can be easily peeled with a pivoting vegetable peeler, the kind you can find at almost any store that carries cooking gadgets. Just slice off the ends with a sharp knife, then slice off skin with the vegetable peeler, rotating it as you go, cutting away from you.

You can also peel hard squashes with a sharp knife. Cut off ends; place on chopping board cut side down, slice skin downwards towards the board. Rotate and continue slicing off skin until the entire piece is bare. Turn over and trim off the small pieces you missed in the first cuts. For long-necked squashes, cut off stem and neck and peel in the same way as the pumpkin, downward towards the chopping board. Scoop out seeds in the remaining rounded part of the squash and discard or save for roasting. Cut the seed bowl into quarters and slice downwards in the same manner. Then cut into size needed for stews, baking or roasting.

Squash, Summer

Summer squashes, like the longneck yellow squash and the scalloped-shaped pattypan squash, can be sliced across, lengthwise, diagonally, or any way you like. There are no seeds to speak of and they have soft, edible skins, so you can cut them to suit your needs.

Zest

The zest is the very tender, oily outer part of a citrus peel. Lemon, lime, and orange zests are commonly added to dishes to give them the subtle, but more "zesty" flavor of the fruit in question. A citrus zester is scraped across the surface of the fruit before it is cut. Sometimes the peel is added as is to the dish; other times it is minced to be less obtrusive. Zest is often used in thin delicate spirals as a garnish to show off a dish.

If you don't have a zester, you can carefully peel a thin outer layer of the fruit with a sharp knife. If you get any of the peel's white inner layer, (the mesocarp) it must be removed or it will make your dish bitter.

Basic Cooking Terms And Techniques

The following is hardly a complete list of cooking techniques, but it will allow you to create the recipes within this book, giving you basic skills to build on. It is understood that you have already washed the herbs and vegetables, and peeled them if called for in the recipe. Again, if you are an experienced cook, you can skip this part.

Bake
Cooking in the oven, covered.

Blanch
Immersing fresh vegetables in boiling water for 30 seconds or until the color deepens.

Boil
Cooking in liquid on relatively high heat until it bubbles aggressively.

Broil
Cooking directly under a heating unit.

Braise

Traditionally, braising means frying food lightly and then cooking with a liquid under low temperature. Rather than frying, in this book we prefer to sauté the food without oil until caramelized, then add liquid.

Caramelize

Cooking vegetables, particularly onions, in oil until they become soft and golden brown. This will tend to make them sweeter. In these recipes oil isn't used. Instead, a little water is added as the vegetable juices begin to brown and cling to the pan. This transfers the brown color to the vegetable, giving it a caramel color and attending sweetness without the use of fat.

Filtered Water

Much of the water we get in our household taps is treated with chlorine to kill unwanted bacteria. The problem with this is it also kills beneficial bacteria. If you are trying to make bread with fermented yeast using chlorinated water, you might very well kill the yeast and never get the bread to rise the way you expect.

Another problem is that chlorinated water tastes like bleach. That alone is enough to ruin a dish you've put your whole heart into creating. If you can afford to buy a filter for your tap you may want to consider installing one, remembering to change it when it is past its expiration date.

If not, cook with spring water if you can. This can be purchased at most grocery stores and large discount shopping centers. I have filters on all my taps in my Virginia home, and in Tennessee we use well water that has been tested and pronounced to be good.

Fold

To 'fold' an ingredient into a wet mixture (like a batter) carefully lift the mixture from the bottom or sides of the bowl and turn it over the ingredient you've added. Repeat until all the ingredients are blended. Folding is a gentler method than stirring, used when you don't want to break up the vegetables you are working with. In non-vegan cooking, it is often employed when adding egg whites to a batter.

Knead

Pressing dough down with your palms, turning and pressing it repeatedly to develop its gluten.

Mix

Combining ingredients by stirring them together.

Parboil

Partially boiling, cooking until the item is still crunchy or only half-done.

Pinch

Referring to dried herbs and spices, a pinch is just enough to hold between a thumb and index finger, less than 1/8 teaspoon.

Roast

Cooking uncovered in the oven.

Simmer

Cooking on low heat with only a few lazy bubbles breaking on the surface.

Sauté

Strictly speaking, sauté means cooking in a little bit of oil until soft. For the purposes of this book, it means cooking on medium heat in a sauté pan or a skillet with a lid until soft, adding a little water if necessary to keep from sticking. It is an oil-free process.

Smash

Crushing beneath the flat side of a chef's knife to break up the fibers in the item being crushed, such as garlic. With root vegetables, like potatoes, smashing means mashing the potato with a potato masher, leaving the skin intact.

Stir

Mixing ingredients with a spoon, fork or whisk in a circular motion, scraping them free from the side of the dish as you go.

A Note About Appliances

Appliances can vary radically in cooking times. I have two ranges in different residences that are virtually the same machine. They are made by the same company and are identical except that one has a convection oven and the other does not. It takes four times longer to broil something in the range without the convection oven, even though the convection feature has nothing to do with the broil feature. However, in the other range, it takes half the time to boil water on the stovetop. Go figure. My point is that it is often necessary to become familiar with the quirks of your appliances and adjust your cooking times accordingly. It is helpful to buy an oven thermometer so you can assure accurate cooking temperatures.

High Altitudes

Living at high altitudes can affect cooking times and possibly even ingredients. In baking you may have to reduce the amount of water in a recipe if you live more than 3,000 feet above sea level because the lowered air pressure affects how cakes and breads perform. You may also need to raise the temperature of your oven an extra 25°F. Recipes that require boiling may take a little longer, as boiling temperature is lower at higher altitudes. The more you practice the better you'll be able to make these simple adjustments in your recipes.

A Few Basic Recipes

While it may be hard to believe that there are some people who really know nothing at all about cooking, I have come to understand there are many busy souls who have never turned on a stove, oven, or microwave in their entire lives. I used to live next door to a woman who in 65 years had never boiled a pot of spaghetti noodles. She came over to my house frustrated because the pasta she had soaked all night long had turned into a bowl of mush! I asked her why she thought she had to soak the pasta beforehand and she said, "It's hard, like beans. You have to soak beans, don't you?"

Since I consider this book a primer for people at all stages of experience in the kitchen, I've added some very simple recipes, such as how to boil pasta and bake a potato, for those who missed this part of their early culinary education. I hope the rest of you can bear with me; obviously you can feel free to skip over recipes you already know.

Additionally I've included recipes I consider to be foundations to creating other recipes. Some dishes require that you complete other basic recipes before you can make the dish.

Making southwestern chile, for example, requires you to have two or three varieties of cooked beans on hand. This sort of thing is a good reason to spend some time in batch cooking. You will already have serving-size portions of ingredients you can just pull out of the freezer whenever you have need of them. If you don't have time to prepare these from scratch, use frozen over canned if that is an option. The flavor will be so much better. (Frozen beans, though, may require additional cooking time.)

Some foundation recipes, such as Tahini Sauce, whip up in a matter of minutes.

The following are a few basic recipes as well as some that will help you to create the recipes in this book. I attempt to demonstrate how you can use the same recipe in other ways to create variety and reduce waste. Many more exist, but these are sufficient for you to get your feet wet.

Note: When preparing basic recipes that are to be used as a part of other recipes, I do not include their preparation and cooking times in the timing of the main recipe. It should be understood that the basic preparation time should be considered in the context of the main recipe and necessary timing adjustments made. Many of the recipes that include other recipes are to demonstrate what can be done with leftover ingredients, so it is presupposed these recipes have already been made and are on hand.

I rarely recommend the use of salt, but I add it as an option in each recipe so you can make your own decision about if you feel you need to include it to make the meal more palatable. It might make the difference in whether you can become accustomed to eating plants rather than animal protein, especially in the beginning. Try to keep your salt consumption below 1/2 teaspoon per day. Once you learn to love plants, then you can work on reducing salt intake. If your doctor has told you to eliminate salt entirely from your diet, then certainly you should follow his instructions.

Saturated fat is another matter. We know from Dr. Vogel's studies that saturated fats immediately affect the function of our endothelial cells. I never recommend adding fat to a diet unless it is in the form of whole foods, such as avocados and nuts, though I will sometimes use a little oil to the surface of a grill or pan to keep food from sticking to them.

A note about the photographs in this book: As an independent publisher, I found it is cost prohibitive to add color pictures to this book. I felt that it was preferable to use black and white photographs than have none at all because it is helpful to know what a particular dish should look like when it is completed. However, color is an integral part of vegetarian cooking and you really can't appreciate the true beauty of these foods in a black and white format. For this reason I have included a page of photographs on my website that will have all of these pictures available in a color format. You can access them by visiting **www.vegginoutandabout.com** and then by clicking on the tab called "Time For Change" in the upper menu bar.

Mirepoix Vegetable Stock

Everyone needs to know how to make a good vegetable stock. Nearly everything that calls for water can be improved by using a good stock instead. Rice cooked with stock is far more delicious than plain rice and it has the additional nutrients of the vegetables from which the stock was made.

The good news is that it is easy, quick, and inexpensive, and you can even make it with just kitchen scraps if you do a lot of cooking with fresh ingredients. The flavor is far superior to store-bought stock and it has not been adulterated with prohibitive quantities of salt and preservatives.

This particular stock can be used whenever a savory dish calls for a liquid. Mirepoix is traditionally a blend of celery, onion and carrot, but you can make any flavored stock you choose by altering the vegetables you use. It will keep in your fridge for up to three days.

Unlike broth and stocks made from animal products, this stock doesn't need to simmer for hours. Once the produce becomes soft, the stock is done. Don't cook it until it becomes a mush. The water should be infused with the flavor and nutrition of the vegetables but the stock should be clear, not cloudy.

You can make a large pot of it and pour it into ice cube trays or three-cup pyrex stackable containers and freeze. Ice cubes are very convenient for when you need only a small amount of stock for a sauce or a gravy. Once frozen, empty cubes into a gallon zip-lock freezer bag and you have stock ready for whenever your recipe calls for it.

Time: 1 hour 15 minutes
Yield: about 8 cups

Ingredients:

4 stalks celery, cut into 4-inch pieces
6 large carrots, ends removed and cut in half
2 large onions, peeled and quartered
12 cups filtered water

Preparation: 7 minutes

1. Wash and prepare vegetables.

Method: a little over an hour

1. Transfer vegetables to a large stock pot with a lid. Cover with water* (about 12 cups) and bring to a rolling boil (20 to 22 minutes).

2. Reduce heat to medium and continue to boil for up to 45 minutes. Leave lid slightly ajar to let steam escape and to avoid boiling over.

3. Strain through a wire mesh into another pot. Discard vegetables. Allow stock to cool. Use immediately, refrigerate or freeze as desired.

*The more concentrated this stock, the more flavorful. It is best to cover the vegetables with only an inch of water above the vegetable line for maximum flavor. However, if you are limited in the amount of vegetables you have on hand and need a large quantity of stock, go ahead and add a lot of water to the pan, regardless of the number of vegetables you have. It will still provide flavor and nutrients and is preferable to plain water.

Note: There is no nutritional data for this recipe since the vegetables are discarded upon completion. We can assume many of the nutrients remain in the liquid but I have no way of accurately measuring them.

Leafy Greens

Because leafy green vegetables are loaded with cancer-fighting antioxidants as well as a variety of important vitamins and minerals, it is wise to incorporate them in our meals whenever possible. They are low in calories and high in fiber and are probably the biggest nutritional bang you can get for your buck. Adding them to beans, grain dishes, and soups are great ways of sneaking greens into your diet. But if you would like the green to be the superstar at the dinner table, these are a few ways you can prepare them.

Massaged Kale

Kale is a delicious and very nutritious green that adds rich color, flavor and interest to salads. But it is very fibrous, which makes it difficult to eat unless it is cooked. Massaging kale is a secret used by professional chefs to break up the fibers, making it softer so it can be eaten raw. It also makes the color more vibrant, which is a plus when adding it to salads and sandwiches, making them satisfying to the eye as well as the palate. It's very easy to do and takes little time and effort. Now the secret is out!

Time: 7 minutes
Yield: 7 cups

Ingredients:
1 bunch curly kale (about 10 ounces)

Preparation: 5 minutes
1.   Wash kale and remove stems.

1. Cut across into 1/4-inch strips or tear into bite-sized pieces.

2. Spin dry in a salad spinner or shake off water and dry with paper towels.

Method: 2 minutes

1. Transfer the kale to a large bowl. Grab a large handful and squeeze it firmly, feeling it crunch within your closed fists.

2. Release the kale, grab another section and repeat. Continually turn the kale so you are always working with a new section.

3. Repeat this process until the all of the kale has become significantly softer and the color has deepened.

Nutritional Data: 1 Cup

Calories: 33, .32g Fat, 6.71g Carbohydrates, 2.21g Protein, Cholesterol: 0, Saturated Fat: .06g, Total Fiber: 1.34g

Steamed Greens

Collards, kale, Swiss chard, mustard greens, beet greens, and virtually any green that doesn't come in a compact head (like cabbage), but rather on individual stems, can be steamed using only the water still clinging to it after it's washed. With this method nutrients are not lost in the cooking water. When the little bit of water has evaporated, the greens are done! This method is very quick and can be accomplished in the last minutes of your dinner preparation, assuring they'll be hot and perfectly cooked when you are ready to serve them to your family.

Time: 8 to 10 minutes
Yield: 2 cups

Ingredients:

1 bunch greens (about 8 ounces)

Preparation: 5 minutes

1. Wash greens and remove stems.

2. Tear into bite-size pieces or cut across into thin strips.

3. Rinse again and shake off excess water but do not spin dry.

Method: 3 to 5 minutes

1. Transfer to a sauté pan with a lid. Cook on medium-high, turning occasionally with a pair of tongs.

2. When all the water has evaporated, the greens should be wilted to perfection. If not, add a tablespoon more water and cook for another minute or two.

Note: For additional flavor and nutrients, try sautéing garlic, onion, ginger, hot or sweet peppers, or other seasonings in the pan before adding the greens.

Grains

Brown, Brown Basmati, Red, Purple And Black Rice

Preparing perfect rice is almost as simple as dumping the ingredients into a pan and turning on the stove. You don't need a fancy rice cooker; all you need is a saucepan with a lid. The varieties are all cooked in the same way; the only difference is the cooking time. The rule of thumb is: 1 part rice to 1 1/2 parts* water. Brown rice takes longer to cook (about 45 minutes) than white rice (15 to 20 minutes). Long and short grained brown rice takes a bit longer than brown basmati. It isn't necessary to add salt.

Brown rice is far superior in flavor and nutrients than white. White rice is so nutrient deficient it really should be avoided. Red, purple and black rice contain the most antioxidants and have wonderful aromatic nutty flavors. They are fun to pair with colorful vegetables and are beautiful to serve.

One of the great things about rice is that it is so versatile. You can add lime and cilantro for a perfect accompaniment to southwestern burritos. You can replace water with vegetable stock or add onion and garlic to enhance the general flavor and nutrition. You can add parsley, basil, and tomato for Mediterranean dishes or turmeric and cardamon for Middle Eastern dishes. Rice can be served with sauces and gravies, or as an ingredient in stuffings and casseroles. Or you can just eat it plain and enjoy its natural nutty flavor. The possibilities are endless. Experiment and enjoy!

Time: 15 to 45 minutes depending on the variety

Yield: 1 cup dry rice equals 3 cups cooked

Ingredients

1 cup rice

1 1/2 cups Mirepoix Vegetable Stock (page 199) or water

Preparation and Method: 25 to 45 minutes

1. Wash rice and pick out any bits that look bad. Drain through a fine-meshed strainer and transfer to a medium-size saucepan with a lid.

2. Add 1 1/2 cups water and bring to a boil.

3. Reduce heat to low and simmer for 25 to 45 minutes (depending on the kind of rice you are preparing) or until all the water has been absorbed and the rice is soft.

4. When it is soft, remove from heat and fluff with a fork. Replace the lid and allow it to rest for 5 to 10 minutes. Serve hot.

*Some chefs use a 2:1 ratio of water to rice. I think that dilutes its flavor and over-expands the rice, altering its texture in a way I don't care for. But I find that there are times when short grain rice may require a little extra water, especially if the rice has been sitting in a cupboard for more than six months. Then I use the 1 3/4:1 ratio; that is, 1 3/4 cups water to 1 cup rice. You can try cooking rice each way and see which you prefer.

Another way to cook rice is to cook it like pasta. Stir the rice into a large pot of boiling water until done, then drain it. I don't care for this method at all because I feel it robs the rice of flavor, gives it a poorer texture, and some of its nutrients are washed down the drain along with the water. Other cooks feel this is the best method ever. Try it and see what you think.

Lime-Cilantro Brown Rice

This tangy rice is excellent in burritos, paired with spicy black beans, or as a side to any southwestern dish. It can also be served as a base for just about any savory bean, adding another dimension to the overall flavor. It is simple to prepare; just make rice as usual and stir in Lime-Cilantro Chutney.

Time: about 35 minutes

Yield: 3 cups

Ingredients:

1 recipe Brown Basmati or any brown rice (page 205)
1 recipe Lime-Cilantro Chutney (page 257)

Preparation and Method: about 35 minutes

1. Prepare rice and chutney.

2. Fold chutney into cooked rice until thoroughly combined.

Nutritional Data: 1 Cup

Calories: 237, 2.73g Fat, 53.6g Carbohydrates, 5.77g Protein, Cholesterol: 0, Saturated Fat: .0g, Total Fiber: 2.97g

Quinoa

Quinoa is a delicious gluten-free substitute for the wheat intolerant. It is also a nice substitute for rice. It cooks quickly by comparison and has a slight crunchy texture.

Time: 20 minutes
Yield: about 3 cups

Ingredients:
1 cup quinoa, (red, white or mixed)
1 1/2 cups Mirepoix Vegetable Stock (page 199) or water

Preparation and Method:
1. Rinse quinoa under running water in a fine-meshed strainer. Transfer to a small or medium sauce pan with a lid.

2. Stir in 1 1/2 cups vegetable stock or water and bring to a boil (about 2 minutes).

3. Reduce heat and simmer for 20 minutes. You'll know it is done when the quinoa grows tiny little tails and all of the water is absorbed. Remove from heat and fluff with fork.

Nutritional Data: 1/4 Pound Dry
Calories: 208, 3.18g Fat, 1.15g, 8.0g Protein, 36.36g Carbohydrates, Cholesterol: 0, Saturated Fat: .4g, Total Fiber: 5.18g

Bulgar Wheat

Cracked wheat is the whole wheat berry that has been broken into small pieces in the milling process. It can take up to 90 minutes to prepare. Bulgar wheat is cracked wheat that has been precooked and dried. This makes it a whole food that cooks quickly. For most recipes calling for bulgar wheat it should be cooked al dente. If you are making a porridge and want a creamier, softer result, add 1/2 to 1 cup extra water and simmer for 15 minutes.

Time: 18 minutes
Yield: 2 1/2 cups

Ingredients:
1 cup bulgar wheat
1 cup Mirepoix Vegetable Stock (page 199) or water

Preparation and Method: 15 minutes

1. In a small saucepan, bring stock or water to a boil (3 minutes).

2. Stir in bulgar wheat. Cover and allow to sit for 15 minutes.

3. Fluff with a fork.

Nutritional Data: 1 Cup
Calories: 190, .52g Fat, 6.88g Protein, 42.48g Carbohydrates, Cholesterol: 0, Saturated Fat: .12g, Total Fiber: 10.24g

Pasta

Pasta Noodles

Pasta cooks according to how thick it is. Angel hair pasta cooks much more quickly than regular spaghetti, which cooks more quickly than linguini, which cooks more quickly than shells or tubes, which cook more quickly than lasagne noodles, and so on. There are many gluten-free varieties available. One pound is enough to feed four people as a main course.

If you like your pasta 'al dente' (a little chewy), which is what most chefs recommend, cook it in the bottom of the cooking range indicated on the package directions. Many chefs recommend adding salt and even oil to the water before adding the pasta. Resist the temptation; both of these ingredients will compromise your health and they make no substantial difference in flavor.

Remember, if you live at a higher altitude it will take a little longer to cook than if you live at sea level.

Time: 30 min

Yield: 1 pound/serves 4

Ingredients:

1 pound linguini (usually 1 package)
4 quarts water

Preparation and Method: 30 minutes

1. In a stock pot, bring 4 quarts water to a rolling boil (about 20 minutes).

2. Carefully add the pasta, just a little in the beginning, because the water will initially create a surge of foam

when you first drop it in. When the foam calms down (about 10 seconds) add the remainder of the pasta.

3. Stir the pasta once it becomes pliable to assure that the pieces do not stick together.

4. Boil, uncovered, until al dente (about 10 minutes). When the end of the cooking time approaches, begin periodically tasting a small piece to determine level of doneness.

5. When the cooked texture suits you, drain in a strainer or colander and toss to loosen, or separate with a large fork to prevent sticking.

6. Transfer to a serving dish and toss in preferred sauce or use for another purpose.

Nutritional Data: 1/4 Pound Dry

Calories: 420, 1.15g Fat, 14.7g Protein, 84.67g Carbohydrates, Cholesterol: 0, Saturated Fat: .31g, Total Fiber: 3.63g

Couscous

Couscous is not a grain as many believe; it is a pasta. There are many kinds of couscous; the size, shape, and type of grain used varies according to its native culture. In the United States the most readily forms available are the French and the Israeli (or pearled) couscous. Buy the whole wheat version if you can find it. (The pearled couscous is not readily available in whole wheat.) Couscous found in the the US is usually already precooked when you buy it so it takes only minutes to prepare. Obviously, if you have wheat allergies or celiac disease, couscous is not for you.

Nutritional Data: 1 Cup
Calories: 175, .18g Fat, 36.46g Carbohydrates, 5.95g Protein, Cholesterol: 0, Saturated Fat: .05g, Total Fiber: 2.2g

French Couscous

French couscous is a tiny crumble-shaped pasta that looks a lot like cracked wheat and its precooked form, bulgar wheat. If you store your grains and pastas in jars, be sure to label them. More than once I've had to call the large health-food chain in the next city to ask them to look up the bin number on the items I just purchased because I couldn't tell the difference between cracked wheat and French couscous. When I buy them in bulk, I've learned to write not only the bin number but the name of the item on the package.

French couscous is one of the quickest and least labor-intensive foods you will find. It only needs rehydrating in hot water. Boil the water, stir in the couscous, let it absorb the water and fluff. That's all there is to it! It is a wonderful quick substitution for rice when you're in a hurry or have forgotten to put rice on to cook in time for dinner.

Time: 10 minutes
Yield: 3 cups

Ingredients:

1 cup couscous
1 1/2 cups Mirepoix Vegetable Stock (page 199) or water

Preparation and Method:

1. In a small saucepan bring 1 1/2 cups vegetable stock or water to a boil.

2. Stir in couscous, making sure it all becomes wet.

3. Remove from heat and let it sit for 5 minutes or until all of the water is absorbed.

4. Fluff with a fork and serve. It is important to fluff couscous because otherwise it will become compact as it absorbs the liquid.

Israeli Couscous

Also known as "pearled couscous," it is larger than French couscous and is shaped like tiny pearls rather than the irregular crumbles of French couscous. It has a creamier texture, which makes it ideal for risotto-type recipes. It is similar to French couscous in that it is made from semolina wheat and is precooked. Because it is larger and more compact it requires a little more time to cook. It will have a slightly chewy texture and should always be cooked al dente. Israeli couscous can be used for main course dishes, salads, sides, and added to soups. It can be served hot, cold, or at room temperature. To make it a little creamier for dishes like couscous pilaf, begin with 1/4 cup more water. Become familiar with this versatile pasta and it will add variety and novelty to your growing repertoire of plant-based meals.

Time: 15 minutes
Yield: 2 cups

Ingredients:
1 cup Israeli couscous
1 cup Mirepoix Vegetable Stock (page 199) or water

Preparation and Method: 15 minutes
1. Bring stock or water to a boil.

2. Stir in couscous; reduce heat and simmer for 5 minutes.

3. Remove from heat and allow to rest for 10 minutes.

4. Fluff with a fork.

Toasted Israeli Couscous

This is my favorite way to prepare Israeli couscous. Roasting gives it a slightly nutty flavor and a more pleasing color. It also creates a less creamy, slightly more chewy texture which makes it more appropriate for salad dishes. You should toast Israeli couscous even if the package says it is already toasted.

Time: about 22 minutes
Yield: 2 cups

Ingredients:
   1 cup Israeli (pearled) couscous
   1 cup Mirepoix Vegetable Stock (page 199) or water

Preparation and Method: 22 minutes

1. In a small dry skillet over medium heat toast couscous 3 1/2 minutes, stirring constantly. Remove from heat and continue to stir in pan for 1 to 2 minutes or until the color is a nice nutty brown. Transfer to a cool dish to stop cooking.

2. Bring a saucepan with 1 cup of stock or water to a boil (about 3 minutes). Stir in couscous; reduce heat and simmer for 5 minutes.

3. Remove from heat and allow to rest for 10 minutes.

4. Fluff with fork.

Roasted Vegetables

The most sure-fire way of bringing out the flavor of vegetables is to roast them. I discovered this one winter when I bought the most anemic Roma tomatoes imaginable for a dinner party I was having that evening. They were the only tomatoes I could find so they would have to suffice. I was certain they were going to taste like cardboard.

I opted to roast them. Cutting them in half, I sprinkled them with a seasoning blend of rosemary, oregano and thyme and roasted them at 400°F, cut side up, for 20 minutes.

I could not believe how delicious they were! My guests went wild for them, grilling me as to where I bought such flavorful tomatoes in the dead of winter. Lesson learned! Roasting brings out the natural sweetness and caramelization of many vegetables as well as intensifying the flavor of most.

If you want a fairly quick meal exploding with flavor, you need only pop a mixture of veggies into the oven and you'll have a delicious meal in no time.

Many vegetables lend themselves well to this technique, particularly potatoes, tomatoes, peppers, eggplants, all the squashes, onions and many more. Some veggies will develop tough or brittle skins if oil is not first rubbed on the surface. I avoid roasting these vegetables and prefer to bake them in aluminum foil to preserve the softness of the skins. The thinner you slice vegetables for roasting, the faster they will cook. However, they will develop a skin so unless you want crispy vegetables cut them a bit on the thick side, cut them in half, or leave them whole.

The following recipes are for ingredients used within other recipes in this book. Experiment with roasting vegetables. You may become as addicted to them as I am.

Roasted Or Baked Garlic

Garlic is one of the most useful and healthy ingredients you can put in your body and there aren't many things as lusciously delicious as roasted garlic. Nearly every culture reveres garlic for its health-protective properties.

Roasted garlic is wonderful spread directly on toast and crostini, in dips and spreads, sauces, soups and marinades. If raw garlic is hard on your stomach, often roasted garlic can be substituted without causing stomach upset.

It is more energy efficient (though not always practical) to cook garlic when you have other things going on in the oven at the same time. It is a simple enough matter to add a few bulbs to a tray of mixed roasted vegetables, roasted whole eggplants or red bell peppers. It seems a shame to heat up an entire oven just to roast a few heads of garlic. Conserving energy when you can is always a good idea.

Use the largest bulbs you can find for roasting garlic. Small bulbs will dry out quickly and will not yield enough of the creamy goodness to make it worthwhile.

Time: 15 to 20 minutes
Yield: As many as you choose to cook

Ingredients:

1 or more bulbs garlic

Preparation: 2 minutes per bulb

1. Peel garlic bulb just enough to gain access to the upper tips of the cloves. With a sharp knife, slice the very top edge of each clove to expose the flesh. Only about 1/8 inch should be exposed before slicing; then all you should see is the exposed cut end. This keeps the garlic bulbs from

exploding. Some people like to cook garlic in aluminum foil. I find the skins, the natural covering of the garlic, is perfectly adequate.

Method: 15 to 20 minutes

1. In a cool oven, place garlic on a cookie sheet and turn to 400°F. When the oven reaches this temperature, turn it off and allow the garlic to cool in the oven. If you notice the cloves are bubbling out of the skins* where you trimmed them, remove them immediately. They are beyond done.

*Depending on the size of the bulb you are roasting, they may cook faster than the other items in your oven. Pay attention so they don't dry out or overcook. They will not collapse like eggplants and bell peppers. They are ready if they are soft when gently pressed. (Use the handle of a wooden spoon or a finger wrapped in a clean, dry kitchen towel as they will be too hot to handle.)

Nutritional Data: 1 Bulb
Calories: 67, .16g Fat, 14.88g Carbohydrates, 2.86g Protein, Cholesterol: 0, Saturated Fat: .04g, Total Fiber: .94g

Roasted Red Peppers

Roasted red bell peppers add a unique flavor to soups, salads, sandwiches, and other dishes that you won't find anywhere else. There are two methods of roasting peppers and choosing the method may have more to do withe how many peppers you need at the time. The stovetop method chars the skin until the entire pepper is black; then the skin is rubbed off and discarded.

The second method is gentler on the pepper and allows you to keep and use the skin. If you are pureeing roasted peppers to add to a sauce, for example, keeping the skins adds flavor and nutrition. If you are adding it to other whole ingredients, the skins will be too tough to use. Always freeze roasted red peppers with the skins on so you have the option of using them or not.

Buy these in late summer at your local farmers' market when the prices are at their lowest. Roast one or two trays of peppers at a time and freeze them in individual freezer bags. This way you'll be assured of having this delicious vegetable (technically a fruit) on hand when the soaring prices at the market take your breath away. Also, in off seasons peppers are shipped in from across the globe, adding to fuel expenditure and contributing to global climate change.

In a pinch you can buy jars of roasted peppers but to avoid added chemical preservatives, salt, sugars, and oil, it's always best to make them yourself.

Nutritional Data: 1 Medium Pepper
Calories: 36, .12g Fat, 7.18g Carbohydrates, 1.18g Protein, Cholesterol: 0, Saturated Fat: .03g, Total Fiber: 2.5g

Stovetop Roasted Red Bell Peppers

When your roasted pepper stores have run out and you are in need one of these tasty gems, a fast way to roast one is directly on a burner on your stovetop. You'll need a pair of tongs for this so you don't burn yourself. I don't recommend roasting small peppers in this fashion. You are likely to burn through the flesh, not just the skins.

Time: about 20 to 30 minutes, depending on size
Yield: 1 pepper

Ingredients:
   1 red bell pepper

Preparation and Method: 15 to 20 minutes

1. Wash pepper.

2. Roast red bell pepper by placing directly onto the grate of a gas burner, exposing it to the flame. Rotate the pepper as it becomes charred and continue roasting, turning with a pair of tongs to expose each side to the flame until the pepper is entirely black. Don't worry, you won't burn the house down; but it is a good idea to have an exhaust fan on during the roasting process.

3. When completely blackened, (12 to 20 minutes) transfer the pepper to a brown paper bag or to a saucepan with a lid so it can steam in its own heat for 5 minutes.

4. Once it's cooled, slide the charred skin off the pepper with a damp paper towel and discard. Rinse the peeled pepper (2 minutes).

5. Cut carefully around the stem with a sharp paring knife. Pull out stem with seeds attached. Discard. With a spoon, scrape out the remaining seeds.

Oven-Roasted Red Peppers

This method is a bit unusual because you do not preheat the oven. Timing will depend on how large your peppers are. If you are cooking very large bell peppers, it will take ten minutes longer than if you're cooking pimentos, carmen red peppers or small red bell peppers. These peppers will cook to perfection using less energy than if you preheated the oven first.

Time: about 1 hour

Yield: As many peppers as you choose to roast

Ingredients:

Red bell peppers

Preparation and Method: about 1 hour

1. Wash peppers and transfer to a cookie sheet lined with a silicone mat or parchment paper.

2. Place the tray of peppers on the middle rack of a cold oven. Set temperature to 400°F.

3. When the oven reaches 400°F, turn it off and allow the peppers to cool inside the oven. If you are cooking large peppers, cook for 10 minutes at 400°F then turn the oven off. Remove stem and seeds as in previous recipe. (If the peppers are still relatively stiff, they need to be cooked longer. If they have wilted, turn the oven off. This is your best barometer for knowing how long to cook them.)

Roasted Or Baked Eggplant

Roasting eggplant is a necessary skill as there are many delicious recipes that call for this versatile nightshade. I like to cook it to the point where you can still use the skin, which contains a considerable amount of nutrients. It isn't necessary to scorch the exterior in order to obtain perfectly roasted eggplants. You can cook as many or as few as you need; the timing is the same. It helps to keep a clay stone on the bottom rack of your oven to hold the temperature at a constant level, but it isn't strictly necessary.

Whether you roast or bake eggplants depends on how you want to use them. If you want to keep the skins soft and edible, bake them wrapped in a sheet of aluminum foil. If the thought of using aluminum next to your food puts you off, you can wrap it first in parchment paper and then in foil. The only difference between roasting and baking is that in roasting, the eggplant is not covered; in baking, it is.

If you only want to scoop out the tender middle and don't care if the skin is charred (for use in dishes like baba ghanoush), then roasting will be the best choice. You can also do a combination of the two, baking until soft then grilling under a flame to achieve a slightly crisp skin.

I use two methods to roast eggplants. The first is to preheat the oven and roast until done; then remove. The second is to place the eggplant into a cool oven so it will begin cooking while the oven is heating up to the proper temperature.

The second is the method I like best, because it uses less energy and you don't have to keep such a close watch over the eggplant. But it does require that you estimate how long it will take an eggplant of a particular size to cook. When the oven reaches the appropriate temperature, you have to decide whether you can turn the oven off or if you should allow the eggplant to continue to cook another five, ten, or fifteen minutes, depending on its thickness. After you've cooked it as long as you judge is needed, you can just turn the oven off and leave it alone. It will complete the cooking process as the oven cools. This is an especially useful method if you are preparing the eggplant for use the next day. Just don't forget to take it out of the oven! After a few attempts you'll get the hang of it.

Time: 1 to 2 hours depending on method
Yield: 1 eggplant

For Roasting:
Method 1 and 2:
Ingredients:
　　1 large eggplant (about 19 ounces)

Preparation: 2 minutes

1.　Wash eggplant.

2.　Pierce all over with the tip of a sharp knife. This will prevent the eggplant from exploding from the pressure of expansion while cooking.

Method 1:
Preheated Oven Method: 1 hour 30minutes to 2 hours

1.　Preheat oven to 400°F (20 to 35 minutes depending on the oven)

2.　Place eggplant on a cookie sheet that has been covered with a silicon mat or parchment paper.

3.　Cook in preheated oven for 45 minutes to 1 hour, making a quarter turn every 15 minutes. It is done when the eggplant is collapsed or is soft when pressed.

4.　Remove from heat and allow to cool.

Method 2:
Cool Oven Method: about 1 hour

1. Place eggplant on a cookie sheet that has been covered with a silicon mat or parchment paper.

2. Transfer to a cool oven and set oven temperature at 400°F.

3. When the proper oven temperature is reached, turn the eggplant over and continue to roast for 20 minutes. If the eggplant is especially thick, like the large Black Beauty variety, you may want to let it cook an extra 5 to 15 minutes. Conversely, if it is long and thin, like a Japanese eggplant, you may not want to continue cooking it at all once it has reached 400°F. You can gauge when the eggplant is done by noting that it is no longer rigid when pressed and the skin has begun to wrinkle.

4. Once you are satisfied that the eggplant is done enough to finish cooking in the cooling oven, turn the eggplant a final 1/4 turn, turn the oven off and allow it to cool. (20 minutes)

For Baking:
1. Snip off stem at the base of the eggplant, but not the cap. Wrap in aluminum foil and place on baking sheet. (There is no need to line the baking sheet for this method.)

Method: 1 to 1 1/2 hours
1. Place pan containing eggplant into either a preheated oven or a cool oven and bake with one of the previous roasting methods.

Nutritional Data: 1 1/4 Pounds
Calories: 131, .69g Fat, 31.24g Carbohydrates, 5.53g Protein, Cholesterol: 0, Saturated Fat: .19g, Total Fiber: 18.36g

Beans

Most beans are cooked pretty much the same way. Soak dried beans overnight and discard the soaking water. Then in fresh water, boil for ten minutes to deactivate potentially harmful lectins. Now you can season and cook as desired.

Fresh beans don't require soaking. They can be rinsed and boiled for ten minutes, then simmered and seasoned.

Lentils are fast-cooking beans that do not require soaking. Boil ten minutes before reducing heat.

Before washing beans, pick out pieces that are broken, withered or simply look bad. Broken pieces cause beans to foam excessively so it's a good idea to remove them, especially if you are using a pressure cooker. (That's the reason it is advised that you never cook split peas or lentils in a pressure cooker. The excessive foaming could stop up the release valve and cause damage to the unit, or worse, create an explosion.)

The easiest way to sift through beans to check for broken pieces is to pour them from a cup into your open palm and let them slide across your hand into a bowl. The damaged pieces become apparent, as do small rocks and debris.

The following are some simple bean recipes that can be used to cook most kinds of beans in a variety of cooking conditions. First determine the kind (fresh or dried) and whether you are planning to freeze them or use them right away. (It is more flexible to add spices when you actually intend to eat them, rather than before you freeze them. Then you are not committed to a flavor profile that could interfere with a future use.)

If you intend to use salt in cooking beans, add it just before serving as a finish. That way you will find you need much less salt than if you added it in the beginning stages of cooking. Try not to use more than you feel is absolutely necessary to make beans palatable for you, no more than 1/2 teaspoon per recipe.

Pressure-Cooked Chickpeas

Far and away my favorite bean, chickpeas (also known as garbanzo beans) are the most versatile bean I've found. They take a bit longer to cook than some other beans. You will want them to reach the soft, buttery texture that makes them melt in your mouth. Don't worry about over-cooking chickpeas. They will seem almost too soft when they are hot but will recover their firmness when left to sit a few minutes.

I think of chickpeas as almost magical beans. They can be added to nearly any dish and can take on any function in a meal; starring as a main course, an unobtrusive side dish, an appetizer, a sauce, a spread on sandwiches or as the main ingredient, a dip for chips or fresh vegetables, and who knows what else! You can also prepare chickpeas in much the same way as my lentils recipe, although cooking time will be increased by 30 to 40 minutes. Or you can speed up the process and cook them to perfection in a pressure cooker.

Make as many as your pot can handle. (Always leave the pressure cooker one-third empty to allow pressure to build.) They freeze extremely well and are always good to have available when you want to throw together a quick hummus dip for guests or to spread on sandwiches for a grab-and-go lunch.

Soak Time: 8 hours or overnight
Cook Time: 50 minutes
Yield: 6 cups

Ingredients:

2 cups dried chickpeas
1 bay leaf
5 cups Mirepoix Vegetable Stock (page 199) or filtered water

1/4 to 1/2 teaspoon salt (optional)

Preparation: 8 hours

1. Place chickpeas in a covered pot with twice the amount of water as you have chickpeas. Let soak for at least 5 hours or overnight. Drain and rinse.

Method: 50 minutes

1. Transfer chickpeas to a pressure cooker. Cover with about 1 inch of vegetable stock or filtered water (4 to 5 cups). Add bay leaf and bring to a boil (10 to 15 minutes). Boil on high, uncovered, for 10 minutes.

2. Replace lid and tighten. Bring to correct pressure, (about 5 minutes) and cook for 25 minutes or according to your pressure-cooker's instruction manual.

Nutritional Data: 1 Cup

Calories: 242, 3.12g Fat, 40.46g Carbohydrates, 12.87g Protein, Cholesterol: 0, Saturated Fat: .42g, Total Fiber: 11.61g

Freshly Shelled Cranberry Beans with Thyme

Cranberry beans are also called October beans. Don't ask me why, they are harvested in August in my area of the country. Regardless, they are wonderfully tasty soup beans and I greedily snatch them up just as soon as they are available at my local farmers' market. These beans are best freshly shelled; the inedible shells are discarded.

This is a basic recipe you can use to cook a variety of fresh beans, especially the lighter varieties, such as limas and white beans, to which you can easily add potatoes, mushrooms, pasta, or any number of grain choices for variety as well as different spices for a change in flavor profiles. A a few leaves of kale, collard greens, or spinach added to the basic recipe works nicely to add colorful phytonutrients. Fresh cranberry beans are lovely prepared simply, with just thyme to flavor it. But you can also add a little parsley, and a sprig of rosemary for another dimension of flavor.

You may wish to cook a large stockpot of these beans to freeze for late fall or early winter when the weather is cool and crisp, just begging for a steaming bowl of beans. After defrosting them, you can then add other fresh ingredients like cooked pasta, green vegetables, potatoes, or grains.

Time: 1 hour

Yield: 6 cups

Ingredients:

4 cups freshly shelled cranberry beans (also known as October beans)

4 cups Mirepoix Vegetable Stock (page 199) or filtered water

2 cups chopped white or yellow onion (about 10 ounces)

1 large bay leaf

3 large cloves garlic, minced

1 tablespoon dried thyme

1/4 to 1/2 teaspoon salt (optional)

Preparation: 10 minutes

1. Wash shelled beans.

2. Peel and chop onion and garlic while bringing beans to a boil.

Method: 50 minutes

1. Transfer beans to a 3- or 4-quart sauce pan with a lid. Add vegetable stock or water and bring to a boil (10 to 12 minutes). Boil on high, stirring occasionally, for 10 minutes.

2. Add bay leaf, onions, garlic, and thyme. Reduce heat and cook 30 minutes, or until tender.

3. Add salt if desired, and adjust seasoning if needed. Serve hot.

Note: Adding 1/4 to 1/2 cup cooked bulgar wheat, pearled barley, or pearled farrow to each serving bowl makes this a hearty meal that will stick to your ribs!

Nutritional Data: 1 Cup

Calories: 460, 1.3g Fat, 83.85g Carbohydrates, 30.66g Protein, Cholesterol: 0, Saturated Fat: .45g, Total Fiber: 33.22g

Steeped Dried Lentils

Lentils cook quickly, as beans go. This is a basic recipe I've included in this book to give you a better option than canned lentils for Cauliflower-Lentil Sloppy Joes. If you do not think you'll use the entire recipe, you can take out what you need and freeze the rest. You can also halve the recipe before cooking, using a whole bay leaf either way.

Time: 50 minutes
Yield: 6 cups

Ingredients:

2 cups brown or green* lentils
4 cups Mirepoix vegetable stock (page 199) or filtered water
1 cup finely chopped onion (1 small onion)
1/4 cup finely chopped celery (about 1 stalk)
1 bay leaf
1/4 to 1/2 teaspoon salt (optional)

Preparation: 10 minutes

1. Prepare vegetables.

2. Wash lentils and remove any bad pieces. Make sure you remove any debris, such as small pieces of dirt or tiny stones.

Method: 30 to 40 minutes

1. Transfer onions to a medium saucepan with a lid. Sauté until vegetables are soft (about 7 minutes).

2. Add lentils, bay leaf and stock. Bring to a boil and cook without a lid for 10 minutes, stirring occasionally.

3. Reduce heat to medium. Cover and cook until soft.

4. Add salt if desired.

*Red lentils are prepared using the same method but will cook more quickly and should be monitored carefully. Overcooking red lentils will result in a mushy bean. Red lentils become yellow when cooked.

Nutritional Data: 1 Cup

Calories: 237, .58g Fat, 41.09g Carbohydrates, 16.84g Protein, Cholesterol: 0, Saturated Fat: .11g, Total Fiber: 20.05g

Spicy Black Beans

This is a fully seasoned recipe that you can use as a side or main ingredient for any southwestern dish. It can also be incorporated with other recipes, such as southwestern chile. Spicy black beans are a marvelous stuffing for burritos with salsa and crisp lettuce. It can also be the main ingredient in a zesty soup! This recipe can be easily doubled.

Time: 1 hour 30 minutes
Yield: 3 cups

Ingredients:

1 cup black turtle beans
1 cup diced onion
1/2 cup diced celery
1/2 cup diced red bell pepper
1/2 cup diced green bell pepper
1 1/2 teaspoons ground cumin
1 tablespoon Southwestern Chile Seasoning
1 teaspoon ground coriander
1/4 to 3/4 teaspoon Chipotle Peppers in Adobe Sauce, depending on how spicy you like it (optional)
1/2 to 1/4 teaspoon salt (optional)
Freshly chopped cilantro for garnish
Fresh lime slices

Preparation: 8 hours or overnight

1. Sort through beans; remove bad pieces and debris. Cover 1 cup dried turtle beans (black beans) with at least 2 cups water and soak overnight.

Method: 1 hour 30 minutes

1. Drain and transfer to a 4-quart saucepan with 3 cups of water.

2. Cover and bring to a fast boil on medium-high heat (about 10 minutes). Remove lid and cook for 10 minutes, stirring occasionally.

3. While beans are cooking, prepare vegetables. Set aside.

4. Add bay leaf, cover, and reduce heat to medium-low, simmering for 30 minutes.

5. Stir in onions, peppers and seasonings, continue simmering until beans are soft, 30 to 40 minutes.

6. Stir in salt, if using. Garnish with freshly chopped cilantro and slices of fresh lime.

Nutritional Data: 1 Cup

Calories: 257, 1.24g Fat, 49.13g Carbohydrates, 14.82g Protein, Cholesterol: 0, Saturated Fat: .28g, Total Fiber: 18.71g

Potatoes

Baked Whole Potatoes, White Or Sweet

Sweet potatoes are one of the healthiest foods you can eat. It is a good idea to keep some in your fridge, for they are a rich source of nutrients as well as a filling carbohydrate that complements most meals. White potatoes are a natural second choice. Carbs are brain food! Enjoy without remorse.

Time: 45 minutes to 1 hour

Yield: 2 potatoes

Ingredients:
2 potatoes,* skin on

Preparation and Method: 45 minutes to 1 hour

1. Preheat oven to 425°F.

2. Wash potatoes and dry with a towel. Pierce skin all over with the point of a sharp knife, at least 15 punctures.

3. Wrap in aluminum foil and place on a cookie sheet in a preheated oven. (If you are concerned about aluminum foil touching your food, wrap first in parchment paper, then in foil.) This will give you a soft potato with a soft skin. If you like a tougher skin, leave the foil off and simply roast the potato whole directly on middle oven rack.

4. Cook for 30 minutes and test for doneness with a fork or a bamboo skewer. If the fork does not easily pierce through to the middle of the potato without resistance, turn potato and cook another 15 to 30 minutes, or until it can be easily pierced.

5. Remove from heat and allow to cool** inside the foil.

*Sweet potatoes cook in the same way as white but may require less cooking time. Check for doneness 15 minutes earlier.

**It's important to allow potatoes to cool before cutting. They become soft while cooking and will firm up somewhat when given time to cool. This will keep them from breaking apart when you want to cut them into medallions or fries.

Microwaved Whole Potatoes, White Or Sweet

I used to avoid using a microwave because of the stories I read and heard on TV and the radio about how microwaves rob vegetables of their phytonutrients. Recent studies not only debunk that myth but indicate that the opposite is true. A group of scientists studied 20 vegetables under 6 cooking conditions and measured the phytonutrient activity in 3 different ways. Vegetables cooked by the microwave method scored higher than any of the other methods tested.[1] Frying is considered the overall worst because of the added oil.

Time: 10 to 12 minutes
Yield: 2 white, red or sweet potatoes

Ingredients:

2 large white, red or sweet potatoes* (12 to 14 ounces), skins on

Preparation: 2 minutes

1. Wash potato, scrubbing the skin thoroughly.

2. Leaving skin on, pierce all over with a paring knife, about a dozen 1/4-inch punctures, 1/4 inch deep.

Method: 5 to 10 minutes, depending on the size of the potato

1. Transfer to a heat-resistant plate and microwave on high for 5 minutes.

2. Test for doneness with a fork or bamboo skewer. If the skewer can go easily to the middle of the potato when pierced, it's done. If not, turn the potato and cook on high for 2 or 3 minutes longer, or when the skewer slides easily through the potato.

3. Allow to cool.** Peel and cut to desired size.

Note: Multiple potatoes will need additional cooking time.

*See page 235, **See page 235

Oven Fries

French fries are an American passion. I've been addicted to them since childhood and had a hard time giving them up when I discovered, as many of us have, how detrimental they are to our health and to our waistlines. I haven't fried a potato in over 20 years, since I realized you can make them just as deliciously in the oven. Whether fixing traditional fries from white Idaho potatoes or from sweet potatoes, the method is the same. If you eat fries often, you can cook several potatoes at once and keep in your fridge, taking them out when you are ready to roast them.

Time: 10 minutes, plus baking time
Yield: 4 cups

Ingredients

2 large (12 to 14 ounces) white, red or sweet potatoes

Preparation: 5 minutes (plus baking or microwaving time)

1. Precook in the oven or microwave (see previous recipes) and allow to cool.

2. Slice into large julienned strips (or sticks) and lay on a baking sheet. I like to use a cooling rack that I've coated with a light layer of oil and placed on top of a baking sheet.

3. Season according to taste* and place on the upper rack of a broiler.

Method: 6 to 8 minutes

1. Broil on high for 3 to 5 minutes on each side. Serve hot.

*White potatoes can be seasoned with a fragrant herbal blend of rosemary, thyme and oregano, plus hot pepper if you like them spicy. Sweet potatoes work well with cinnamon, nutmeg, or Indian spice blends.

Nutritional Data: 1 lb. White Potato

Calories: 421, .44g Fat, 11.34g Protein, 95.93g Carbohydrates, Cholesterol: 0, Saturated Fat: .16g, Total Fiber: 9.98g

Nutritional Data: 1 lb. Sweet Potato

Calories: 408, .45g Fat, 9.12g Protein, 93.94g Carbohydrates, Cholesterol: 0, Saturated Fat: .15g, Total Fiber: 14.97g

Cauliflower

Steamed Cauliflower

Cauliflower is a vegetable that goes with everything. It has a very mild flavor and therefore can be seasoned to complement any meal. It can be mashed, grated, creamed, sautéed, baked, and broiled — to name only some of the marvelous ways cauliflower can be prepared. Often I drop whole florets into soups and stews, but I also like to steam cauliflower as a first step and then bake it, broil or purée.

Time: 8 to 13 minutes
Yield: about 8 cups

Ingredients:

1 whole large cauliflower (1 1/2 to 2 pounds)

Preparations: 3 minutes

1. Slice off stem and outer leaves of cauliflower and discard. Following the contours of the stem, remove branches. Cut core into 1/2-inch pieces.

2. Rinse cauliflower florets and pieces under cold running water to remove any grit, dirt, or bugs you might find.

Method: 5 to 10 minutes

1. Transfer to a large sauté pan or a skillet with a lid. Add 1/2 cup of water and steam on medium heat until the cauliflower has softened. If you intend to roast, bake, or broil the cauliflower, cook it only until the outsides are tender and the stems are still firm, since they will be cooked further in the oven (about 5 minutes). If you are

pureeing the cauliflower, cook until tender (7 to 10 minutes).

Pureed Cauliflower Mashed Potatoes

Cauliflower can be steamed and pureed to resemble mashed potatoes for an easy way to sneak vegetables onto your family's dinner plate. After all, who doesn't love mashed potatoes? You can also toss it with a little nutritional yeast and freshly cooked fettuccine for a flavorful Fettuccine Alfredo. You can even divide the puree in half and make two delicious meals from one effort! Cauliflower Fettuccine Alfredo sauce can be added to mashed or smashed potatoes in place of butter and cream, making it a satisfying accompaniment to a meal that can be enjoyed completely without remorse!

Time: 15 minutes

Yield: 4 cups

Ingredients:

1/2 recipe Steamed Cauliflower (page 238)
1 to 2 teaspoons garbanzo bean miso
1/4 teaspoon salt (optional)

Preparation and Method:

1. Transfer all ingredients to a blender. Work in batches if necessary. Puree until smooth.

Nutritional Data: 1 Cup
Calories: 29, .01g Fat, 2.05g Protein, 5.82g Carbohydrates, Cholesterol: 0, Saturated Fat: .07g, Total Fiber: 2.14g

Sautéed Balsamic Portobello Mushrooms

Portobello mushrooms have a wonderful meaty texture and are often used as a meat replacement in plant-based cuisine. The balsamic vinegar brings out their flavor, but you can omit it if it competes with other flavors in your meal.

It's almost a crime to use oil in sautéing mushrooms. With a little encouragement they release their own juices making oil unnecessary. Portobellos absorb liquids easily, which is why they should be brushed rather than washed to remove any debris clinging to them, unless package directions tell you otherwise. If you wash them, you should remove the lid halfway through the cooking process to allow their liquid to evaporate and add about ten minutes to their cooking time. Still, they may need encouragement to release their juices by adding a tablespoon of water at a time. This also prevents their sticking to the pan.

Time: about 15 minutes
Yield: 1 cup or 10 slices

Ingredients:

2 fresh portobello mushrooms about 5 inches in diameter
3 tablespoons water
1 tablespoon balsamic vinegar

Preparation and Method: about 15 minutes

1. Brush mushrooms with a soft brush or a damp paper towel.

2. Slice into 4 or 5 pieces.

3. Transfer to large sauté pan or skillet with a lid.

4. Add 1 tablespoon water, cover and sauté on medium heat. Gently stir periodically.

5. As the mushrooms begin to stick, add another tablespoon water and continue cooking. Repeat this until mushrooms have released their juices and have become soft.

6. Remove lid and continue cooking on medium heat until the mushroom water has resorbed or evaporated.

7. When mushrooms are soft and dry, add vinegar. Stir gently until mushrooms have absorbed it. Remove from heat and use for intended purpose.

Nutritional Data: 1 (5-inch) Mushroom

Calories: 29, 0.2g Fat, 2.17g Protein, 5.27g Carbohydrates, Cholesterol: 0, Saturated Fat: .06g, Total Fiber: 1.31g

Beets

I've included several recipes for cooking beets in this section because beets have a reputation of being a pain to cook. They can take a long time, but they are not difficult to prepare. Beets are remarkably versatile and can be added to many dishes to enhance color, flavor, and nutrition. Choose the method that works best for you and add this antioxidant-rich vegetable to your repertoire of delicious recipes. Many root vegetables can be cooked in the same way, adjusting cooking times to the thickness and character of the vegetable.

Pressure-Cooked Beets

This is my favorite way to cook beets because it is quick and easy and requires little of my attention. Since every pressure cooker is different, refer to the directions that accompany your pressure cooker for proper cooking times. I always cook beets in groups of three or four because that's usually the way they are sold, with their green stems still attached. Don't discard the leaves. Steamed beet leaves are delicious!

Time: 22 to 35 minutes
Yield: 3 or 4 beets

Ingredients:
1 1/2 cups water
3 to 4 medium beets (washed, leaves and stems removed)

Preparation: 5 minutes

1. Remove leaves and stems about 1/2 inch from the root. Set aside for another use.

2. Scrub beet roots gently under cold water with a nylon scrub pad.

Method: 30 to 35 minutes

1. In pressure cooker, pour in 1 1/2 cups water. Set in steamer basket. Arrange whole beet roots in basket. Cover and lock lid. Bring to up to pressure (7 to 12 minutes, depending on the type of pressure cooker).

2. When the pressure cooker is up to maximum pressure, reduce heat enough to keep it pressurized but not enough to cause the steam to be suddenly expelled. Each pressure cooker is different, so refer to your model's instructions.

3. Cook 15 to 25 minutes, depending on your pressure-cooker. Turn off heat and allow pressure to dissipate or place cooker under cold running water. Unlock lid and test beets by pushing a bamboo skewer through the middle of the beet. If it goes all the way in, the beets are ready. If not, repeat the process by re-locking the lid of the pressure cooker and bringing the pressure up again. Make sure there is at least a cup of water in the bottom of the pressure cooker. Cook another 5 or 10 minutes, then allow to cool and depressurize. When you can easily pierce with a skewer, the beets are done.

4. Transfer to a plate and allow to cool. Discard water. Note that the water will be red. This is mostly from the stems of the beets, not the roots. The beets can be easily scraped clean at this point with the edge of a sharp knife. You can peel them with your fingers if you don't mind the stains. (Your fingers will stain temporarily. Contrary to what you

may have heard the color does not cling to your fingers for very long.) You can also rub off the skins with a damp paper towel. The beets can now be used for your intended purpose. You can grate them, cut them into wedges or cubes, slice them and marinate them if you wish, or just eat them as they are.

Steeped Whole Beets

It doesn't matter how many beets you are cooking or how large or small they are. The process is the same. Timing is completely dependent on the size of the beets you are cooking.

Time: 55 minutes
Yield: 3 beets

Ingredients:

3 medium beets

Preparation: 5 minutes

1. To steep beets, cut off the leaves about 1/2 inch from the roots. Wash the beets well and set leaves aside for another purpose.

Method: 50 minutes for 3 beets, 2 1/2 to 3 inches in diameter at the widest point.

1. Place the whole, unpeeled beets in a saucepan with a lid. Choose the size of the pan according to the size and number of the beets you will be cooking. They should cover the bottom of the pan, but do not stack them on top of one another. If your pan is too large, reduce the amount of water.

2. Barely cover the beets with water. If you have a variety of sizes, choose a medium-size beet as your gauge. Cover and bring to a full boil.

3. Allow to boil rapidly until all the water has evaporated. Test by pushing a fork into the center of the beet. If it goes through easily, the beets are done. If not, add a little more water and continue cooking until the fork enters easily. Make sure all the water has evaporated. Do NOT walk away from the stove while you are steeping or steaming anything! You don't want to walk away and burn them a the last moment.

4. When the beets can be pierced through, they are done. Allow them to cool.

5. To peel the beets, cut off the root and tip ends. Then, simply slide the skin off by grasping the beet in your hand and gently rub off the whole skin in one piece. Another way is to wrap the beet in a paper towel and pull off the skin; it should slide off easily. Or you can scrape off skins with a paring knife. Then slice, dice, or julienne them according to your needs.

Microwaved Whole Beets

By far the quickest way to cook beets is in the microwave. The amount of time will depend on the size of your beets and how many you cook at one time.

Time: 10 minutes
Yield: 3 beets

Ingredients:

3 firm medium beets, skins on

Preparation: 2 minutes

1. Trim stems and leaves about 1/2 inch from the top of the beets. Set aside leaves for another use.

2. Wash beets gently with a nylon scrubber. Pierce skin several times (about a dozen) all over beet. Remove tail. (It is important to cut off the long tail-like end of the beet because it will cook much quicker than the rest of the beet. In the microwave, it could actually catch on fire. It's best to cut it off in advance to remove that possibility.)

Method: 5 to 7 minutes (depending on the size of your beets and the variability between microwave ovens)

1. Place beets on a microwave-safe plate and cook on high for 3 minutes. Test with a fork.

2. If the beets can't be easily pierced, turn and cook another 3 minutes. Test for doneness again and cook another minute or two if necessary.

3. Remove peel as described in previous recipe when cool enough to handle.

Nutritional Data: 1 Beet

Calories: 35, 0.1g Fat, 1.32g Protein, 7.84g Carbohydrates, Cholesterol: 0, Saturated Fat: .02g, Total Fiber: 2.3g

Marinated Beets

Marinated beets are wonderfully flavorful and are so naturally sweet and delicious they are almost decadent. If you need them in a hurry, marinating them for just a couple of hours will produce a tasty result. But it is better to allow them to soak overnight to fully absorb the marinade's flavors. They will last three or four days in the fridge in an air-tight container. These are fantastic served as a side dish, layered on a sandwich or stuffed into pita pockets.

Time: 10 minutes plus overnight marinade
(assuming beets are prepared ahead of time)
Yield: 2 1/2 cups

Ingredients:

3 whole beets, cooked and sliced (pages 242-245)
Juice of 1 orange (1/3 to 1/2 cup)
2 tablespoons minced fresh ginger
2 tablespoons balsamic vinegar

Preparation and Method: 10 minutes

1. Juice orange. Peel and mince ginger

2. In a measuring cup, combine orange juice and balsamic vinegar.

3. In a glass three-cup container with a lid, (Pyrex rectangular storage containers work great for this.) arrange beet slices in a single layer. Sprinkle with some of the ginger, and pour a little of the orange juice mixture on top. Repeat layering until all the beets and juice are used. Cover and set in refrigerator overnight, or for at least 2 hours.

Serve chilled.

Nutritional Data: 1/2 Cup

Calories: 55, 0.14g Fat, 1.71g Protein, 12.29g Carbohydrates, Cholesterol: 0, Saturated Fat: .03g, Total Fiber: 2.71g

Sauces And Such

Homemade Barbecue Sauce

A good barbecue sauce makes becoming plant-based an easier endeavor. You can prepare a wide variety of dishes that make you forget you aren't eating meat. Added to veggie burger ingredients, it gives them a sweet and savory flavor. It can also serve as a tangy burger spread for something more flavorful than mayonnaise. Generously coat vegetables and cook on a grill, or sear under a broiler flame. Do the same with Tofu, Tempe or Seitan, in strips or cutlets. They can then be enjoyed as a side or as the main ingredient of a vegetarian sandwich with oven fries and green vegetables on the side.

This recipe makes a large batch, suitable for an outdoor party. You can reduce the recipe in half if you prefer less. It also freezes well, which makes it available anytime you might want it. We love it so much, we use it up quickly, even though there are just the two of us in our household. There are several steps and numerous ingredients in this recipe. Don't let that put you off; it pulls together quickly and is not difficult to prepare.

Whenever possible, buy organic ingredients. In this recipe it is especially important since conventionally grown peppers may be extremely toxic, having been heavily treated with pesticides. This applies particularly to hot peppers, which can be even more toxic than bell peppers. We tend to overlook this in seasonings, but there is no reason to believe that non-organic cayenne and chili powders are any less toxic just because they have been dried and ground into a powder. Always buy organic when purchasing any kind of pepper. Organic brown sugar is available in most grocery stores and easy to find. Organic molasses can be found at most large health food stores. I've not yet found a source for organic cocoa.

Time: 50 to 60 minutes
Yield: 5 to 5 1/2 cups

Ingredients:
Fresh Ingredients:

3 cloves garlic, smashed and allowed to rest 10 minutes
3 cups chopped onion (1 large onion)
1/2 cup chopped celery (about 2 stalks)
1/2 cup chopped green bell peppers (about 1/2 medium pepper)
1/2 cup chopped Roasted Red Pepper (page 219)
1 tablespoon orange zest

Prepared Ingredients:

1/4 cup apple cider vinegar
1 (6-ounce) can tomato paste
1 (14-ounce) can chopped tomatoes
1/3 cup brown sugar
1/2 cup molasses

Spices and Seasonings:

1/4 teaspoon ground cloves
1/2 teaspoon turmeric
1 tablespoon garlic powder
1 teaspoon cinnamon
1 teaspoon red chili pepper
1/2 teaspoon salt
1/2 teaspoon pepper
1 tablespoon southwestern chile powder blend
1 tablespoon cocoa powder

Preparation: about 15 minutes

1. Combine spices and seasonings into a small bowl. Set aside.

2. Chop vegetables.

Method: 35 to 45 minutes

1. In a medium saucepan add onion, celery, garlic, and bell peppers. Cover and cook on medium heat, stirring often, until soft and translucent adding a little water if needed to prevent scorching.

2. Transfer to a high-powered blender and blend until smooth.

3. Return vegetable mixture to sauté pan. Cover and cook on low heat, stirring often. (Don't bother cleaning the blender, we'll use it again.)

4. Measure vinegar, brown sugar, and molasses and pour into blender. Add tomato paste and chopped tomatoes. Blend on high until smooth. Stir into the vegetable mixture.

5. Pour 1 1/2 cups water into blender and blend on high to loosen the remaining barbecue mixture. Stir into the sauce mixture.

6. Stir in spices and seasonings.

7. Cover, and simmer for 10 to 20 minutes.

Nutritional Data: 1/2 Cup

Calories: 150, .43g Fat, 2.53g Protein, 36.84g Carbohydrates, Cholesterol: 0, Saturated Fat: .15g, Total Fiber: 3.43g

Tahini Sauce

Tahini sauce is delicious over just about any grain dish. It also makes a nice salad dressing. This will keep three days in your refrigerator and reheats well. You can make it to the consistency you desire by adjusting the amount of water you use.

Time: 10 minutes

Yield: 3/4 cup

Ingredients:

3 tablespoons tahini (sesame seed paste)
2 teaspoons white miso (garbanzo bean or soy miso)
1 teaspoon Mitoku sweet brown rice vinegar (If you can find only brown rice vinegar, add 1 teaspoon organic sugar.)
1 tablespoon fresh lemon juice
1 tablespoon brown sugar
1/2 cup filtered water

Preparation and Method: 10 minutes

1. In a blender on medium-high speed, blend all ingredients until smooth.

2. If you have a high-powered blender, like a Vita-mix, use the high setting and blend until the mixture is as thick as heavy cream, and warm. Add just enough water to thin to a nice creamy sauce.

For Stovetop: add 5 minutes

1. If you don't have a Vita-mix, transfer the sauce to a small saucepan and carefully heat on medium-low until thickened, adding water until you achieve a warm sauce

with the texture of cream. Use a flame-tamer if you have one. Stir frequently as nut sauces tend to burn easily.

Note: As with many sauces and gravies, it is necessary to heat the ingredients with a liquid for the materials to meld and transform into the creamy texture required for the dish. Constant stirring prevents the sauce from lumping and/or scorching. Then more liquid may be added to adjust the creaminess to the viscosity you prefer.

Nutritional Data: 1/2 Cup

Calories: 116, 7.71g Fat, 2.57g Protein, 9.99g Carbohydrates, Cholesterol: 0, Saturated Fat: 1.13g, Total Fiber: 1.41g

Ginger-Lime Salad Dressing

Chia seeds and flaxseeds perform well as thickening agents in salad dressings and will give them a creamy texture without the need for oil. This dressing is one I created for my Massaged Kale and Chickpea Salad but it works well with most salads. This will mix up quickly in a high-powered blender. If you have a typical kitchen blender, you may want to allow the ingredients soak for 15 minutes after processing and then blend again.

Time: 12 to 22 minutes

Yield: 1/2 cup

Ingredients:

1 tablespoon whole chia seeds
Juice of 1 orange (1/3 to 1/2 cup)
Juice of 1/2 lime (about 2 tablespoons)
1 teaspoon minced ginger (you can reduce this if you like it less spicy)
2 medjool dates (pitted) or 1 to 2 teaspoons date sugar (You can also use organic white or brown sugar if necessary.)
1 teaspoon balsamic vinegar

Preparation: 5 minutes

1. Juice orange and lemon; mince ginger.

2. Remove pit from medjool date by slicing it lengthwise down one side and pulling out the seed. Discard seed.

Method: 7 to 17 minutes (depending on speed of blender)

1. Place all ingredients in blender and blend on high for one minute.

2. Let the mixture rest for 5 minutes and blend again. If you don't have a high-powered blender, allow to rest for 15 minutes before blending the second time.

Nutritional Data: 1/4 Cup

Calories: 121, 1.8g Fat, 1.81g Protein, 27.12g Carbohydrates, Cholesterol: 0, Saturated Fat: .23g, Total Fiber: 4.13g

Mango-Avocado Salsa

Most of the work in this dish is in the peeling and chopping of ingredients. Tossing it all together takes only seconds. It's a wonderful accompaniment for Spicy Black Bean Burritos.

Time: 30 min

Yield: about 4 cups

Ingredients:

1 1/2 cups diced mango
1 cup diced ripe avocado
1 medium minced jalapeño pepper
1/3 cup diced green bell pepper
1/2 cup diced red bell pepper
1/3 cup diced red onion*
2 tablespoons lime juice (or to taste)
1 to 2 tablespoons chopped cilantro
1 teaspoon organic sugar (optional)

Preparation and Method: 30 minutes

1. Prepare vegetables and juice lime.

2. In a medium bowl, toss all ingredients together.

*If you aren't a fan of onion, you can reduce this amount or you can substitute green onion.

Nutritional Data: 1/2 Cup

Calories: 60, 2.6g Fat, .79g Protein, 9.48g Carbohydrates, Cholesterol: 0, Saturated Fat: .41g, Total Fiber: 2.28g

Lime-Cilantro Chutney

This recipe is an excellent accompaniment to beans and rice to give them a little pizzaz. It is also an essential ingredient in Lime-Cilantro Brown Rice.

Time: 15 minutes
Yield: 1/2 cup

Ingredients:

1 cup (1 ounce) cilantro leaves and some small stems
Pinch (less than 1/8 teaspoon) organic ground chipotle pepper
Zest of 1 lime
1 lime, juiced
4 garlic cloves
1/8 teaspoon salt (optional)

Preparation and Method: 15 minutes

1. Make sure the cilantro is clean and dry. Combine all ingredients except for the lime zest in a food processor until fine but not quite creamy.

2. Add lime zest and salt (if using) and pulse a couple times. If you like, you can add additional lime to taste.

Nutritional Data: 1/2 Cup
Calories: 36, .15g Fat, 1.55g Protein, 9.21g Carbohydrates, Cholesterol: 0, Saturated Fat: .02g, Total Fiber: 1.22g

Lemon-Cilantro Salsa

This is a quick salsa that goes with just about any bean dish. It can be served on top of the beans or on the side. This salsa can be prepared in a few minutes just before serving.

Time: 10 minutes

Yield: 1 cup

Ingredients:

1 tablespoon chopped cilantro
1 clove smashed and minced garlic
1/2 cup diced diced tomato
1/4 cup diced green onion
1/4 cup diced green bell pepper
1 tablespoon fresh lemon juice
1/8 teaspoon salt (optional)

Preparation and Method: 10 minutes

1. Prepare vegetables, garlic first, and juice lemon.

2. Toss all ingredients together in a small bowl. Serve.

Nutritional Data: 1/2 Cup
Calories: 19, .12g Fat, .92g Protein, 4.57g Carbohydrates, Cholesterol: 0, Saturated Fat: .03g, Total Fiber: 1.25g

Ubiquitous Plant-Based Dairy Recipes

There are recipes you can find almost anywhere and are mainstays of plant-based cuisine. You can find versions of them in nearly every vegan resource imaginable. I've included my take on these classics in a separate category, as these are not what I would consider "stand alone" recipes but are often used in conjunction with others. I refer to them time and again throughout the recipe portion of this book, as well as in other cookbooks that I am in the process of writing.

While these recipes are delicious and healthier alternatives to dairy, it is important to experience them without the expectation that they will taste exactly like the products you are replacing. They won't. But they will allow you to enjoy favorite foods that call for dairy products. Vegan ricotta cheese won't taste like the dairy ricotta cheese you are used to, but stuffed into pasta shells or a calzone you'll find that the flavor is close enough to allow you enjoy these comfort foods without sacrificing your health. Give your tastebuds a chance to adjust to these dairy-free recipes. Before long you'll forget all about dairy.

A Note About Nuts

When making raw sauces, soups and creams with nuts, it is a good idea to soak them for several hours, discarding the soaking liquid afterwards. Soaking helps to make the nuts less bitter by releasing tannins which are then discarded with the soaking water. You can speed up this process a little by soaking them in hot water. Soaking also makes nuts creamier when blended, producing a more authentic texture to vegan creams and cheeses.

Cashew Cream

Cashew cream is a marvelous substitute for heavy cream. It can be used to make béchamel sauces for pasta dishes, creamy soups, condiments, whipping cream for desserts and more. It all depends on what you add to the basic recipe. This cream also thickens when heated, which makes it a wonderful base for a cream sauce.

Time: 3 to 6 minutes (depending on the speed of your blender) plus at least 5 hours soaking time
Yield: about 1 to 1 1/3 cup

Ingredients:

1/2 cup raw cashews

1 teaspoon garbanzo bean or organic light soy miso (optional)

1/2 to 3/4 cup water*

Preparation: 5 hours or overnight

1. Soak cashews at for at least 5 hours or overnight. Drain and discard liquid.

Method: 3 to 6 minutes

1. Transfer to a blender. Add fresh water and miso. Blend until smooth and creamy.

*The less water you use the thicker the cream. Like real cream, cashew cream will thicken as it heats so keep that in mind when making cream sauces. You can make the thicker version and dilute with water as needed during the cooking process. But if you are making a casserole, like Creamy Scalloped Potatoes, you will want to begin with a thinner cream because you will not have the opportunity to stir in water to thin it as it is cooking.

Nutritional Data: 1/4 Cup

Calories: 76, 5.32g Fat, 2.46g Protein, 4.48g Carbohydrates, Cholesterol: 0, Saturated Fat: 1.05g, Total Fiber: .45g

Cashew Cream Cheese

Cream cheese made from cashews can be expensive to make. Varieties of pre-made vegan cream cheeses are available more economically in your local grocery or health food stores. I prefer to make them myself despite the expense because I can control what goes into my finished product. Many of the commercial pre-made products offered contain palm oil or coconut oil, which I prefer to avoid since they contain saturated fats.

There are many ways to make cashew cream cheese. The most tangy and authentic take days to prepare and involve a fermentation process. This version is quick and easy and very similar to the dairy cream cheese you can find in most grocery stores. This version has a refrigerated life of 3 or 4 days.

Time: 8 to 15 minutes, plus 5 hours soaking time
Yield: 1 1/2 cups

Ingredients:

1 1/4 cups cashews*, soaked at least 5 hours or overnight
Juice of 1 to 2 lemons (2 1/2 to 5 tablespoons)
1 tablespoon apple cider vinegar
1/4 teaspoon salt
1 to 2 tablespoons freshly minced dill (optional)

Preparation: 4 minutes

1. Drain cashews and discard liquid.

2. Juice lemon(s).** Remove seeds.

3. Chop dill.

Method: 4 to 11 minutes

1. Add cashews to the carafe of a high-powered blender, food processor, or regular blender. Add lemon juice, apple cider vinegar, and salt. Scrape down sides as needed, blending until smooth.

2. Transfer to a bowl with a lid and add your choice of herbs, or enjoy it plain. Cover and transfer to refrigerator for at least 2 hours to set and for flavors to meld.

Spread on crackers, breads, or fresh fruit and vegetables slices.

*It is difficult, if not impossible, to reduce this recipe because if you use less than 1 cup of nuts the blender's blade can't grind them. It is actually better to make a larger batch if you can use the cheese within a few days. 1 cup of nuts is the minimum amount needed to process smoothly; 1 1/4 cups is ideal.

**How many lemons you use is a matter of personal taste. While I prefer mine to have a little bite, you might like a milder flavor. If you add extra lemon, you may want to add just an extra pinch of salt. Always keep in mind that you don't want to exceed your daily limit of 1/2 teaspoon salt. Lemons will vary in the amount of juice they produce depending on the variety, the size, its age, and so forth. It is better to measure by the tablespoon rather than by the number of lemons used.

Note: If you are using a standard kitchen blender, you may have to add as much as 1/4 cup water, a tablespoon at a time and blend on high for up to 11 minutes, stopping every 30 seconds or so to scrape down the edges. It will not bring it to the same creamy consistency that a high-powered blender like a Vita-mix will accomplish in 3 to 4 minutes, but it will be creamy enough to enjoy. After adding up to 3 tablespoons water, you can achieve a very creamy consistency using a food processor, but it will not have the density of cream cheese; it will reach a consistency somewhere between cream cheese and whipped butter. A high-powered blender will render the best results. Even if you are using a high-powered blender, you may prefer the consistency of a whipped cream cheese. Adding a little extra water (up to 1/4 cup) or extra lemon juice will allow you to achieve this consistency.

Nutritional Data: 1/4 Cup
Calories: 238, 16.64g Fat, 7.76g Protein, 14.12g Carbohydrates, Cholesterol: 0, Saturated Fat: 3.29g, Total Fiber: 1.47g

Cashew Parmesan Cheese

Italian food just doesn't seem the same without a sprinkle of good parmesan cheese to complete the dish. No worries; this vegan version has just the right amount of cheesiness and body to satisfy even the fussiest eater. Ready to eat in less than 5 minutes, all you need is a food processor and you are good to go. This cheese is best for white sauces, such as Cauliflower Fettuccine Alfredo.

This is one recipe in which I don't soak the nuts. When using such a small amount, tannins shouldn't be an issue. But if you are concerned about this, you can soak them, drain, and then dry them ahead of time in your dehydrator or oven before using.

Time: 5 minutes

Yield: 1 cup

Ingredients:

1/2 cup cashews

1/2 cup nutritional yeast

1/4 teaspoon salt

Preparation and Method: 5 minutes

1. Measure all ingredients and transfer to the bowl of a food processor.* Pulse a few times to break up the cashews, then turn on high and process for 1 or 2 minutes.

2. Stop and scrape bowl to loosen pieces that will surely have stuck to the bottom of your bowl. Process again until mixture has a fine grainy texture. Use immediately or keep refrigerated for up to a week.

*Alternatively you can grind all ingredients together with a mortar and pestle.

Nutritional Data: 1 Tablespoon

Calories: 34, 1.83g Fat, 2.1g Protein, 2.27g Carbohydrates, Cholesterol: 0, Saturated Fat: .33g, Total Fiber: .81g

Tofu Sour Cream

Some things just aren't the same without a dollop of sour cream. You don't have to give up this timeless favorite. Go ahead and enjoy your baked potatoes, tacos, soups and dips. With this healthy version, you'll have no regrets. This recipe can be easily doubled.

Time: 6 minutes
Yield: 1 1/8 cups

Ingredients:

1/2 brick (7 ounces) firm organic tofu
Juice of 1 1/2 lemons (about 4 tablespoons)
1 1/2 tablespoons unsweetened pineapple juice
1/2 teaspoon apple cider vinegar
1/8 teaspoon salt (optional)
Chives or green onions (optional)

Method:

1. Blend in food processor until thick and creamy.

2. Scrape into serving bowl and chill for at least 2 hours.

Serve with chopped chives or green onions, if desired.

Nutritional Data: 1/4 Cup

Calories: 43, 1.96g Fat, 4.01g Protein, 2.87g Carbohydrates, Cholesterol: 0, Saturated Fat: .23g, Total Fiber: .44g

Tofu Cottage Cheese

This version of vegan cottage cheese is especially good in baked items, such as lasagna, stuffed pasta shells, and manicotti. It really doesn't taste like cottage cheese, nor ricotta cheese in the creamier version. But it will give you the texture, and the flavor is delightful. You can use this recipe in any dish that calls for cottage cheese.

Time: 10 minutes
Yield: 2 1/2 cups

Ingredients:

1 brick (14 ounces) firm tofu
2 tablespoons freshly chopped dill
2 to 3 tablespoons lemon juice
1 teaspoon apple cider vinegar
1/4 teaspoon salt

Preparation: 5 minutes

1. Wash and chop dill (the feathery leaves, not the stems).

2. Juice lemon

Method: 5 minutes

1. Drain tofu and squeeze between two paper towels to remove excess water. Crumble with hands into a glass bowl until it resembles the consistency of large curd cottage cheese.

2. Gently fold in dill weed, lemon and vinegar. Sprinkle with a little salt to balance tartness.

3. Let sit for half an hour for flavors to meld.

Note: For a Ricotta cheese substitute, add all ingredients to a high-powered blender or food processor, and pulse to a creamier consistency.

Nutritional Data: 1/2 Cup

Calories: 68, 3.5g Fat, 7.11g Protein, 2.48g Carbohydrates, Cholesterol: 0, Saturated Fat: .4g, Total Fiber: .67g

Vegan Mayonnaise

There is no need to expose your body to processed mayonnaise when this recipe is so easy and so delicious. The chia seeds give it a little body and the other ingredients provide flavor. There is nothing in this recipe that isn't good for you so enjoy it liberally.

Time: About 20 minutes (plus soak time)
Yield: 1 1/2 cups

Ingredients:

    1/2 brick (7 ounces) firm tofu

    1 tablespoon white chia seeds

    1 tablespoon lemon juice

    2 teaspoons whole grain mustard

    2 teaspoons garbanzo bean miso or mellow white soy miso

    1/4 teaspoon umeboshi vinegar (optional, see resources)

    1/4 teaspoon salt

Preparation: 15 minutes

1. Drain tofu and discard water. Wrap in a clean dish towel or paper towel and squeeze out remaining water.

2. Soak chia seeds in 3 tablespoons water for 15 minutes.

Method: 4 minutes

1. Combine all ingredients in a blender and blend on high until smooth.

Note: You can use black chia seeds for this recipe but it will give your mayonnaise a slightly darker, muddier color that you might not find as appetizing for dishes like potato salad, though I've found some people actually prefer this color. Either way, it is fine as a sandwich spread.

Nutritional Data: 1/4 Cup

Calories: 43, 2.1g Fat, 3.21g Protein, 2.34g Carbohydrates, Cholesterol: 0, Saturated Fat: .22g, Total Fiber: .9g

❧ 16 ❧

HEALTHY RECIPES TO GET YOU STARTED

This chapter is a sampling of recipes to give you an idea of the variety of foods you can enjoy on a WFPB diet. They range in difficulty level from simple to a bit more complex. None of them are particularly difficult, though several involve more steps than you may find comfortable. They may also contain ingredients that are unfamiliar to you. All the ingredients in these recipes can most likely be found at one or more of your local markets. Take your time, read through the entire recipe first so there will be no surprises along the way. Don't let long ingredient lists intimidate you. By organizing your ingredients into several steps this becomes not only manageable, it's easy.

As in the previous chapter, I took the liberty of giving very detailed instructions, assuming you have no experience at all in the kitchen. If you are an experienced cook, by all means ignore these basic instructions and begin wherever you feel most comfortable.

Be brave, go forth and conquer!

Breakfast

Breakfast Cereal With Fresh Fruit

Fresh fruit and rolled oats are just what the doctor ordered for first thing in the morning to start the day with a burst of flavor and powerful antioxidants. With cholesterol-lowering oats and loads of fiber, this meal is quick and satisfying. Many refer to rolled oats as a raw food, but they are actually steamed before they are rolled.

We like the thick rolled oats for their chewiness, but suit yourself as to how thick or thin you like it. In the winter you may want to cook them first just for the warming quality of oats. Add a little cinnamon and a few raisins for sweetness. Then add the fruit and flaxseeds on top and skip the milk altogether. This is the breakfast Rich and I have almost every day. We never tire of this delicious nutritional powerhouse.

Time: 10 minutes
Yield: 2 servings

Ingredients:

1/2 cup organic thick rolled oats
1/4 cup organic raisins
1 1/4 cups organic strawberries
1/3 cup organic blueberries
1 tablespoon flaxseeds, ground
1 banana
1/2 cup (30-calorie) unsweetened almond milk
cinnamon to taste (Ceylon cinnamon is best, see resources.)

Preparation and Method: 10 minutes

1. Grind flaxseeds in a coffee grinder. This will expand with grinding to a heaping tablespoon.

2. Divide ingredients into 2 bowls as you prepare. First, place oats in the bottom of a cereal bowl.

3. Mix the flaxseeds and the oats. This will prevent the flaxseeds from clumping.

4. Cut strawberries and bananas to desired size and add to bowl with remaining ingredients.

5. Pour almond milk on cereal and enjoy.

Nutritional Data: 1 Bowl
Calories: 344, 6.03g Fat, 10.05g Protein, 66.03g Carbohydrates, Cholesterol: 0, Saturated Fat: .76g, Total Fiber: 10.24g

Cooked Oats (Oatmeal)

In the winter, we prefer the warmth of cooked oatmeal. This method is quick and easy and does not overcook the oats. If you prefer more of a mush, cook a little longer, adding a little more liquid if needed.

Time: 10 minutes
Yield: 2 servings

Ingredients:

1/2 cup organic thick rolled oats
1/4 cup organic raisins
1 1/4 cups organic strawberry pieces
1/3 cup organic blueberries
1 tablespoon flaxseeds, ground
1 sliced banana
Cinnamon to taste
1/2 to 1 cup (30-calorie) unsweetened almond milk (optional)

Preparation and Method: 10 minutes

1. While oats are cooking, slice banana and cut up strawberries to desired size.

2. In a small saucepan, add raisins and one cup water. Cover and bring to a boil.

3. Stir in the oats. Reduce heat and cook for 2 to 3 minutes or until desired consistency is reached.

4. Stir in flaxseeds and top with a sprinkle of cinnamon, strawberries, blueberries and banana slices. Add almond milk if desired.

Nutritional Data: 1 Bowl

Calories: 337, 5.41g Fat, 10.05g Protein, 66.16g Carbohydrates, Cholesterol: 0, Saturated Fat: .76g, Total Fiber: 10.32g

Banana Spelt Pancakes With Pecans

Pancakes are a delicious and satisfying comfort food. I don't make them often, but when I do I enjoy them without guilt. There is no reason to add eggs to pancakes, nor milk for that matter. I prefer water to soy or nut milks because the flavor of the grain and the fruit are dominant, rather than the flavor of the milk. These pancakes are light and fluffy and ready to eat in only 15 minutes. What's not to love?

Time: 15 minutes
Yield: 6 to 7 pancakes (4 to 4 1/2 inches)

Ingredients:

1 cup organic unbleached all-purpose flour
1 cup organic whole spelt flour
1/2 teaspoon salt
1 tablespoon baking powder
1/2 teaspoon cinnamon
1/3 cup coarsely chopped pecans
1 medium banana, mashed
1 1/2 cups filtered water
1 teaspoon 100 percent pure vanilla extract

Method: 15 minutes

1. In a medium mixing bowl, stir together first 5 ingredients.

2. Mash the banana to a pulp with a fork. Add to dry ingredients.

3. Measure water in a two-cup measuring cup. Stir in vanilla.

4. With a large spoon, stir vanilla/water mixture into dry ingredients. Don't over-mix, stir together just until all the ingredients are incorporated. Make sure there is no flour stuck to the bottom of the bowl. Set aside while heating the skillet. This short resting period is important to achieve fluffy pancakes.

5. Place a large non-stick skillet* on stove and turn heat to medium-high.

6. After a minute, add a drop of water onto the skillet. If it sizzles the skillet is hot enough. If not, wait another 30 seconds and try again. Spoon pancake mixture onto skillet to make 3 pancakes, 4 to 4 1/2 inches in diameter. Reduce heat to medium and cook for about 2 minutes or until the pancakes' edges begin to firm up and little air bubbles or

holes form on top. Turn pancakes and cook another minute or two on the other side.

7. Serve immediately topped with fresh fruit and 100 percent pure maple syrup,** heated or at room temperature.

*You can cook all the pancakes at once if you use 2 skillets on separate burners. Then everything is hot and ready at the same time.

**You'll find if you serve the maple syrup on the side in a small bowl for dipping you'll use much less than if you pour it directly over the pancakes.

Nutritional Data: 3 Pancakes
Calories: 209, 4.78g Fat, 5.94g Protein, 38.47g Carbohydrates, Cholesterol: 0, Saturated Fat: .4g, Total Fiber: 4.43g

Soups

New England Clamless Chowder

Whether or not you are a fan of clam chowder, if you enjoy decadently creamy potatoes and are craving comfort food, this is a dish you will love. It doesn't have the fishy taste of clams, but the shiitake mushrooms provide the color and chewiness of clams and enhance the character of this dish as a potato stew. This is a perfect transition dish if you miss seafood.

Time: 25 minutes
Yield: 7 cups

Ingredients:

1 cup cashews, soaked for at least 5 hours or overnight

2 tablespoons white garbanzo bean miso (Master Miso brand is the most readily available.)

1 teaspoon tomato paste (optional)

2 cups diced yellow or white onion, 1/4-inch dice

4 cups diced Yukon Gold potatoes, skins on, 1/2-inch dice

1/2 cup diced celery, 1/8-inch dice (1 stalk)

1/4 cup diced red pepper, 1/4-inch dice

1 cup dried shiitake mushrooms, broken into 1/4-inch pieces

1/2 to 1 teaspoon dried thyme leaves

Preparation: 1 hour, plus soaking time

1. Drain cashews and discard liquid.

2. Break dried shiitake mushrooms into small pieces.

3. In a small saucepan, cover shiitake mushrooms with an inch of water and bring to a boil. Turn off heat and allow to soak for 30 minutes to 1 hour. An alternative method is to microwave the mushrooms in water on high for 1 to 2 minutes or until boiling. To keep all of the mushrooms submerged, it it helpful to set a bowl within a bowl, with the bottom bowl containing the mushrooms and water and the top bowl acting as a weight. Allow to soak for 30 minutes to an hour. Drain and reserve liquid.

4. While the mushrooms are soaking, dice onions, celery, and bell peppers. Place in large skillet or sauce pan with a lid.

5. Cut potatoes into 1/2-inch cubes and rinse. Cover with water to prevent discoloration.

Method: 20 to 25 minutes

1. Drain potatoes and transfer to a medium saucepan with 1/2 inch water.

2. Bring to a boil. Reduce heat to medium and cook for 10 minutes or until the potatoes are fork tender. Drain, reserving liquid.

3. At the same time cook onions, celery, and bell peppers until soft (about 10 minutes). Add drained mushrooms and heat through. Add potatoes.

4. Discard cashew soaking liquid and transfer the nuts, miso, and tomato paste to a blender. Add 1 cup of liquid, using all of the reserved mushroom water and some of the potato liquid. Blend on high speed until creamy, adding more potato water if you feel it is too thick (about 2 minutes).

5. Add the cashew cream to the potato mixture, folding in to incorporate. Add thyme and cook for 2 minutes, thinning to desired consistency with potato water, or just plain water if you've exhausted your supply. Salt and pepper to taste. Serve hot.

Nutritional Data: 1 Cup

Calories: 200, 7.67g Fat, 5.52g Protein, 27.96g Carbohydrates, Cholesterol: 0, Saturated Fat: 1.53g, Total Fiber: 4.24g

Curried Soup With Yellow Split-Peas
And Sweet Potatoes

*This recipe is creamy and a little chunky at the same time.
The sweet potato adds a rich sweetness that is tempered by the
savory flavors of curry. Add a green salad and a slice of whole
grain bread and you'll have a hearty balanced meal.*

Time: 45 minutes (plus soaking time)
Yield: 6 cups

Ingredients:

1 1/4 cups dried yellow split-peas
4 cups Mirepoix Vegetable Stock (page 199), or filtered water
1 teaspoon crushed and minced fresh garlic
1 teaspoon minced fresh ginger
1 large sweet potato (about 1 pound)
1/2 teaspoon cinnamon
1 tablespoon curry powder
1/8 teaspoon black pepper
1 tablespoon date sugar* (optional)
1/4 teaspoon salt (optional)

Preparation:

Times overlap as part of the preparation occurs while beans are cooking. The cooking time assumes the beans have been soaked overnight or at least 5 hours.

1. Wash split peas. Remove stones, bad pieces and debris. Cover with 3 inches of water and soak overnight. Drain and discard water.

Method: 2 hours

1. Transfer split peas to a large saucepan. Add 4 cups stock or water, cover, and bring to a boil (10 to 12 minutes). Boil on high, uncovered, for 10 minutes. Reduce heat, cover, and simmer until beans are soft (2 hours).

2. While the beans are cooking, peel and cut the sweet potatoes into small chunks. In a separate small saucepan with a lid, add the sweet potato, ginger, garlic, and 1/2 inch water. Bring to a boil then reduce heat. Simmer for 10 minutes, or until the potatoes are fork tender.

3. Transfer to a blender or use an immersion blender. Blend until smooth adding cinnamon, black pepper, curry powder, and a little water if needed. If you want a creamier soup blend the split peas as well. If you choose to do this the cooking time will be reduced by more than half. Be sure to blend until the mixture is perfectly creamy. You may want to blend the split peas first in two batches, then blend the sweet potato before combining. For a soup with more texture do not puree the split peas.

4. Combine pureed potatoes and split peas. Add date sugar. Simmer on low another 10 minutes. Adjust seasonings to taste, add salt, if using, and more vegetable stock or water to thin if necessary. Simmer 5 minutes more. Serve hot.

*The addition of date sugar is optional. The natural sweetness of sweet potatoes is often enough. Buying them organic and in season nearly always ensures a good sweet potato. Date sugar is a whole food; it is nothing more than dried ground up dates. You can purchase it in most large grocery stores, most health food stores or order it on line. Feel free to add a little if it isn't sweet enough to suit you. Alternatively, you can blend in a couple of whole dates (making sure to remove the seeds.) or a little organic cane sugar.

Nutritional Data: 1 Cup
Calories: 217, .56g Fat, 12.24g Protein, 43.44g Carbohydrates, Cholesterol: 0, Saturated Fat: .04g, Total Fiber: 13.73g

Appetizers/Salads

The first three dishes in the salad category can be served as a starter or appetizer as well. I learned to make these dishes from a lovely Iraqi gentleman who had been Saddam Hussein's personal chef for 20 years. His recipes have quite a lot of oil and one of them contains yogurt. I have created healthier versions by removing the oil, reducing the salt, and by substituting vegan cashew cream cheese for yogurt.

Mediterranean Hummus

Hummus is a vegetarian staple. It is creamy and satisfying and wonderfully healthy. It's beans!

If you are cooking for only a couple of people, you can easily cut this recipe in half. Another option is to divide the

finished hummus into 3 portions. The first portion can be a thicker spread for sandwiches, crackers or crostini, the second can be diluted with reserved bean-water to make a traditional hummus dip for fresh veggies, chips or flat-bread. The third can be further diluted, and with additional seasonings can become a sauce for grains, vegetable dishes, or even pastas.

Hummus can also be used as a base by adding various seasonings as well as different vegetable combinations.

Time: 15 minutes
Yield: 2 cups

Ingredients:

4 to 6 cloves fresh garlic
2 cups cooked garbanzo beans
2 tablespoons bean liquid*
2 tablespoons tahini**
Juice of 2 lemons*** (5 tablespoons, more or less to suit your tastes)
1/2 teaspoon salt

Preparation: 10 minutes

1. This recipe presupposes you have Pressure-Cooked Chickpeas on hand (page 226). You can substitute canned, but discard liquid and rinse. Use fresh water or Mirepoix Vegetable Stock (page 199) to thin the mixture rather than canned bean liquid.

2. Peel garlic. Juice lemons.

Method: 5 minutes

1. For a thicker mixture suitable for sandwich spreads, place garlic cloves in food processor and spin until all pieces are clinging to the side of the bowl. Add drained beans to

blender bowl. Add tahini, lemon juice, and salt. Process until all ingredients are well blended.****

2. For traditional hummus, dip add a little bean stock, 1/8 cup at a time, and puree until you reach desired consistency. Remove desired amount and place in a covered dish. Refrigerate.

3. To make a sauce, add more bean stock and puree until you reach desired consistency. Use on grain, vegetable or pasta dish.

*This refers to the liquid from freshly cooked chickpeas. If you are buying canned chickpeas, drain the water and rinse thoroughly. For the additional liquid you'll need in your recipes, use homemade vegetable stock or filtered water.

**If you have the equipment to grind your own seeds, it is better to make your own fresh tahini as you need it. Nut butters go rancid fairly quickly while the seeds hold up over time.

***If you are not a fan of lemon, you can reduce this amount. If you prefer a stronger lemon flavor, you can certainly add more. I often use 3 lemons.

****If dividing, take out the desired amount you need for a spread, dip, or sauce and place it in a clean storage bowl with a lid. Refrigerate until ready to use.

Nutritional Data: 1/2 Cup
Calories: 175, 5.43g Fat, 8.03g Protein, 24.39g Carbohydrates, Cholesterol: 0, Saturated Fat: .78g, Total Fiber: 6.63g

Baba Ghanoush

Baba Ghanoush is creamy, luxurious spread to serve as an appetizer for dipping fresh vegetables, pita wedges, or other flatbread, or with baked chips or crostini. It also makes a delicious sandwich spread that complements nearly any plant-based sandwich ingredient. Stuff it into pita pockets, use in burrito wraps, or spread it on toast; baba ghanoush is a fine addition to your collection of plant-based recipes. That it is simple to prepare is just a bonus!

The timing below presupposes you have already made the Roasted Eggplant, Roasted Garlic, and the Cashew Cream Cheese, all of which can be made the day before.

Time: 15 to 20 minutes
Yield: 1 1/2 cups

Ingredients:

1 large (about 18 ounces) Roasted Eggplant (page 222)
1/3 packed cup whole fresh mint leaves (1/2 ounce)
Juice of 1 lemon (about 3 tablespoons)
1 medium bulb (6 or 8 cloves) Roasted Garlic* (page 217)
1/2 teaspoon ground cumin
1 tablespoon tahini (sesame seed paste)
1/4 cup Cashew Cream Cheese (page 262)
1/4 teaspoons salt

Preparation and Method: 15 to 20 minutes

1. Wash mint leaves and shake or spin dry; remove stems and discard. Add to bowl of food processor.

2. Scrape soft eggplant pulp from its skin and add to the bowl of a food processor. (If you prefer, you can use the whole eggplant, skins and all (if the skin is soft), but discard the stem.)

3. Add remaining ingredients and blend for a minute or two or until creamy.

4. Transfer to serving dish. Serve chilled or at room temperature.

*Rather than roasting a whole garlic, you can make slits in the sides of the eggplant and force garlic cloves into them. The garlic will cook along with the eggplant. (Add 5 minutes to the cooking time to peel garlic and stuff the slits.)

Nutritional Data: 1/2 Cup

Calories: 148, 5.43g Fat, 8.03g Protein, 17.82g Carbohydrates, Cholesterol: 0, Saturated Fat: 1.34g, Total Fiber: 6.97g

Middle-Eastern Tabbouleh

Tabbouleh is a middle-eastern favorite that is full of gorgeous green antioxidants. Usually this dish is made with a little olive oil but since we now understand the damage oil does to our endothelial cells, this recipe is oil free. Lemon juice with just a pinch of salt is enough to make the vegetables in this dish sing. Whenever I use pure lemon juice as a dressing, I

always add just a touch of salt because it rounds out the flavor and takes away the pucker-tartness of the lemon. Because of the salt, even this small amount, the ingredients will quickly begin to release their natural juices. So prepare it just before serving and enjoy it while it is fresh. Serve it with store-bought or fresh homemade pita bread and you'll have a hit on your hands!

Time: 20 to 30 minutes

Yield: 4 3/4 cups

Ingredients:

3/4 cup water
1/4 cup Bulgar Wheat (page 209) or Quinoa (page 208)
Juice of 1 to 2 lemons
3 medium cloves garlic
2 bunches flat-leaf parsley (6 ounces)
1 packed cup fresh mint leaves (1 1/2 ounces)
1 1/4 cups finely diced ripe tomato (8 ounces)
3/4 cup finely diced cucumber, seeds removed (4 ounces)
1/4 cup finely diced red onion (1.3 ounces)
1/4 teaspoon salt

Preparation and Method: 15 to 20 minutes

1. Prepare Bulgar Wheat or Quinoa. While the grain is cooking, prepare vegetables.

2. Place flat side of a chef's knife on each garlic clove, with the blade turned away from you, and whack it with the palm of your hand, releasing the peel. Remove the peel and transfer garlic to a food processor: pulse until minced.

3. Wash mint and parsley and spin dry in a salad spinner; or shake off water then wrap in a clean kitchen towel or a paper towel to remove excess water. Remove all but the smallest stems from each and transfer leaves to a food processor. Discard stems. Pulse until the herbs are finely chopped but not creamy.

4. Cut tomato into a fine dice. Do the same with the red onion and cucumber.

5. Transfer parsley concoction to a large bowl. Add chopped tomatoes, cucumber, and bulgar wheat or quinoa.

6. Toss with lemon juice and salt. Serve immediately.

Note: If you don't have a food processor, you can mince the garlic and chop the mint and parsley by hand. It will take a few minutes longer but you'll achieve the same delicious results.

Nutritional Data: 3/4 Cup

Calories: 50, .33g Fat, 2.38g Protein, 11.13g Carbohydrates, Cholesterol: 0, Saturated Fat: .09g, Total Fiber: 3.06g

Main Course Salads

Massaged Kale And Chickpea Salad

A perfect use for leftover chickpeas and marinated beets, this salad is so beautiful you'll be tempted to hang it on the wall. It is also so tasty and satisfying you'll want to make it often. With all the color in this salad you can be sure it has plenty of cancer-preventive antioxidants. Your body and your tastebuds will thank you for this one.

Time: 20 to 25 minutes
Yield: 2 Salads

Ingredients:

2 cups Massaged Kale (page 202)
1 cup Marinated Beets (page 247)

1 cup Pressure-Cooked Chickpeas,* drained (page 226)
1 to 2 clementines, mandarin oranges, or tangerines
2 ounces walnuts, coarsely chopped
1/2 cup Ginger-Lime Salad Dressing (page 254)
Orange and lime zest for garnish

Preparation: 12 to 22 minutes

1. Peel clementines and break into segments.

2. Chop walnuts.

3. Make Ginger-Lime Salad Dressing and gather other ingredients so they are at hand.

4. Zest orange and lime.

Method: 3 to 5 minutes

1. Distribute 1/2 of kale onto each of 2 salad plates. Toss with 2 tablespoons Ginger-Lime Salad Dressing.

2. In the middle of the kale, scatter 1/2 cup marinated beets.

3. Arrange 1/2 cup chickpeas atop the beets.

4. Tuck clementine segments into the kale in an attractive arrangement.

5. Top with walnuts and drizzle with remaining salad dressing.

6. Garnish with zest of lime and orange.

*You can cook chickpeas on your stovetop if you don't have a pressure cooker, though it will take longer. Or you can substitute canned chickpeas, drained and rinsed.

Nutritional Data: 1 Salad
Calories: 564, 21.5g Fat, 17.94g Protein, 81.62g Carbohydrates, Cholesterol: 0, Saturated Fat: 2.316g, Total Fiber: 17.71g

Kate Strong's Rainbow Salad

This is a recipe I'm delighted to share with you. It was contributed by Kate Strong, our newest writer for Veggin' Out And About! Not only is Kate a world-class athlete, she has owned a bed and breakfast in Australia and is no stranger to the kitchen. Try this salad and discover what good tastes like! This dish is packed with calories, fiber and other healthy nutrients, as well as the "good" fats, which makes it a perfect fuel for high-intensity training, but may be too rich for those leading more sedentary lifestyles.

Reprinted by permission of Kate Strong, Photographer

Time: 25 minutes
Yield: 4 "regular" people, 3 hungry triathletes

Ingredients:

Soy dressing:

125ml (4.2 ounces/about 1/2 cup) soy sauce, unsalted
1 red chili
1 (2 x 4 inch) clump of minced wheatgrass
1 handful fresh coriander
Zest and juice of 1 lemon
2 cloves minced garlic
3 kaffir lime leaves, coarsely chopped (optional, can substitute
1 tablespoon lime zest)

Dukkah:

220g (7.8 ounces) sesame seeds
440g (15.5 ounces) hazelnuts
10 teaspoons whole cumin seeds
10 teaspoons whole coriander seeds
1 tablespoon pepper

Salad:

2 carrots
1 beet
1/4 cucumber
1/4 diced red onion
1 handful pepitas (pumpkin seeds)
5 stalks asparagus, sliced at an angle
1/2 red capsicum (pepper)
5 large kale leaves, roughly chopped
400g (14 ounces) cooked Quinoa (page 208)
Juice of 1 lemon
Dukkah for garnish (This is an Egyptian spice blend.)

Soy Dressing Method:

1. Dice and chop all ingredients; add to an airtight glass jar with soy sauce. Refrigerate.

   Note: The longer you leave it the better it tastes: I make mine 4 weeks prior to using!!!

Dukkah method:

1. Lightly pan fry sesame seeds for 3 minutes. Add to large mixing bowl.

2. Roast hazelnuts in oven set at 180°C (350°F) for 5 minutes. Remove from heat and place in colander. Cover colander tightly, stand over sink (or in garden, even better!) and shake hard removing the husks from the nuts.

3. Pan fry the cumin and coriander seeds for about 4 to 5 minutes. Once the seeds start to pop, remove from the heat.

4. Grind coriander, cumin and pepper using a mortar and pestle and add to the sesame seeds.

5. Using a food processor, blend the hazelnuts until the desired consistency. I like to have a few medium-sized pieces of nuts for added crunch and add to the sesame mix bowl.

6. Mix all ingredients thoroughly and store in an air-tight container.

Salad Method:

1. Using a mandolin, cut into thin strips the carrots, beet & cucumber. Transfer vegetable strips and the diced red onion to a large bowl.

2. Gently stir in the soy dressing. Allow to marinade for 10 minutes.

3. Add the pepitas, diced capsicum, sliced asparagus to the bowl.

4. Stir in the lemon juice.

5. Distribute quinoa on plate and arrange salad on top of quinoa. Garnish with dukkah.

Nutritional Data: 1 Salad (1/4 recipe)
Calories: 1301, 95.88g Fat, 40.08g Protein, 79.11g Carbohydrates, Cholesterol: 0, Saturated Fat: 9.68g, Total Fiber: 27.58g

Toasted Israeli Couscous Salad With Fresh Herbs

As fresh as springtime, this salad is savory and satisfying. Lime complements the tomatoes, peppers, and cucumbers and pairs naturally with both mint and cilantro. The couscous adds carbohydrates for satiety and balances the tang of the lime. A little salt is critical to reduce the pucker of the limes. Just a pinch is all you need.

Time: 15 minutes
Yield: 4 cups

Ingredients:

2 cups cooked Toasted Israeli Couscous (page 215)
2 tablespoons minced mint
2 tablespoons minced cilantro
Juice of 3 limes (1/3 to 1/2 cup)
1 cup diced cucumber
1 cup diced sweet yellow pepper, 1/4-inch dice
1 cup diced sweet red pepper, 1/4-inch dice
3 small red tomatoes, 1 1/2 inches in diameter, cut in 1/2 inch pieces (about 2/3 cup)
1/4 teaspoon salt

Preparation and Method: 15 minutes

1. Prepare couscous and allow to cool.

2. Mince cilantro and mint, dice cucumber and peppers and cut up tomato.

3. Juice lime.

4. Toss all ingredients together with lime juice and 1/4 teaspoon salt.

Nutritional Data: 1 Cup

Calories: 189, .14g Fat, 6.41g Protein, 40.52g Carbohydrates, Cholesterol: 0, Saturated Fat: .05g, Total Fiber: 3.94g

Side Salads

Warm Potato-Dill Salad

This dish is easy and so delicious. It is wonderful as a side dish served warm, but can also be refrigerated and served chilled as well. It's a great pot-luck dish for most any occasion. This keeps about three days in your fridge so you can make it the day before with no worries.

Time: 20 minutes
Yield: 4 cups

Ingredients:

4 cups (about 1 1/2 pounds) diced Yukon Gold potatoes, (1/2-inch dice)
3 green onions, sliced crosswise into 1/8-inch rounds
3 tablespoons chopped fresh dill
1/2 cup Vegan Mayonnaise* (page 271)

Method: 20 minutes

1. Wash potatoes carefully, using a nylon scrub pad. Cut into large dice, about 1/2-inch cubes. Rinse and transfer to a medium saucepan with a lid. Add 1/2 cup water and bring to a boil. Reduce heat to simmer and cook for 12 to 15 minutes or until fork tender.

2. While potatoes are cooking, chop dill and slice green onions. Set aside.

3. When the potatoes are done, drain and return to the sauce pan.

4. Fold in vegan mayonnaise, taking care to preserve the shape of the potatoes. Don't over-mix!

5. Carefully fold in onions and dill, leaving a few small fronds of whole dill on top as a garnish.

Serve warm or chilled.

*You can substitute Vegenaise if you like, but it will increase the fat and calories of this dish. To the Vegenaise, add 1/2 teaspoon organic tamari and 1 teaspoon whole grain mustard. Stir to combine, then add to recipe.

Nutritional Data: 1 Cup
Calories: 125, 1.07g Fat, 3.83g Protein, 26.02g Carbohydrates, Cholesterol: 0, Saturated Fat: .11g, Total Fiber: 4.75g

Italian Orzo With Cherry Tomatoes And Fresh Basil

This delightful pasta salad is summer goodness in a bowl! Fresh basil and ripe cherry tomatoes are combined with the salty bite of Kalamata olives, capers, and a splash of lemony garlic. Ready to eat in 15 minutes from the time your water comes to a boil, what's not to love? I like to keep a cold pasta dish in the fridge for my husband to snack on. This is one of his favorites.

Time: 25 minutes
Yields: 9 cups

Ingredients:

1 pound orzo (small rice shaped pasta)
1 pint box* (11ounce) cherry tomatoes, sliced into halves
2 tablespoons capers, plus a little of the juice
20 Kalamata olives, quartered
1 cup packed fresh basil leaves, cut into chiffonade
1 large garlic bulb, smashed and minced
3 large lemons, juiced (1/3 cup)
1/4 teaspoon salt**

Preparation and Cooking: 25 minutes

1. Separate garlic cloves. Smash with the flat edge of a chef's knife. Remove skins and mince. Set aside.

2. Bring a large saucepan or stock pot of water to a boil. Stir in orzo and cook uncovered 6 to 8 minutes or until al dente.

3. While the water is boiling and the orzo is cooking and cooling, wash and slice tomatoes. Slice olives. Have capers handy. Juice lemons and chiffonade basil.

4. When the orzo is ready, drain in a fine-meshed strainer. Allow to cool. You can accelerate the cooling process by running cold water over the pasta while it's in the strainer. Drain well and transfer to a large bowl.

5. Mix the garlic and lemon juice*** together. Pour over orzo mixture and toss until fully incorporated. Salt to taste.

6. After the orzo has cooled, add basil, olives, and capers along with a tablespoon of the caper liquid. Toss to combine.

Serve at room temperature or chilled.

*Volume and liquid measurements are not always equal. A pint of cherry tomatoes (11 ounces) is not the same as a pint of water (16 ounces).

**Whenever I use a lot of lemon in a dish, I find that it needs to be tempered by a little salt. Salt removes the sour puckering quality of lemon and softens the edges while still allowing the citrus flavor to shine. If you are salt-sensitive or if your physician suggests you limit your salt intake, you may wish to reduce the amount of salt and possibly the amount of lemon you use in this recipe. Always consider the amount of salt you have eaten in a given day and the amount of salt per person when making seasoning decisions. Most of the food I prepare requires no added salt at all so I have some wiggle room in the occasional dish in which I do choose to use it.

***The amount of lemon is a personal choice. I sometimes use the juice of 3 lemons because I enjoy the citrus overtones in this dish.

Nutritional Data: 1 Cup

Calories: 223, 2.9g Fat, 7.17g Protein, 42.63g Carbohydrates, Cholesterol: 0, Saturated Fat: .01g, Total Fiber: 3.07g

Main Course Recipes

Quinoa With Carrots, Corn And Peas

This dish is healthy, colorful, and fragrant; pleasing to both the eye and the palate. It has layers of complex flavors finished with the citrus tang of fresh lemon juice. Add a side of cooked greens or a green salad and you will have all the nutrients you could desire.

The long ingredient list for this recipe may seem overwhelming. As you transition to a plant-based lifestyle you'll find yourself using these spices over and over again, reducing the cost of each individual dish. Measure them into a small bowl at the beginning of the cooking process to avoid the frantic search for a particular spice when it is called for. Organization is key in preparing this dish. No need to panic;

this recipe is not difficult. Take it one step at a time and in only 25 minutes you'll have a wonderfully flavorful meal to share with your family.

Time: 25 minutes

Yield: 7 cups

Ingredients:

Spice Blend:

1/4 teaspoon ground cardamom

1 teaspoon ground cinnamon

1 teaspoon ground coriander

1 teaspoon ground cumin

1/2 teaspoon ground turmeric

1/4 teaspoon ground chili pepper (You can substitute cayenne.)

1/4 teaspoon salt (optional)

1/4 teaspoon black pepper

Main Ingredients:

3 cups cooked Quinoa (page 208)

1/2 cup sliced almonds

1/4 cup finely chopped fresh mint

1 small yellow onion, julienned

1 teaspoon minced fresh garlic

1 teaspoon minced fresh ginger

3 cups carrot slices cut 1/8-inch on the diagonal (about 4 medium carrots)

1/2 cup organic corn, fresh or frozen

1/2 cup baby green peas

1/2 cup golden raisins plus water to cover

Juice of 1/2 lemon (Use the whole lemon if you like a less sweet and more bright flavor.)

Method: 25 minutes, including preparation

Most of your preparation is done while the quinoa is cooking, so the entire process takes only 25 minutes.

Preparation:

1. Prepare quinoa and vegetables and raisins. Cover carrots with water to prevent discoloration.

2. Measure all your spices into a small bowl. Stir to combine.

3. Juice lemon and set aside.

Method:

1. In a dry skillet, sauté onions until nearly translucent (about 8 minutes). Add garlic and ginger and sauté another minute. Add 1/4 cup water (Use the water from soaking the raisins.) and carrots. Cover and cook until the color of the carrots has deepened. The carrots should still be a little crunchy. Add the corn, peas, and raisins. Add spice mixture, a tablespoon at a time, stirring to incorporate.

2. Fold in quinoa making sure the spices are incorporated in it. Turn off heat and allow to sit for a couple minutes. While the quinoa is resting, prepare almonds by roasting in a dry pan over medium heat turning constantly with a spatula. Don't worry if they don't brown evenly. It is better to have a few undercooked than have any of them burned.

3. Fluff quinoa with a fork. Toss with lemon juice and fresh mint. Sprinkle with almonds. Serve hot.

Nutritional Data: 1 Cup

Calories: 245, 5.68g Fat, 8.16g Protein, 43.2g Carbohydrates, Cholesterol: 0, Saturated Fat: .61g, Total Fiber: 7.01g

Creamy Penne Pasta With Broccoli

Penne Pasta is always a favorite at our house. My Italian-American husband loves it and, I have to admit, so do I. Bursting with bright fresh flavors, you'll want to make this all the time.

You have to be a bit of a multi-tasker to prepare this dish seamlessly. The preparation and cooking steps overlap. How quickly this meal is prepared is a matter of organization and practice. I can complete this dish in 40 minutes, but for beginners it often takes closer to an hour. Take the time you need and enjoy the process. It is easier than it looks. Once you get the hang of it, preparing this dish will be a breeze.

Time: 40 minutes to 1 hour
Yield: 9 cups

Ingredients:

1 pound penne pasta (cooked according to package directions)
1 can diced tomatoes
1 recipe Cashew Cream (page 260)
1 tablespoon dried basil
1 teaspoon dried oregano
1/2 teaspoon dried thyme
1/4 teaspoon cayenne pepper (optional)
4 cups broccoli (about 2 large stalks), cut into florets, stems into sticks (1-inch long/1/4-inch wide)
1/2 teaspoon salt (optional)
6 to 8 fresh basil leaves for garnish

Preparation and Method: 40 minutes to 1 hour

1. In a large saucepan or stock pan bring 4 quarts of water to a boil. The rest of the preparation can be done while the pasta water is coming to a boil (about 20 minutes).

2. While the pasta water is heating, wash broccoli and cut florets into bite-sized pieces. Peel stem and cut into small bite-size sticks. Set aside.

3. Chiffonade basil by rolling leaves into a cigar shape and cutting across to make thin ribbons. Set aside.

4. Add diced tomatoes to a blender and pulse. This should be a fairly smooth puree with texture, not watery. Transfer to a medium saucepan with a lid and heat on medium-high, stirring occasionally.

5. Prepare Cashew Cream. Remove lid and stir cream into tomatoes. Add another 1/4 cup water to the blender and pulse a few times to release any cashew cream still adhering to the walls of the blender. Stir this into the tomato mixture.

6. Stir in dried basil, oregano, thyme, cayenne pepper, and salt. Cook, uncovered, on medium heat until edges begin to bubble, stirring frequently. Reduce heat to simmer. Cashew cream burns easily, so do not neglect to stir the sauce. If it becomes too thick, add a little water. This should be thinner than most pasta sauces; not as thick as a gravy but thicker than a soup. Once you've cooked this a time or two you'll get a feel for what works best.

7. When the pasta water is boiling, drop in broccoli pieces and cook until their colors brighten (about 30 seconds). Remove with a strainer or slotted spoon, draining off water at the same time, and set aside in a bowl.

8. When the broccoli is blanched, add the pasta to the water and cook until it is al dente (about 10 minutes). Drain it in a sink by pouring into a colander or large strainer with a pan underneath it to reserve water. Toss to remove all the water and return to pan.

9. Combine all the contents of the creamy tomato sauce with the pasta. (It may seem that this is too much sauce for the pasta. Don't worry, it is just the right amount.) Fold to combine.

10. If the broccoli has cooled, dunk it in the reserved pasta water for 5 to 10 seconds to reheat. Drain in strainer.

11. To serve, spoon pasta onto separate plates and garnish with basil chiffonade. Arrange broccoli on top. Serve hot.

Nutritional Data: 1 Cup
Calories: 256, 3.88g Fat, 9.4g Protein, 46.1g Carbohydrates, Cholesterol: 0, Saturated Fat: .61g, Total Fiber: 4.35g

Cauliflower Fettuccine Alfredo
With Pink Peppercorns

Who doesn't love Fettuccine Alfredo? Rich and creamy to the point of decadence, the traditional recipe is made with heavy cream and butter. This healthy version allows you to indulge in this timeless comfort food free of guilt. Fruity pink peppercorns give it a dash of color and a piquancy that is much milder and sweeter than black pepper. It is simple to prepare. Serve as a main course with a salad or as a side. Either way, it hits the spot!

Time: 30 minutes
Yield: 3 cups

Ingredients:

1/2 medium cauliflower, cut into florets (5 cups)
1/2 cup water
1/2 pound fettuccine noodles
1 teaspoon garbanzo bean miso
1 tablespoon nutritional yeast
1/4 cup Cashew Cream Cheese (page 262)
1 teaspoon whole pink peppercorns for garnish (You can substitute a pinch of black pepper.)
Salt to taste (optional)
Cashew Parmesan Cheese (page 265)

Preparation and Method: 30 minutes

1. Boil pasta and drain according to directions (page 210).

2. While the pasta water is boiling, steam cauliflower in a saucepan on medium-high heat with 1/2 cup water until tender (page 238).

3. Add cauliflower, cashew cream cheese, nutritional yeast, and mizo to a blender and puree until smooth. Use a little of the cauliflower water or filtered water if it seems too thick (2 minutes).

4. Transfer to a medium saucepan.

5. Heat through and adjust consistency by adding a little water if needed.

6. Toss with fettuccine noodles. Sprinkle with pink peppercorns and Cashew Parmesan Cheese. Serve hot.

Nutritional Data: 1 1/2 Cups

Calories: 659, 11.15g Fat, 28.53g Protein, 113.02g Carbohydrates, Cholesterol: 0, Saturated Fat: 1.83g, Total Fiber: 14.2g

Coconut Curry With Indian Spices

This dish smells as good as it tastes. The aromas will drive your family and dinner guests wild while they are awaiting this treat. Again, don't be intimidated by the number of ingredients needed. You'll use these spices over and over. Measuring them out in advance into small bowls will prevent mistakes. It is easy to forget a spice if it isn't handy. If you prepare the rice in advance, it will save you some time when you are scrambling to get food on the table. It is also very good served with French whole wheat couscous, which only takes 10 minutes to prepare. It is also excellent served over linguini.

Note that the cinnamon stick, bay leaf, and cardamom pods are for flavor and should not be eaten. Pick the cinnamon and bay leaf out before serving; the cardamom pods will be harder to find so just warn your guests that they are not to be eaten. They won't hurt them, but the seeds are very fibrous and have a

woody texture. Plus, biting into them may give your guests a jolt of cardamom flavor that could be overpowering.

Time: 35 to 40 minutes
Yield: 7 cups, plus rice

Ingredients:
Prepare in advance:

1 1/2 cups organic brown or red rice (page 205), whole wheat French Couscous (page 213), or linguini (page 210)

3 cups Mirepoix Vegetable Stock (page 199) or filtered water

2 1/2 cups Pressure-Cooked Chickpeas,* drained (page 226)

Spice Blend:

1/2 teaspoon ground turmeric

1 tablespoon garam masala

1/2 teaspoon ground hot chili powder (You can substitute cayenne.)

1/8 teaspoon ground black pepper

1/2 teaspoon salt (optional)

Main Ingredients:

2 cups diced onion (1 large onion)

2 bay leaves

6 cardamom pods

1 (3-inch) cinnamon stick

2 tablespoons minced garlic

2 tablespoons minced ginger

1 can organic coconut milk

6 ounces baby spinach, washed and spun dry

1 pint cherry tomatoes, cut in half (1 3/4 cups or about 40)

1 tablespoon lemon juice

Preparation: about 20 minutes

1. Prepare vegetables.

2. Transfer drained, cooked chickpeas to a bowl. Set aside.

3. Set aside cinnamon stick and cardamon pods. Measure remaining spices into a small bowl. Set aside.

Method: 15 to 20 minutes

1. In a dry skillet, sauté onion with bay leaves, cardamom pods, and cinnamon until soft and translucent, stirring frequently (about 10 minutes).

2. Stir in ginger and garlic. Sauté 2 minutes, adding a little water a tablespoon or two at a time if necessary to prevent scorching.

3. Add turmeric, garam masala, ground chili powder, and black pepper. Stir until spices are fully incorporated with the onion mixture.

4. Stir in coconut milk, tomatoes, and chickpeas. Cook for 5 minutes or so on medium heat until sauce is bubbling and tomatoes have wilted. Adjust spices to taste.

5. Just prior to serving, remove saucepan from heat and fold spinach** into mixture until wilted.

6. Stir in lemon juice and serve immediately over rice, couscous, pasta or grain of choice.

*You can cook chickpeas on your stovetop if you don't have a pressure cooker, though it will take longer. Or you can substitute canned chickpeas, drained and rinsed.

**Don't over-cook the spinach. It should be added no more than 5 minutes before serving. Spinach becomes a little slimy if allowed to cook for too long. Heat it only until it is wilted.

Nutritional Data: 1 Cup

Calories: 265, 12.73g Fat, 9.23g Protein, 32.54g Carbohydrates, Cholesterol: 0, Saturated Fat: 9.84g, Total Fiber: 9.37g

Steamed And Roasted Stuffed Acorn Squash

Stuffed acorn squash is fantastic any time but it is especially welcome during the Thanksgiving and Christmas holidays when turkey takes center stage in many American homes. This dish is cooked mainly on top of the stove and for only the last 15 minutes in the oven. It not only cooks more quickly than baking or roasting alone, but I believe you end up with a more flavorful result.

Time: 50 minutes
Yield: 2 halves, stuffed
Serves 2 as a main course, 4 as a side dish

Ingredients:

2 oranges, juiced with pulp

3 tablespoons maple syrup, divided

1 cup water

1 large organic acorn squash

1 large red delicious apple*, seeded and chopped into 1/4-inch cubes, (about 2 cups)

1/4 cup chopped walnuts

1/4 cup raisins, preferably golden organic

1/2 teaspoon ground cinnamon

1/4 teaspoon ground nutmeg

Method: 35 to 50 minutes

Preheat oven to 375°F

Prep time: 10 minutes

Stovetop: 15 to 25 minutes, depending on the size of your squash

Oven time: 10 to 15 minutes

1. Cut acorn squash in half, from stem to pointed tip. With a spoon, scrape out all the seeds and seed pulp until there is a clean hollow where the seeds were.

2. In a large covered skillet or saucepan, mix the water, orange juice, and 1 tablespoon maple syrup. Stir to combine.

3. Arrange squash in pan, cut side down. Arrange the raisins in the pan around the squash. Cover and bring to a boil. Allow to boil on high until tender. (If the water boils away too quickly add a little more, 1/4 cup at a time.) This will take 15 to 25 minutes, depending on the size of your squash. When it is tender and can easily be pierced with a fork or bamboo skewer, remove the lid and allow most of

the liquid to boil away. Do not allow the thick liquid or the raisins on the bottom of the pan to burn.

4. While the squash is steaming, chop apples and toss with cinnamon, nutmeg, walnuts, and 2 tablespoons maple syrup. Set aside. Once the squash is tender, transfer to a casserole dish or other baking dish with sides. Turn the squash cut side up. Scoop remaining liquid and the raisins out of the pan and add to the apple mixture. Fill the cavities in the acorn squash with this mixture.

5. Roast, uncovered, in a preheated oven for 10 to 15 minutes. The apples should develop a caramel glaze and should still be firm. Do not allow to burn. Serve hot.

*Though Red Delicious isn't typically a cooking apple, I like it in this recipe because it is sweeter than most apples and one of the most nutritious. Also because you are only wilting the apple rather than fully cooking it, it will continue to hold its shape and still have a little bit of a crunch.

Nutritional Data: 1/2 Squash
Calories: 444, 9.95g Fat, 5.53g Protein, 89.89g Carbohydrates, Cholesterol: 0, Saturated Fat: 1.18g, Total Fiber: 8g

Pearled Couscous
With Butternut Squash, Haricots Vert, And Sage

Roasted butternut squash and green beans with hints of maple, sage, and tarragon create a dish that is subtly flavored yet packed with healthy phytonutrients. It is a gorgeous dish to serve to family and friends. While it may take little extra time to prepare, it is not difficult. Served as a main course or a side dish, this one is sure to please.

Time: about 30 minutes
Yield: 7 cups

Ingredients:

4 cups cooked Israeli Couscous (page 214)
1 tablespoon chia seeds
3 tablespoons water
1/4 cup water
1/4 cup maple syrup
1 butternut squash (1 1/2 pounds)
1 cup French green beans (You can use any kind of snap bean or flat bean.)
1/2 cup diced sweet red bell pepper or carmen pepper (a long sweet pepper with a gorgeous deep red color)

Spices:

1 teaspoon tarragon, divided
1 teaspoon poultry seasoning
1 teaspoon rubbed sage
1/8 teaspoon pepper
1/4 teaspoon salt (optional)

Preparation: 17 minutes (includes soaking time)

1. Prepare chia dressing by soaking chia seeds in 3 tablespoons of water for 15 minutes. Transfer to a blender with 1/4 cup water and maple syrup. Blend until smooth (2 minutes).

2. While the seeds are soaking, remove squash skin with a vegetable peeler. Slice in half and remove seeds with a spoon and discard. Slice the squash into long pieces, about 1/4-inch thick. Slice crosswise into 1 1/2-inch pieces (7 minutes).

3. Cut green beans on the diagonal, about 1 1/2 inches long. Alternatively, you can snap them (3 minutes).

4. Dice red pepper.

Method:

1. Prepare couscous.

2. Place squash into a large sauté pan or frying pan with a lid along with 1/4 cup water. Arrange in one layer if possible. Cook on medium heat for 5 to 7 minutes until squash can be pierced with a fork. Remove lid and continue to cook until all the water has evaporated.

3. At the same time, in a separate pan with a lid, add 1/4 cup water. Cover and steam green beans until they have deepened in color and softened (5 to 7 minutes).

4. Combine the beans with the squash. Stir in red pepper and continue cooking 2 minutes.

5. Sprinkle with 1/2 teaspoon rubbed sage, 1/2 teaspoon dried tarragon leaves, 1/2 teaspoon poultry seasoning, and salt if using.

6. Toss vegetables with couscous, remaining tarragon, sage, and maple syrup mixture. Remove from heat and serve.

Nutritional Data: 1 Cup

Calories: 260, .55g Fat, 7.34g Protein, 56.87g Carbohydrates, Cholesterol: 0, Saturated Fat: .09g, Total Fiber: 5.46g

Bulgar Wheat With Broiled And Sautéd Vegetables

This is a delicious way to get both grains and colorful vegetables into your diet. Serve it as is or on a bed of pureed cauliflower. The ingredient list may seem daunting, but all those fresh veggies and spices are what makes this dish so yummy. Just follow the steps and you'll have a new favorite in no time!

Time: 50 minutes to 1 hour
Yield: 5 cups

Ingredients:

Step 1:

1 cup diced onion
1 cinnamon stick
1 bay leaf
6 cardamom pods

Step 2: Broiled Vegetables

1 cup small tomato wedges
1 cup sliced yellow squash (1/4-inch slices)
1 cup sliced zucchini (1/4-inch slices)

Step 3:

1/3 cup diced green bell pepper
1/3 cup diced diced red bell pepper
1 tablespoon crushed and minced garlic
1 tablespoon minced ginger

Step 4:

2 teaspoons cumin
1/8 teaspoon black pepper
1/2 teaspoon salt (optional)
1 cup Mirepoix Vegetable Stock (page 199) or water

Steps 5 and 6:

1 cup bulgar wheat

Step 7:

1/3 cup toasted almonds

Step 8:

2 to 3 tablespoons chopped fresh mint

Preparation: 12 to 15 minutes

1. Wash and cut vegetables as directed. Chop mint.

2. Arrange tomatoes and squash on a foil-lined cookie sheet or a warming rack placed on a cookie sheet.

Method: about 30 minutes

1. In a large sauté pan or saucepan with a lid, place bay leaf, cardamom pods, cinnamon stick, and diced onions. Cover and sauté on medium heat, stirring frequently until translucent (about 7 minutes).

2. While onions are sautéing, transfer cookie sheet with tomatoes and squashes to the top rack of an oven. Turn broiler on low if you have that option. Broil 4 to 10 minutes or until barely browned. Turn over and cook on the other side. Don't allow the vegetables to over-cook. Broil just long enough to make them tender, not crisp. Remove from oven and allow to cool. When cool enough to handle, cut squash and zucchini slices into 4 quarters.

3. When the onions are translucent, stir in peppers, ginger, and garlic. Cook for another 2 or 3 minutes until peppers are softened but still slightly crunchy. Add a little water a tablespoon at a time if necessary to prevent scorching.

4. Stir in cumin, black pepper. and salt if using. Add vegetable stock or water. Bring to a boil (about 2 minutes).

5. Stir in bulgar wheat, making sure all of it becomes wet.

6. Reduce heat and simmer, covered, for 15 minutes.

7. While the wheat is steeping, roast slivered almonds in a small frying pan on medium heat with no oil. Turn constantly with a spatula until the almonds are a light

brown (4 to 5 minutes). Don't worry if they don't brown evenly. When they are ready, remove from heat and transfer to a cool dish.

8. After the wheat has been steeping for 15 minutes, test for doneness. It should be a little chewy but not hard. If it isn't ready, remove from heat and fluff with a fork. Cover and allow to rest for 5 minutes. Toss with broiled vegetables, mint, and almonds. Serve hot.

Nutritional Data: 1 Cup

Calories: 186, 4.08g Fat, 7.01g Protein, 33.74g Carbohydrates, Cholesterol: 0, Saturated Fat: .47g, Total Fiber: 9.32g

Saffron Brown Rice And Summer Vegetables

Saffron adds an excitement to rice, infusing it with both a pleasing flavor and a decorative yellow hue. In addition, saffron appears to be one of those spices that are protective against Alzheimer's disease. Add summer vegetables, crisp snow peas, and a little bite of green olives and you have a party on your palate!

This recipe stands alone as a main course or can be used as a stuffing for other vegetables like stuffed bell peppers, Swiss chard, or cabbage rolls. Because the stock or water is boiled 5 minutes before the rice is added, I've increased the liquid an extra 1/4 cup to allow for evaporation.

Time: 45 to 50 minutes
Yield: 6 cups

Ingredients:

1 cup brown basmati rice
1 1/2 cups Mirepoix Vegetable Stock (page 199) or water
1/4 teaspoon saffron
1/2 cup diced onion
1/4 cup diced green bell pepper
3/4 cup diced carrot
1 1/2 cups yellow squash that has been cut into 3/4-inch irregular pieces
1/4 cup quartered or sliced green olives, with or without pimentos, plus 2 tablespoons of the olive brine*
1/2 cup snow peas, strings removed
1/3 cup roasted cashews
1/4 to 1/2 teaspoon salt (optional)

Preparation: 10 minutes

1. Wash rice and drain.

2. Wash vegetables. Peel and cut onion, peel and dice carrot, dice green pepper, cut up yellow squash, quarter or slice olives.

Method: 35 to 40 minutes

1. Bring 1 1/2 cups stock or water to a boil (about 5 minutes).

2. Add saffron and continue to boil on medium heat for 5 minutes.

3. Add rice and bring back to a low boil. Lower temperature and simmer for 25 to 30 minutes. *While the rice is cooking do the next steps.*

4. After the rice has been steeping 15 minutes, transfer bell pepper, onion, and carrot to a large sauté pan or frying pan with a lid. Sauté 5 to 7 minutes, stirring often. Stir in 1/8 cup water, add remaining veggies and continue cooking another 3 to 5 minutes.

5. Roast cashews on low heat in a dry fry pan on until brown and fragrant, turning almost constantly (3 to 4 minutes).

6. When the rice is soft and all the water has been absorbed, remove from heat. Fluff with a fork, then cover, letting it stand for 5 minutes.

7. Fold saffron rice mixture into the vegetable mixture, turning gently to coat. Fold in olives and the olive brine. Toss with roasted cashews and salt, if using.

*Brine is the salty liquid created in the canning process and in which the olives are preserved.

Nutritional Data: 1 Cup
Calories: 182, 4.93g Fat, 4.97g Protein, 32.67g Carbohydrates, Cholesterol: 0, Saturated Fat: .07g, Total Fiber: 3.01g

Sides

Dutch Stamppot

My friend Dave returned from Europe raving about a dish he had tried in the Netherlands called Dutch Stamppot, which literally means "stamped pot." I played around with the ingredients he described to me and this is my interpretation of this national dish. It is so delicious I could eat it every day! You can serve it as a side dish or as the main course. I often whip up a batch of this to eat by itself when I am craving some comfort food that is filling and nutritious.

This may seem like you are juggling a lot of steps at one time, and you are. This is really more easily managed than it may seem. Take it one step at a time, everything you need is right there within reach.

Time: 25 minutes

Yield: 6 cups

Ingredients:

1 1/4 cups finely diced sweet yellow or white onion (about 6 ounces)

2 cloves garlic, crushed and minced

2 (10 ounce) diced Yukon Gold potatoes (3 3/4 cups)

2 (5 ounce) carrots (1 1/2 cups)

1/4 teaspoon salt (optional)

2 to 3 tablespoons Tofu Sour Cream (page 267) or Cashew Cream Cheese (page 262)

1 bunch kale, cut into 1- to 2-inch pieces

Preparation: 10 minutes

1. Prepare vegetables. Peel onion and carrots, cut into 1/8-inch dice. Cut potatoes into 1/4-inch dice. Peel and mince garlic and cut kale into 1- to 2-inch pieces.

Method: 15 to 17 minutes

1. Add the potatoes and carrots to a medium saucepan with an inch of water. Bring to a boil. Reduce heat and simmer, covered, for 10 to 12 minutes or until vegetables can easily be pierced with a fork.

2. While the potatoes and carrots are simmering, transfer onions to a large saucepan or flat-bottomed skillet* with a lid. Cover onions and sauté until translucent, 3 to 5 minutes, stirring frequently. Add garlic and stir another minute. If the sides of the pan begin to brown, reduce temperature and add a small amount of water (a tablespoon at a time) to release the caramelization.

3. When the potatoes and carrots are fork tender, drain and transfer to pan with onions. Add Tofu Sour Cream or

Cashew Cream Cheese, salt and pepper. With a potato masher,** mash all ingredients together until mashed but not too creamy. You still want to have a slightly chunky consistency. Transfer back into the saucepan you used to cook the potato mixture.

4. Wash out your flat-bottomed skillet and return to burner. Rinse kale and shake it out a little over the sink. There should be droplets of water still on it. This is all the water you'll need to wilt the kale without losing its flavor and nutrition into excess water. Transfer to skillet, cover and cook on medium-high until kale is wilted and has darkened in color (about 3 minutes). Using a pair of tongs or a large spoon, periodically turn the kale so it wilts evenly and the bottom doesn't burn. Fold mashed potato mixture into kale with a large wooden spoon. Serve hot.

This is very good with sliced fresh ripe organic tomatoes as a side.

*A flat-bottomed skillet will make mashing the potatoes easier.

**It is difficult to mash potatoes with the skins still attached, aka "smashed potatoes," if you are using a potato masher that has a grid type surface. It is better to use a potato masher that resembles a snake or a a series of "S" curves, making it less likely to become clogged. This also allows you to make your potatoes as creamy or as chunky as you like as opposed to the grid-style masher, which tends to create a creamier texture.

Nutritional Data: 1 Cup
Calories: 118, 0.5g Fat, 3.82g Protein, 26.71g Carbohydrates, Cholesterol: 0, Saturated Fat: .08g, Total Fiber: 5.08g

Creamy Scalloped Potatoes
With Mushrooms And Caramelized Onions

*This is one of the favorite comfort foods of my childhood.
and is the one dish my mother prepared that I eagerly
anticipated, my mouth watering at the very thought of it. With
layers of onions and potatoes in a rich creamy sauce, she also
added thick layers of ham. Of course, since ham is no longer
on the menu, I've substituted mushrooms for the meaty texture.
This version is a little different than my mother's but it is just
as good.*

Time: 1 hour 20 minutes
Yield: 1 8 x 8 pan/Serves 6

Ingredients:

3 1/2 to 4 cups sliced mushrooms (16 ounces)

5 cups thinly sliced Yukon Gold potatoes (about 1 1/2 pounds - You can substitute russet potatoes.)

2 1/2 cups thinly sliced onion for layering

1 1/2 cups sliced onion for caramelizing

3 cups Cashew Cream, plus 1/4 cup water (page 260)

2 to 3 teaspoons dried thyme (Adjust this seasoning to suit you. If you are not a fan of thyme try other herbs such as dried basil, dill or fresh sprigs of rosemary.)

1 teaspoon salt (optional)

pepper to taste (optional)

Preparation: 20 minutes

1. Prepare cashew cream; adjust recipe by using 1 cup soaked cashews, 1 tablespoon garbanzo bean miso, 1 teaspoon salt (optional) and 1 1/4 cups water

2. Clean and slice mushrooms; transfer to a sauté pan with a lid. Cover and cook on medium-low heat until mushrooms release their juices. It is important to allow the mushrooms to expel their water. Otherwise it will be released in the casserole and create a soupier dish than intended. Remove lid and continue to cook on medium-high until the liquid evaporates. Set aside.

3. While the mushrooms are cooking, peel and slice the smaller onion into half rings; separate with your fingers. In a separate skillet with a lid, sauté onion until caramelized a golden brown. Add a little water as you need it to prevent sticking. Keep a measuring cup with 1/2 cup of water near your cooking area for this purpose.

4. Slice potatoes and submerge in a large bowl of cold water to remove starch and prevent discoloration. Set aside.

5. Peel and slice larger onion into thin half-rings. Separate with your fingers; set aside.

Method: about 1 hour

1. Evenly spread 1/2 cup of the cashew cream onto the bottom of an 8-inch baking dish.

2. Drain the potatoes and place a single layer on the bottom of a casserole dish. Loosely arrange a layer of mushrooms on top. Then arrange a layer of onion slices.

3. Sprinkle with a little thyme and a pinch of salt (if using).

4. Pour 1/2 cup cashew cream over the 3 layers.

5. Repeat layers until all the ingredients have been used. The final layer should be potatoes. Sprinkle with thyme, pepper and salt (optional).

6. Finally, top with grilled onions. Cover tightly with a lid or aluminum foil and place casserole on a cookie sheet into a preheated oven. Bake for 45 minutes to an hour or until a fork or bamboo skewer slides easily through all layers.

Nutritional Data: 1 Serving

Calories: 265, 9.12g Fat, 9.17g Protein, 38.69g Carbohydrates, Cholesterol: 0, Saturated Fat: 1.85g, Total Fiber: 6.52g

Caramelized Cabbage And Onions With Apples And Golden Raisins

Caramelizing a vegetable is traditionally achieved by sautéing it in a little oil until it is soft and golden brown. Since the addition of oil is unhealthy and unnecessary, use a little water in small increments instead to prevent burning. Thus the same sweet result is achieved without damage to our precious endothelial cells.

Even if your family generally doesn't like cabbage you may discover they really love this dish. The sweetness of the onions and cabbage is intensified by the apples and raisins. A splash of sweet marsala wine unites the flavors, creating a dish that is something special.

Time: about 30 minutes
Yield: 4 cups

Ingredients:

6 cups thinly sliced cabbage
3 cups sliced onion
1/4 cup golden raisins
1 cup water, including raisin water
1 1/4 cups diced apple
1 tablespoon minced ginger
1/4 cup sweet marsala wine
1/4 teaspoon salt (optional)

Preparation: 5 to 6 minutes

1. Barely cover raisins with boiling water, or place in a small microwave-safe bowl, cover with water and microwave on high for 30 seconds. Set aside.

2. Wash cabbage and cut into quarters. Remove stem by cutting along the contour. Slice across cabbage to make thin strips. Separate with your fingers. Rinse.

3. Remove onion skin and cut in half, then across into half-rings. Separate with your fingers.

4. Peel and mince ginger; wash and dice apple.

Method: about 20 minutes

1. In a large sauté pan with a lid, place cabbage strips with a little water still clinging to them. Sauté, uncovered, on medium heat until the cabbage begins to wilt and caramelization begins to form in the pan juices (about 10 minutes). Add a little water and stir, pulling the caramelization onto the cabbage until it is as soft and as caramelized as you like (10 to 20 minutes). You will need to keep an eye on it, once the cabbage begins to caramelize it can burn very easily. Keep a cup of water by the stove stirring in only a tablespoon or two at a time as

needed to prevent burning and to incorporate the caramelization of the pan juices into the cabbage. The same technique is used with the onion.

2. This recipe works better if the cabbage and onions are sautéd at the same time, but in different pans. This prevents the crowding of the vegetables and encourages caramelization rather than steaming, which is what happens under crowded conditions. Transfer the onion strips to a separate pan with a lid. Cover and sauté on medium-high heat until the onion and its juices begin to slightly brown. Add a tablespoon of water and continue cooking in this way until the onion is soft and has a nice caramel color. Add ginger and apple and continue to sauté until the apple is semi-soft and the mixture is fragrant with ginger.

3. When the cabbage is the cooked the way you like it, fold into the onion mixture until all ingredients are combined.

4. Fold in marsala. Serve hot or at room temperature.

Nutritional Data: 1 Cup

Calories: 131, .25g Fat, 2.86g Protein, 30.67g Carbohydrates, Cholesterol: 0, Saturated Fat: .13g, Total Fiber: 5.62g

Beets Steeped In Pineapple Juice And Ginger

Beets are one of the most versatile vegetables to be found. Like golden squashes, dark greens, sweet potatoes, and sweet corn, they are beautiful arranged on a plate with other colorful vegetables, and they are naturally sweet and delicious. Beets come in many varieties from dark ruby red to striped to golden. I never met a beet I didn't adore.

This is an easy way to cook beets and the sauce is fantastic. The ginger gives it just the right amount of kick. You have to pay attention to them, especially towards the end of the cooking process, as they are easily burned once the sauce has caramelized.

Time: 30 to 35 minutes
Yield: 2 cups

Ingredients:

3 medium to large beets, peeled and cut to desired size and shape according to intended use
2 tablespoons freshly minced ginger
2 (6 ounce) cans unsweetened pineapple juice
2 tablespoons balsamic vinegar
1 teaspoon fresh lemon juice

Preparation: 10 minutes

1. Prepare vegetables.

Method: 20 to 25 minutes

1. In a 12- to 14-inch sauté pan or frying pan with a lid, arrange beets in single overlapping layers until you've used them all. Sprinkle ginger over the top and add pineapple juice.

2. Cover and cook on medium-high heat until the beets can be easily pierced with a fork, most of the pineapple juice has evaporated and what is left is a thick caramelized syrup in the bottom of the pan. Carefully stir in lemon juice and balsamic vinegar. They can burn very easily at this point so work quickly while taking care that you don't break up the tender beets.

3. Fold gently to coat with remaining syrup.

4. Remove from heat and transfer to a serving dish. Serve hot or at room temperature. These are also quite good chilled.

Nutritional Data: 1/2 Cup
Calories: 64, .12g Fat, 1.12g Protein, 15.05g Carbohydrates, Cholesterol: 0, Saturated Fat: .02g, Total Fiber: 1.56g

Barbecued Cauliflower Florets

Cauliflower is one of those vegetables that can become almost anything. You can make sauces from it, faux mashed potatoes, steam, bake, broil, stir fry — seemingly endless variations. This method is one of my favorites and takes only minutes to prepare. Cauliflower prepared this way will surprise and delight guests.

Don't expect it to become crunchy. It is still cauliflower and its flesh will be soft to the bite. The flavor, however, is fantastic!

Time: about 1 hour

Yield: 5 cups

Ingredients:

1 whole large cauliflower (1 1/2 to 2 pounds)
1 1/2 cups Homemade Barbecue Sauce (page 249)

Preparations: 3 minutes

1. Slice off stem of cauliflower. Following the contours of the stem, remove branches. Reserve stem for another purpose or for making stock.

2. Rinse florets under cold running water to remove any grit, dirt or bugs you might find.

Method: 45 to 50 minutes

1. Transfer to a large sauté pan or a skillet with a lid. Add 1/4 cup water and steam on medium heat until the cauliflower has softened but is not cooked completely through (5 to 7 minutes). This will make roasting it much quicker.

2. Coat each floret with barbecue sauce (5 to 7 minutes). The easiest way to do this is to put the barbecue sauce in a bowl and dunk each piece into the sauce. Shake loose excess and lay on a lined cookie sheet or a cookie sheet with a rack. (I often use metal cooling racks for this.)

3. Place cookie sheet or rack under a broiler on low heat until one side is just barely browned, then turn and repeat on the other side.

4. Alternatively, place florets on a silpat or parchment paper lined cookie sheet on the middle rack of an oven preheated to 400°F. Roast for 30 minutes or until browned.

Note: A whole barbecued cauliflower makes a lovely presentation, though it doesn't always cook all the way through as intended. You can have an equally beautiful presentation and a more reliable result by slicing the cauliflower in half and then steaming it before applying the sauce. (You will have to brush it on rather than dunk it.) Roast at 400°F, cut side down, until brown.

Nutritional Data: 1 Cup

Calories: 332, .45g Fat, 4.61g Protein, 30.03g Carbohydrates, Cholesterol: 0, Saturated Fat: .22g, Total Fiber: 5.28g

Lunch Or Anytime

Spicy Black Bean Stuffed Sweet Potatoes With Lemon-Cilantro Salsa

Sometimes a quick meal is just the ticket. If you have some left-over black beans or have some tucked away in the freezer, this is a fast, filling and delicious meal that you may find yourself preparing often. Perfect for a packed lunch or for a healthy dinner without the fuss, this nutritional powerhouse is a no-brainer!

Time: 15 minutes
Yield: 1 stuffed potato

Ingredients:

1 whole Microwaved Sweet Potato (page 235)
1/2 to 3/4 cup Spicy Black Beans (page 232)
1/2 cup Lemon-Cilantro Salsa (page 258)
1 tablespoon Tofu Sour Cream, optional (page 267)
Sliced green onions for garnish

Preparation and Method: about 15 minutes

1. Heat sweet potato and black beans in microwave.

2. Prepare salsa.

3. Cut sweet potato down the middle lengthwise without cutting through bottom skin. With your thumbs on one end and your forefingers on the other, squeeze the ends towards the middle of the potato until the cut has opened and a pocket has formed in its middle.

4. Fill the pocket with Spicy Black Beans.

5. Top with a dollop of vegan sour cream and a few slices of green onion.

6. Serve with Lemon Cilantro Salsa

Nutritional Data: 1 potato

Calories: 332, 1.54g Fat, 15g Protein, 68.63g Carbohydrates, Cholesterol: 0, Saturated Fat: .03g, Total Fiber: 19.47g

Lentil And Cauliflower Sloppy Joes

This recipe is an example of how you can make several meals from one recipe. We made the barbecue sauce in a previous recipe. Then we prepared a recipe for barbecued Cauliflower Florets. Now, we'll take the leftover cauliflower and barbecue sauce and make something new. Kids will love these Sloppy Joes. They are sweet and savory, have loads of protein and hold up well in a bun. These are Sloppy Joes children can handle without getting sauce all over themselves, which will make Mom happy. They can be served with sweet or white potato oven-fries and a green salad or a cooked green vegetable for a fully balanced meal.

Time: 15 minutes
Yield: 3 cups

Ingredients:

1 1/2 cups Homemade Barbecue Sauce (page 249)
3/4 cup Steeped Dried Lentils, green or brown (page 230)
1/2 cup raw cauliflower,* finely grated or chopped into small pieces, about the size of rice (optional).

Method: 10 to 15 minutes

1. Add cauliflower and lentils to a medium sauté pan and cook until cauliflower is soft. Add a little water if needed.

2. Add barbecue sauce and heat through.

3. Toast burger bun. Top with barbecue mixture. Devour!

*Cauliflower is included in this recipe to demonstrate what you can do with leftover cauliflower pieces, like the edible stem. You can omit it if you like or add more than 1/2 cup. It isn't critical to the recipe.

Nutritional Data: 1 Cup (not counting bun)

Calories: 221; .69g Fat, 7.34g Protein, 49.71g Carbohydrates, Cholesterol: 0, Saturated Fat: .28g, Total Fiber: 9.33g

Dagwood Sandwich

This is my favorite sandwich of all time. I call it a Dagwood sandwich because it is tall and bulky and can be a little messy to eat. You can control the mess by slicing your veggies very thin. As I mentioned earlier, this is my "go to" meal for when I don't feel like cooking but want to enjoy something delicious and nutritious.

The soft sweet cooked vegetables pair beautifully with slightly crisped roasted yellow squash and crunchy cucumber. Topped with Mediterranean Hummus or Baba Ghanoush, the combination is out of this world! This recipe presupposes you have prepared these ingredients beforehand and have them in your fridge. Keeping them handy allows you to add nutrients, flavor, and color to whatever dish you may be creating, be it a sandwich, soup, stew, or salad. You'll find you never run out of demand for these staples. (I used to add fermented veggies to this sandwich but in light of recent health concerns regarding fermented products, I've omitted them.)

Time: 10 minutes
Yield: 1 sandwich

Ingredients:

3 slices Marinated Beets (page 247) or Beets Steeped In Pineapple Juice And Ginger (page 342)
3 slices cooked sweet potato (pages 234-235)
3 slices roasted yellow squash or zucchini
3 slices organic cucumber
2 to 3 tablespoons Mediterranean Hummus spread (page 287), Baba Ghanoush (page 290), or Cashew Cream Cheese (page 262)
1 whole grain hamburger bun or 2 slices whole grain bread

Preparation: 5 to 8 minutes

1. Prepare vegetables.

2. Toast bun or bread in a wide-slot toaster. (optional)

Method: 2 minutes

1. On each piece of bread, spread hummus, baba ghanoush or cashew cream cheese.

2. On the bottom slice, arrange slices of marinated beets, then slices of cooked sweet potato, then slices of yellow squash or zucchini and, finally, cucumber.

3. Cap the sandwich with the top piece of bread. Cut in half to make it easier to eat, especially if you using sliced bread rather than a bun.

4. Serve with a side of steamed greens, corn on the cob, Italian Orzo or any number of veggie accompaniments.

Nutritional Data: 1 Sandwich

Calories: 279, 4.13g Fat, 12.34g Protein, 49.52g Carbohydrates, Cholesterol: 0, Saturated Fat: .85g, Total Fiber: 9.85g

Vegan Chicken Pita Pocket

If you or your guests are craving the taste and texture of chicken but don't want to stray from your commitment to a plant-based lifestyle, this dish might save the day. Pita pockets stuffed with vegan chicken-free strips from Beyond Meat will give your diners something that will taste like the real thing. This recipe is delicious served with any number of plant-based accompaniments.

Time: about 10 minutes
Yield: 2 (6-inch) pita pockets

Ingredients:

1 (6-inch) pita bread
4 tablespoons Cashew Cream Cheese (page 262)
1 medium Roasted Red Pepper (page 219)

6 apple slices (about 1/4 medium apple, cut thin)
8 Beyond Meat vegan chicken-free strips
5 artichoke hearts (jarred or canned)
4 to 6 romaine leaves, cut into 1/4-inch strips (about 2 cups)

Preparation: 5 minutes

1. Slice apple; drain and slice artichoke hearts in half. Halve roasted red pepper.

2. Wash romaine lettuce and shake or spin dry; cut across the leaves to make thin strips.

3. Divide the ingredients so you have equal amounts for each pita half.

Method: about 5 minutes

1. Heat chicken-free strips in microwave for 40 seconds or heat on stovetop for 2 to 3 minutes.

2. Heat pita in microwave for 15 seconds. Remove and slice in half across the bread making 2 equal half circles. Carefully open the pita along the cut side, taking care not to tear it.

3. Spread bottom layer with 2 tablespoons of Cashew Cream Cheese.

4. Layer inside of pita with lettuce strips, apple slices, chicken-free strips, artichoke halves, roasted pepper, and finally romaine lettuce.

Nutritional Data: 1 Pita Pocket
Calories: 313, 11.02g Fat, 19.84g Protein, 36.92g Carbohydrates, Cholesterol: 0, Saturated Fat: 1.48g, Total Fiber: 6.7g

Balsamic Portobello Wrap
With Roasted Red Peppers

Portobello wraps offer a meaty texture and loads of flavor. You can't go wrong with this marriage of roasted red bell peppers and vegan cream cheese, chewy kale and the sweetness of fresh grapes. If you have roasted peppers in your freezer and vegan cheese on hand, this dish comes together quickly. Using store-bought burrito wraps will also save time.

Time: 8 to 10 minutes
Yield: 2 wraps

Ingredients:

1 recipe Sautéed Balsamic Portobello Mushrooms (page 240)
1 Roasted Red Pepper (page 219)

4 to 6 romaine leaves, cut into 1/4-inch strips (2 cups)
4 tablespoons Cashew Cream Cheese (page 262)
13 grapes
2 extra-large flour tortillas

Preparation: 3 minutes

1. Wash romaine and spin or shake dry, then pat with a paper towel to remove any remaining moisture. Cut across the leaves to make thin strips.

2. Wash grapes and slice lengthwise, from stem to bottom.

3. Have all ingredients readily available before preparing wrap.

Method: 5 to 7 minutes

1. Heat tortillas in microwave for 5 seconds. Or in a flat skillet on medium heat, cook the wrap for a few seconds on each side until heated through. Alternatively, don't heat them at all.

2. In the middle of the wrap, about 2 inches from each side and 3 or 4 inches across, depending on the size of the wrap, layer cream cheese, romaine, red peppers, mushrooms, and grapes, in that order.

3. Fold in the sides to partially cover the ingredients. Then roll the side closest to you over the filling. Continue to roll, tucking in both the filling and the sides as you go, until the wrap is a solid tube.

4. Slice on the diagonal across the middle of the wrap.

Nutritional Data: 1 Wrap

Calories: 376, 11.39g Fat, 12.39g Protein,54.31g Carbohydrates, Cholesterol: 0, Saturated Fat: 2.14g, Total Fiber: 3.66g

Spicy Black Bean Burrito With Lime-Cilantro Rice And Mango-Avocado Salsa

A great next-day use for Spicy Black Beans is a lunch burrito that is sure to please. Layer with Mango-Avocado Salsa, Lime-Cilantro Brown Rice and crispy lettuce leaves for a combination of flavors that the fussiest eater will enjoy. You can even add some vegan cheddar for those who think they can't live without cheese on their wrap. Multiply this recipe by as many people as you are serving.

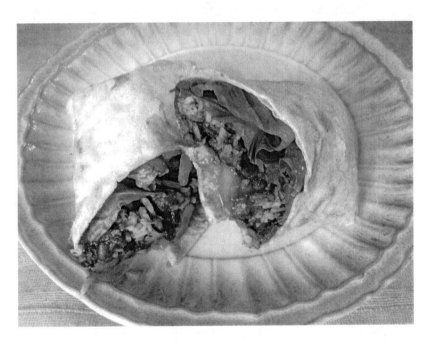

Time: 10 minutes
Yield: 1 burrito

Ingredients:

1 extra-large flour tortilla
1 cup romaine lettuce (cut across to make 1/4-inch ribbons)
1/3 cup Spicy Black Beans (page 232)
1/3 cup Mango-Avocado Salsa (page 256)
1/3 cup Lime-Cilantro Brown Rice (page 207)

Preparation: 5 minutes

1. Heat burrito wrap in microwave for 5 seconds, or in a flat skillet on medium heat cook the wrap for a few seconds on each side until heated through. Alternatively, don't heat it at all.

2. In a microwave or in separate small saucepans, heat the rice and the black beans.

Method: 5 minutes

1. Place wrap on a plate. In the center, arrange the lettuce in a mound.

2. With a slotted spoon, place a serving of black beans, rice, and salsa in equal portions atop the lettuce. The amount should be adequate to the size of the wrap you are using. (about 1/3 cup for a large burrito)

3. Fold the bottom and top sides of the wrap towards the center, covering up a portion of the rice, beans and salsa.

4. Then fold over the side of the wrap closest to you (again towards the center), tucking in the filling as you roll the wrap to the other side to make a long, enclosed tube.

5. Cut across the center and serve with fold sides down.

Nutritional Data: 1 Burrito

Calories: 413, 6.29g Fat, 14.14g Protein, 77.10g Carbohydrates, Cholesterol: 0, Saturated Fat: .89g, Total Fiber: 9.71g

Dessert

We are not a big fans of desserts in our household. Occasionally Rich and I will indulge when we are out dining with friends, but this is rarely something we do at home. Instead we've learned to enjoy fresh fruit when we are craving something sweet, or hot chocolate made with almond milk when the weather is especially cold. I have intentionally not put much effort into making vegan desserts as, more often than not, they are permeated with coconut oil or some other form of saturated or processed fat. Remember, just because something is vegan doesn't mean it is healthy. French fries and soda are technically vegan and they are seriously unhealthy foods, if they can be called foods at all. Desserts loaded with sugar, buttery icing (even if it is vegan butter) and other fats will pack on the pounds just as quickly as their animal-based counterparts.

The following recipes are ones that I make for guests when something sweet is called for and I don't want to send my friends into diabetic comas with heavy desserts. These are all fruit-based with just enough sugar and spice to make them special.

Ginger Poached Pears With Brandy

This dish is very easy and quick to prepare, yet is as delicious as it is elegant. Ginger gives it just the right amount of bite to offset the sweetness of the honey. It is always a hit at any dinner, special or simple. Having a few extra pears on hand can save the day when you have unexpected dinner guests.

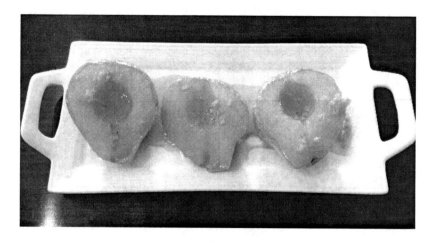

Time: 15 minutes

Yield: 4 pear halves

Ingredients:

2 ripe Bartlett pears

1/4 cup raw honey (You can substitute 2 tablespoons organic granulated sugar or brown sugar if you prefer.*)

2 tablespoons freshly minced ginger

1 teaspoon freshly squeezed lemon juice

3/4 cup filtered water

1 to 2 tablespoons raspberry-balsamic vinegar, brandy, coffee or chocolate liqueur, or whatever you prefer (optional)

Preparation: 5 minutes

1. Wash pears and cut in half lengthwise from stem to the rough fibrous cavity at its bottom.

2. With a melon baller, cut out seeds to form a smooth, round cavity where the seeds were.

Method: 10 minutes

1. Place pears, cut side down, in a 12-inch flat-bottomed skillet with a lid. Add ginger, brown sugar or honey, and water. Cover and bring to a boil. Boil until water becomes syrupy and pears can be easily pierced with a fork. If the mixture threatens to become too dry before the pears are fully cooked, add a little more water.

2. Transfer pears, cut side up, to a serving dish or individual dessert plates. Drizzle with the ginger and pan syrup mixture.

3. Fill pear cavity with flavored vinegar, brandy or liqueur of choice. Serve.

*Date sugar doesn't work well in this recipe. It is preferable to sugar in many instances, since it is a whole food, but it doesn't dissolve well and will give this type a dish a grainy texture.

Nutritional Data: 1/2 Pear

Calories: 156, 0.1g Fat, 0.7g Protein, 41.47g Carbohydrates, Cholesterol: 0, Saturated Fat: .02g, Total Fiber: 4.52g

Pan Seared Or Roasted
Cinnamon-Pineapple Rings

This yummy dessert is so easy you'll wonder why you never thought of it before. Serve it on a plate as a side, arrange on a small plate cut into wedges, or with two or three rings per person. The pan-searing method is quickest but the roasted method has a little better flavor in my opinion. Whatever way you choose to prepare it, it's just the right amount of sweet at the end of a meal without the heaviness of a rich dessert.

Time: 12 to 25 minutes (depending on method)
Yield: About 10 Pineapple Rings

Ingredients:

1 fresh ripe medium-size pineapple cut into rings (You can substitute unsweetened canned pineapple.)
1/4 teaspoon cinnamon
1 tablespoon light brown sugar

Preparation: 5 minutes

1. Preheat oven to 400°F. (roasted method only)

2. Remove top and bottom of the pineapple with a sharp knife and discard. Turn pineapple, cut side down, and slice off skins from top to bottom in one cut. Repeat, rotating until all the skin is removed. Shave off corners that still contain some of the eyes.

3. Lay the pineapple on its side and cut across into 1/4-inch discs.

4. Cut out the center core of each pineapple ring with a knife, following the contour of the core, or punch it out with a small round cookie cutter. (You can find cookie cutter sets on-line or at specialty baking stores. The one I use for this is 1 1/2 inches in diameter.)

5. In a small bowl combine the brown sugar and the cinnamon.

Pan Seared Method: 7 to 8 minutes

1. Place pineapple rings in a large non-stick skillet. Sprinkle rings with cinnamon/sugar mixture pinched between your fingers.

2. Turn and sprinkle the other side.

3. Cover and cook on medium-high heat for 5 minutes. Turn, replace lid, and cook on other side for 2 minutes or until the sugars begin to caramelize.

4. Remove from heat. Serve.

Roast Method: 20 minutes

1. Arrange pineapple rings on a silpat or parchment paper covered cookie sheet. Place in preheated oven; cook for 5 minutes. Remove from oven and turn rings over.

2. Sprinkle with cinnamon/sugar mixture and return to oven to cook for another 5 minutes.

3. Remove from oven; turn rings over and sprinkle lightly with cinnamon/sugar mixture.

4. Return to oven and cook another 10 minutes or until pineapple is beginning to caramelize and become slightly brown. Serve warm.

Nutritional Data: 2 Rings

Calories: 97, .11g Fat, .98g Protein, 25.62g Carbohydrates, Cholesterol: 0, Saturated Fat: .02g, Total Fiber: 2.6g

Baked Or Microwaved Apples

The smell of apples baking has the ability to transport us to simpler times, filling our kitchens with aromas of cinnamon and brown sugar, reminiscent of Thanksgiving and Christmas holidays. There's no need to wait; you can enjoy this treat any day of the year. In the microwave it takes less than 10 minutes from start to finish. In the oven, your guests will have to wait a little longer but they will be tantalized by the delicious fragrances wafting from the kitchen as they enjoy the main course.

Time: 10 to 30 minutes
Yield: 1 apple/2 servings

Ingredients:

1 firm baking apple (such as Granny Smith or Ambrosia)
2 teaspoons raisins
2 teaspoons chopped walnuts or pecans
1/4 cup maple syrup
1/8 teaspoon cinnamon
1/4 teaspoon nutmeg

Preparation: 5 minutes

1. Cut apple in half from stem to fibrous cavity on the bottom. With a melon baller or a teaspoon, remove the core. Pull off stem.

2. Fill each cavity with half the raisins, nuts, and maple syrup.

3. Sprinkle half the cinnamon and nutmeg over the tops of each apple half.

Microwave Method: 3 to 5 minutes

1. Place apple haves, cut side up, in a microwave-safe dish. Cook on high for 3 minutes. Test with a fork and cook longer if needed.

2. Transfer to a serving plate and pour pan juices over the apple halves. Serve hot.

Baking Method: 20 to 30 minutes, plus time to preheat oven

1. Preheat oven to 400°F

2. Transfer apple halves to an oven-safe dish with a lid, or cover tightly with aluminum foil.

3. Place dish in center rack of the oven and bake for 20 minutes. Test with a fork for doneness. If necessary, cook a few minutes longer until the apple can be easily pierced with a fork.

4. Transfer to a serving plate and pour pan juices over the apple halves. Serve hot.

Note: While microwaving is faster, the oven method provides a richer flavor and better preserves the integrity of the apple. The peel may break and separate from the flesh. That's normal and should be expected.

Nutritional Data: 1/2 Apple

Calories: 174, 1.7g Fat, .74g Protein, 41.94g Carbohydrates, Cholesterol: 0, Saturated Fat: .25g, Total Fiber: 2.6g

BIBLIOGRAPHY

Chapter One

1. Campbell, T. Colin, Ph.D., Campbell, Thomas M. II, "The China Study: The Most Comprehensive Study of Nutrition Ever Conducted and the Startling Implications for Diet, Weight Loss and Long-term Health," Published by BenBells Books, Inc, 2006
   1. pp. 37- 67
   2. pp. 61- 62
   3. p. 7
   4. p. 36

Chapter Two

1. Ceres C. Romaldini, Hugo Issler, Ary L. Cardoso, Jayme Diament, Neusa Forti, "Risk factors for atherosclerosis in children and adolescents with family history of premature coronary artery disease,", Jornal de Pediatria - Vol. 80, N°2, 2004

2. Smith, Jeffrey, "Doctors Warn: Avoid Genetically Modified Food," Institute for Responsible Technology: Dec 20, 2013 http://www.responsibletechnology.org/gmo-dangers/health-risks/articles-about-risks-by-jeffrey-smith/Doctors-Warn-Avoid-Genetically-Modified-Food-May-2009

3. Channa Jayasumana, Sarath Gunatilake, and Priyantha Senanayake,"Glyphosate, Hard Water and Nephrotoxic Metals: Are They the Culprits Behind the Epidemic of Chronic Kidney Disease of Unknown Etiology in Sri Lanka?" International Journal of Environmental. Research and Public Health 2014, 11

4. Samsel, Anthony, Seneff, Stephanie, "Glyphosate, pathways to modern diseases II: Celiac sprue and gluten intolerance," Interdisciplinary Toxicology. December 2013; 6(4): 159–184.

5. Chavkin, Sasah, "Sri Lanka bans Monsanto herbicide citing potential link to deadly kidney disease," The Center For Public Integrity, http://www.publicintegrity.org/ 2014/03/13/14418/sri-lanka-bans-monsanto-herbicide-citing-potential-link-deadly-kidney-disease, March 13, 2014

6. ColomboPage News Desk, Sri Lanka, "Sri Lanka lifts ban on sale of glyphosate," http://www.colombopage.com/ archive_14A/May13_1399920230CH.php, May 13, 2014

7. GM Watch, "Sri Lanka lifts ban on sale of glyphosate," http://www.gmwatch.org/index.php/news/archive/ 2014/15433-sri-lanka-lifts-ban-on-sale-of-glyphosate, May 13, 2014

8. Malone, Andrew, "The GM genocide: Thousands of Indian farmers are committing suicide after using genetically modified crops;" The Daily Mail, 2 November 2008, http:// www.dailymail.co.uk/news/article-1082559/The-GM-genocide-Thousands-Indian-farmers-committing-suicide-using-genetically-modified-crops.html

9. Union of Concerned Scientists, "About Us," www.National Headquarters, Brattle Square, Cambridge, MA 02138-3780. www.uscuas.org/about/

10. Union of Concerned Scientists, "Does UCS Have A Position On GE?" http://www.ucsusa.org/food_and_agriculture/our-failing-food-system/genetic-engineering/ November 7, 2012

11. Grieve', Carol, "Dr. Don Huber: GMOs and Glyphosate and Their Threat to Humanity," http://foodintegritynow.org/2014/04/08/dr-don-huber-gmos-glyphosate-threat-humanity/ April 8, 2014

12. Samsel, Anthony and Seneff, Stephanie, "Glyphosate, pathways to modern diseases II: Celiac sprue and gluten intolerance." 12 November 2013 http://www.ncbi.nlm.nih.gov/pmc/articles/PMC3945755/

13. Environmental Working Group: http://www.ewg.org/foodnews/, EWG's 2014 Shopper's Guide to Pesticides in Produce™ (April 2014)

14. Vogel RA, Corretti MC, Plotnick GD, "Effect of a single high-fat meal on endothelial function in healthy subjects," American Journal of Cardiology. 1997 Feb 1;79(3):350-4. http://www.ncbi.nlm.nih.gov/pubmed/9036757

15. Vogel RA, Corretti MC, Plotnick GD, "The postprandial effect of components of the Mediterranean diet on endothelial function," Journal of American College of Cardiology, 2000 Nov 1;36(5):1455-60, http://www.ncbi.nlm.nih.gov/pubmed/11079642

16. USDA, Agricultural Research Service, Basic Report: 04053, "Oil, olive, salad or cooking," National Nutrient Database for Standard Reference, Release 26 http:// ndb.nal.usda.gov

17. Esselstyn, Jr., Cauldwell, MD, "Prevent and Reverse Heart Disease, The Revolutionary, Scientifically Proven, Nutrition-based Cure," Published by the Penguin Group, 2007
    1. p. 115
    2. p. 19
    3. p. 15
    4. p. 90
    5. p. 22
    6. p. 91

18. Esselstyn Jr, Caldwell B, MD; Gendy, Gina, MD; Doyle, Jonathan, MCS; Golubic, Mladen, MD, PhD; Roizen, Michael F., MD, "A way to reverse CAD? Though current medical and surgical treatments manage coronary artery disease, they do little to prevent or stop it, nutritional intervention, as shown in our study and others, has halted and even reversed CAD." The Journal of family Practice | July 2014 | Vol 63, no 7

Chapter Three

1. Tuso, Philip J., MD; Ismail, Mohamed H., MD; Ha, Benjamin P, MD; Bartolotto, Carole, Ma, RD, Excerpt from abstract: "Nutritional Update for Physicians: Plant-Based Diets," Permanente Journal 2013 Spring;17(2): 61-66

2. Australian Dietary Guidelines; "Australian Dietary Guidelines — providing the scientific evidence for healthier Australian diets," (2013) (PDF 2MB) NHMRC Ref N55, http://www.eatforhealth.gov.au/guidelines

3. Gregor, Michael, MD; "Do Vegetarians Get Enough Protein? Nutritional quality indices show plant-based diets are the healthiest, but do vegetarians and vegans reach the recommended daily intake of protein?" NutritionFacts.org, Jun 6, 2014, Volume 19

Chapter Five

1. Gregor, Michael, MD; "Beans, Beans, They're Good For Your Heart: Legumes such as lentils, chickpeas, beans and split peas may reduce cholesterol so much that consumers may be able to get off their cholesterol-lowering statin drugs, but to profoundly alter heart disease risk we may have to more profoundly alter our diet." NurtritionFacts.org, August 29, 2014/Volume 20 http://nutritionfacts.org/video/beans-beans-theyre-good-for-your-heart/

2. Miyai K1, Tokushige T, Kondo M; Iodine Research Group, "Suppression of thyroid function during ingestion of seaweed "Kombu" (Laminaria japonoca) in normal Japanese adults," NutritionFacts.org, Sep 9, 2011/volume 5, http://nutritionfacts.org/video/too-much-iodine-can-be-as-bad-as-too-little/

3. US Food and Drug Administration; "Bad Bug Book Foodborne Pathogenic Microorganisms and Natural Toxins Handbook, Phytohaemagglutinin" http://www.fda.gov/

food/foodborneillnesscontaminants/ causesofillnessbadbugbook/ucm071092.htm, Page Last Updated: 08/05/2013

Chapter Six

1. https://www.youtube.com/watch?v=npP8maVti7o Morey eel - Ron & Valerie Taylor.mpg

Chapter Seven

1. Lisle, Doug, Ph.D, co-author, "The Pleasure Trap," excerpt from lecture for VSH, Vegetarian Society of Hawaii, http:// www.youtube.com/watch?v=nxf4kj8Rb6Y)

2. Campbell, T. Colin, Ph.D., Campbell, Thomas M. II, "The China Study: The Most Comprehensive Study of Nutrition Ever Conducted and the Startling Implications for Diet, Weight Loss and Long-term Health," Published by BenBells Books, Inc, 2006, pp 228-229

3. Gregor, Michael, "Vitamin B-12 Necessary For Arterial Health: The cardiovascular benefits of plant-based diets may be severely undermined by vitamin B-12 deficiency." NutritionFacts.org, December 20, 2013/Volume 16, http:// nutritionfacts.org/video/vitamin-b12-necessary-for-arterial-health/

Chapter Nine

1. Chen, Rosalind Chia-Yu 1, Lee, Meei-Shyuan 2,3, Chang, Yu-Hung 4 and Wahlqvist, Mark L, Cambridge, "Cooking

frequency may enhance survival in Taiwanese elderly," Journals Online-Public Health Nutrition / Volume 15 / Issue 07 / July 2012, pp 1142 - 1149 May 2012

Chapter Eleven

1. Gregor, Michael, "Waistline Slimming Food: A biological understanding of why soy may result in less abdominal fat." NutritionFacts.org, October 15, 2009/Volume 3, http://nutritionfacts.org/video/waistline-slimming-food/ http://nutritionfacts.org/video/best-cooking-method/
2. Physicians Committee For Responsible Medicine, Food For Life of Cancer Project. http://pcrm.org/health/cance-resources/ask/ask-the-expert-soy

3. Gregor, Michael, "Is Kimchi Good For You? Epidemiological evidence that kimchi consumption may significantly increase cancer risk." NutritionFacts.org, December 16, 2010/Volume 4, http://nutritionfacts.org/video/is-kimchi-good-for-you/

4. H. Yu, J. Y. Hwang, J. Ro, J. Kim, and N. Chang. "Vegetables, but not pickled vegetables, are negatively associated with the risk of breast cancer." Nutr Cancer, July 2010,62(4):443-453, http://www.ncbi.nlm.nih.gov/pubmed/20432165

5. L. Jian, D. H. Zhang, A. H. Lee, and C. W. Binns. Do preserved foods increase prostate cancer risk? British Journal. Cancer, May 4, 2004, 90(9):1792-1795, http://www.ncbi.nlm.nih.gov/pmc/articles/PMC2409746/#!po=5.55556

6. Gregor, Michael, Breast Cancer Prevention: "Which Mushroom Is Best?" NutrionFacts.org, September 21, 2011/Volume 5, http://nutritionfacts.org/video/breast-cancer-prevention-which-mushroom-is-best/

7. Cornicopia Institute, "Carrageenan: How a "Natural" Food Is Making Us Sick," http://www.cornucopia.org/carrageenan-2013/ March 2013

Chapter Twelve

1. Gregor, Michael, MD," How can I preserve the anti-cancer effects of cooked garlic?" http://nutritionfacts.org/questions/what-are-the-anti-cancer-effects-of-garlic/, NutritionFacts.org, November 8, 2012

Chapter Thirteen

1. Gregor, Michael, MD, "Nuts May Help Prevent Death: Just a few small servings of nuts a week may increase our lifespan and lower cancer risk." NutritionFacts.org, March 19, 2014/Volume 17, http://nutritionfacts.org/video/nuts-may-help-prevent-death/)

2. Gregor, Michael, MD, "Nuts and Obesity: The Weight of Evidence Nut consumption does not appear to lead to the expected weight gain." NutritionFacts.org, August 17, 2012/Volume 10, http://nutritionfacts.org/video/nuts-and-obesity-the-weight-of-evidence/

3. Gregor, Michael, MD, "Boosting the Bioavailability of Curcumin," NutritionFacts.org, January 20, 2014/Volume

15, http://nutritionfacts.org/video/boosting-the-bioavailability-of-curcumin/

4. Shoba Gl, Joy D, Joseph T, Majeed M, Rajendran R, Srinivas PS. "Influence of piperine on the pharmacokinetics of curcumin in animals and human volunteers." Planta Med. 1998 May; 64 (4): 353-6

5. M. Rose, J. Lewis, N. Langford, M. Baxter, S. Origgi, M. Barber, H. MacBain, and K. Thomas. "Arsenic in seaweed: forms, concentration and dietary exposure." Food Chem.Toxicol, 45(7):1263-1267, 2007. NutritionFacts.org, September 24, 2007/Volume 1, http://nutritionfacts.org/video/avoiding-iodine-deficiency-2/

Chapter Fifteen

1. Gregor, Micahel, MD, "Best Cooking Method: Which are the gentlest cooking methods for preserving nutrients and which vegetables have more antioxidants cooked than raw." NutritionFacts.org, September 10, 2010, http://nutritionfacts.org/video/best-cooking-method/

RESOURCES

Books

"The China Study: The Most Comprehensive Study of Nutrition Ever Conducted And the Startling Implications for Diet" by T. Colin Campbell, Thomas M. Campbell II, Howard Lyman and John Robbins (May 11, 2006)

"Prevent and Reverse Heart Disease: The Revolutionary, Scientifically Proven, Nutrition-Based Cure" by Caldwell B. Esselstyn Jr. M.D. (Feb 1, 2007)

"The McDougall Plan" by John A. McDougall and Mary A. McDougall (Oct 22, 1983)

"The Starch Solution: Eat the Foods You Love, Regain Your Health, and Lose the Weight for Good!" by John McDougall and Mary McDougall (May 8, 2012)

"Dr. Dean Ornish's Program for Reversing Heart Disease" by Dr Dean Ornish (Sep 22, 2010)

"Dr. Neal Barnard's Program for Reversing Diabetes: The Scientifically Proven System for Reversing Diabetes without Drugs" by Neal Barnard (April 1, 2008)

"Power Foods for the Brain: An Effective 3-Step Plan to Protect Your Mind and Strengthen Your Memory" by Neal Barnard (Feb 19, 2013)

"Peter Reinhart's Whole Grain Breads: New Techniques, Extraordinary Flavor" by Peter Reinhart (September 1, 2007)

"The Bread Baker's Apprentice: Mastering the Art of Extraordinary Bread Hardcover" by Peter Reinhart (November 14, 2001)

"The Vegetarian Flavor Bible: The Essential Guide to Culinary Creativity with Vegetables, Fruits, Grains, Legumes, Nuts, Seeds, and More, Based on the Wisdom of Leading American Chefs" by Karen Page – October 14, 2014

Documentaries And DVDs

Forks Over Knives
Genetic Roulette
Supersize Me
Food Inc.
Fast Food Nation
Fat Sick & Nearly Dead
Earthlings
Vegucated
Cowspiracy

Websites

www.vegginoutandabout.com - *Veggin' Out and About!* Our food and travel website directs consumers to vegan friendly restaurants and markets. Also, we interview people involved in interesting and beneficial activities pertaining to the advancement of both local and global plant-based movements, environmental sustainability, and the protection of animals.

www.nutritionfacts.org - Dr. Michael Gregor's website will tell you nearly everything you want to know regarding current research on food and nutrition.

www.pcrm.org - Physician's Committee For Responsible Medicine

www.drmcdougall.com - Dr. McDougall's Health & Medical Center, excellent resource for recipes, workshops and clinics

www.ucsusa.org - Union of Concerned Scientists

www.ewg.org - Environmental Working Group

www.jeffnovick.com - Jeff Novick's website - cooking videos and nutrition information

www.happycow.net - food and travel website

www.yelp.com -food and travel website

www.tripadviser.com - food and travel website

Food Products And Equipment Resources

www.naturalimport.com - Natural Imports carries a wonderful assortment of high quality Japanese foods, like misos, seaweeds, tamari, plum vinegars, etc.

www.vitamix.com - excellent high powered blender

www.harvestessentials.com - Excalibur dehydrator

www.v-dog.com - excellent vegan dog food

www.breadtopia.com - wonderful resource for baking artisan breads, also carries baking supplies

www.mountainbreezenaturals.com - bulk organic Ceylon cinnamon (Buy this over cassia cinnamon, which contains a high level courmarin, which can be toxic to the liver in high doses.)

www.ethiopianspices.com - bulk Ethiopian spices

I purchase a lot of items on-line, most often at www.amazon.com. The following is a list of items I've found particularly useful over the years and the companies who sell them through Amazon. You may also buy directly from the companies in most cases.

Paderno World Cuisine A4982799 Tri-Blade Plastic Spiral Vegetable Slicer by Paderno World Cuisine

2 to 3 Year Old Kaffir Lime Tree in Grower's Pot, 3 Year Warranty by Lemon Citrus Tree

Zwilling J.A. Henckels Twin Sharp Duo Knife Sharpener by Zwilling J.A. Henckels

Zwillilng J.A. Henckels Twin Four Star 8-Inch High Carbon Stainless-Steel Chef's Knife by Zwilling J.A. Henckels

Wusthof Classic 7-Piece Cutlery Set with Storage Block - Professional quality cutlery set with only the pieces you'll use.

Kuhn Rikon 3-Set Original Swiss Peeler, Red/Green/Yellow - very inexpensive set of swivel peelers, fantastic for peeling hard squashes, like butternut.

Stovetop Smoker - The Original Camerons Stainless Steel Smoker with Wood Chips - Works over any heat source, indoor or outdoor by Camerons Products

OliveNation Pink Peppercorns 16-ounce by JR Mushrooms & Specialties

Boyajian Pure Lemon Oil 5-ounce size by Boyajian (Use only 1 drop of this, it is very powerful!!)

WMF Perfect Plus 6-1/2-Quart Pressure Cooker by WMF

Prestige Deluxe Stainless Steel Mini Handi Pressure Cooker, 3.3-Liter by Prestige

Flame Tamer Simmer Ring Aluminum Heat Diffuser Distributer gas stove top stovetop with Wood Handle by Maxi-Aids

Roland Dried Green Flageolets, 17.6-Ounce Boxes (Pack of 4) by Roland

Frontier Mustard Seed, Yellow Mustard Whole Certified Organic, 16-Ounce Bags (Pack of 2) by Frontier

Frontier Mustard Seed, Brown Mustard Whole Certified Organic, 16-Ounce Bags (Pack of 3) by Frontier

Danish Dough Whisk, large and small sizes - this is indispensable for stirring doughs and thick batters.

ACKNOWLEDGEMENTS

I'd like to thank so many people involved in the creation of this project; family, friends, and neighbors who tasted my food and offered valuable feedback, read portions of my manuscript and offered insights and encouragement. There are too many of you to name; you know who you are. Thank you, from the bottom of my heart.

Especially, I'd like to thank author, Nora Percival, who at 100 years of age tirelessly edited this work and made me fight for every sentence I wanted to preserve. She adds color to the world simply by being a part of it. Nora, I hope you live forever.

I would like to thank all the physicians, nurses and other medical professionals who worked so hard to keep me alive. I wish I could single each of you out. Thank you for giving me back my life.

I'd also like to thank T. Colin Campbell whose book, *The China Study*, sent me down the path to recovery and restored health.

A special thanks to artist Debbie Grimm who lent me many of her exquisite pottery pieces for food photographs for this book and forthcoming cookbooks. I'm grateful also to the talented costume designers of the Barter Theater, who sampled my food, gave me valuable feedback, and created for me an assortment of lovely napkins for food photography.

I'd also like to acknowledge High Country Writers of Boone, NC, whose members were always available for constructive criticism and support. You guys are the best!

Last, but certainly not least, with all my heart, I thank my husband and partner, Rich Bussone, whose indefatigable humor, kindness, wisdom and love make all things possible. I love you, Bucko of the World!

ABOUT THE AUTHOR

Danielle Bussone is a free-lance writer, a certified wellness coach, and an avid cook. After discovering the healing powers of food, she became fascinated with creating dishes that were not only health-promoting but bursting with flavor. Danielle completed Cornell University's certification program in plant-based nutrition, in conjunction with the T. Colin Campbell Foundation.

She and her husband Rich, co-founded *Veggin' Out And About!*, a food and travel blog for plant-based diners. Danielle serves as a restaurant reviewer and writer for *Veggin' Out And About!*, as well as editor for contributors from across the globe.

Danielle is currently working on several cookbooks of plant-based cuisines from the US and around the world. Danielle and Rich divide their time between SW Virginia and East Tennessee, where they live with two dogs and two cats, collectively known as their "Beloved Monsters." In her spare time she writes fiction and is currently working on a novel based in New Orleans.

You can follow Danielle's blog and/or contact her at www.vegginoutandabout.com.

VEGGIN' OUT AND ABOUT!

VOAA provides reliable vegan food resources readers can visit with confidence. From fledgling efforts, we have grown to include volunteer restaurant reviewers from across the globe. We also interview people doing interesting and laudable deeds involving plant-based nutrition, the sustainability of our natural resources and the protection of animals.

VEGAN VERIFIED AND APPROVED BY

Veggin' Out and About!

Restaurant and Market Guide For The Veggie Loving Traveler
www.vegginoutandabout.com

Our overarching goal is that of furthering the efforts of the whole foods plant-based movement, which aims to reduce the impact of consuming animals on our health, our children's health and that of future generations, reduce the effects of animal consumption to our planet's sustainability as well as reduce or eliminate the needless suffering and slaughter of other sentient beings.

Look for our decal on the doors of restaurants you visit and let us know of other worthy establishments we should review. Please join us as we travel the United States and the globe in search of delicious and health-promoting foods as we go *Veggin' Out And About!*

CPSIA information can be obtained at www.ICGtesting.com
Printed in the USA
LVOW06s1640310815

452226LV00019B/905/P

9 780615 794792